Charles Godfrey Leland

The Egyptian Sketchbook

Charles Godfrey Leland

The Egyptian Sketchbook

ISBN/EAN: 9783741136283

Manufactured in Europe, USA, Canada, Australia, Japa

Cover: Foto ©Thomas Meinert / pixelio.de

Manufactured and distributed by brebook publishing software
(www.brebook.com)

Charles Godfrey Leland

The Egyptian Sketchbook

ERRATA.

Page 70, line 22, *for* Herodities, *read* Heroddities.

Page 174, line 23, *for* "mortema birrit," *read* "mortem aburit."

Page 178, line 11, *for* wriggled, *read* wiggled.

Page 190, line 10, and page 196, line 10, *for* "secula seculorum,"
read "sæcula sæculorum."

CONTENTS.

THE EGYPTIAN SKETCH-BOOK.

INTRODUCTION.

I WENT to Egypt expecting to see visions and dream
dreams of Pharaohs, Amenophs, Ptolemies, ibises,
Osirises, scarabæi, and all of the tremendous terrors
and archæological agonies in which Antiquity was
born, the result of it all being very much like that of
a story which I recently heard narrated by an artist
friend, who often tells a very good one. Three young
painters had often heard, what the American Page
had proved, that by carefully peeling the picture of a
great artist coat by coat, one may learn all his secrets
of colour. So, having raised their last available cent,
and brought themselves, by closely screwn sacrifice, down
to the level of the bottom dollar (for I intend to write
when I please in American), they invested the results in
an undoubted Titian—a Virgin—which they laid on a
table, and proceeded to remove the outer varnish by
means of friction with the fingers; which varnish very

A

soon rose up in a cloud of white dust, and acted much as a shower of snuff would have done,—to say nothing of dusting their jackets.

They thus arrived at the naked colours, which had by this time assumed a very crude form, owing to the fact that a certain amount of liquorish tincture, as of Turkey rhubarb (*tinct. rhabarbara*), had become incorporated somehow with the varnish, and to which the colours had been indebted for their "golden warmth."

. This brought them to the *glazing proper*, which had been deprived of the evidence of the age or antiquity by the removal of the *patinæ*, or little cups which had formed in the canvas between the web and the woof.

The next process was to remove the glaze from the saffron robe, composed of yellow lake and burnt sienna. This brought them to a flame colour, in which the modelling had been made. They next attacked the robe of the Virgin Mary; and having taken away the crimson lake, were astonished to find a greenish drab. When they had thus in turn removed every colour in the picture, dissecting every part by diligent care, loosening every glaze by solvents too numerous to mention—including alcohol and various adaptations of alkali—they had the ineffable satisfaction of feeding their eyes on the design in a condition of crude, blank chiaroscuro. Blinded by enthusiasm—yet having made careful notes of all they had done—they flew valiantly at the white and black with pumice-stone and potash; when lo and behold! something very rubicund appeared, which further excavations declared was the tip of the red——nose of King George the Fourth!

The Titian for which they had sacrificed so much was a false god!

I, in like manner, went at my Egypt full of the spirit of antiquity—thinking of nothing less modern than the Ptolemies or Hypatia—expecting to unroll the ancient mummy by going from century to century, as from one inscribed cerecloth to another, or, as the artists did with their picture, from varnish to glaze, and from glaze to sketch. But what was the result? As soon as the varnish dust of antiquity had vanished, what remained, and what almost entirely occupied me, was a very modern Egypt indeed. Perhaps I went too deeply —like the German who scraped away a Monk-Latin chronicle, being of the faith that something classical and Roman was inscribed beneath, and only found that he had come to a deed of 1801, which had been written on the other side! * He had gone clear through.

Years ago I gave some study in books and pictures to the glories of Thebes and Luxor, Dendera and Karnak, to Birch, Brugsch, Bononi, Champollion, *et cetera*, and believed it was the best preparation I could make for what was called the Land of Misr—and which most travellers describe as the Home of Misery.

* Everybody who writes on Egypt uses the palimpsest simile. This is the best I could do with it. It is almost played out now. I wonder how the next man will get it into shape, and glue it, so as to stand up.

Perhaps I was mistaken, for there is something in the country beside the ruins. What principally impressed me when I came to Egypt was Egypt itself, as it really is—and not its old clothes—as will be found in the following pages.

CHAPTER I.

SOME one once compared the out-letting of a black congregation from a negro church in Philadelphia to the outpouring of an upset bottle of Day and Martin's blacking; and the immense multitude of creamy-blanche burnus-clad Arabs streaming towards the steamship at Marseilles, as I approached it, made that vessel seem at a distance like a tub being filled with human whitewash. It was a very poor steamer, not even one of the regular Messageries craft, rather less than a New York and Brooklyn ferryboat ; and yet two hundred and twenty of these Arab pilgrims, on their way from Algiers to Mecca *via* Marseilles and Alexandria, were packed on deck on board of her ; and we of the first-class cabin paid the same price as if we had taken passage on a boat of the same line of twice the accommodation and thrice the comfort. They do not manage *these* things better in France.

I learned one Arab word between the door of the dock and the gangway plank, while going about one hundred feet; and had I only continued learning Arabic at the same rate, I should be deeply learned in it now. This word was *Shꝛoyé!* literally, "A little!" but signifying, "Give way a bit! room there!" These holy men were all terribly loaded with immense pig or goat-skins of water; and he who has never studied the latter objects can have no idea of their appalling ugliness. Black and hairy, with ears and noses, legs and tails dripping with water, and flapping and nodding from side to side as they were shaken, with a motion like life, they looked like dying devils being carried home to breathe their last, or vagabond fiends who, having ventured on a cold bath, found it did not agree with them. Other Hajis carried coarse bags with curious stripes, or immense packs of matting, made from palm leaves; but everything was strange and wild African. I did not see a single article among them that did not appear to have been made in the desert, afar from factories, uninfluenced by counting-houses. I was struck, indeed, by the fact that none of their chattels seemed to have been bought at all of anybody. And as they crowded in a steady press, every man of them overloaded, they gently cried to one another, "*Shꝛoyé!*"

Having secured my state-room or cabin, I went on the upper-deck, from which, as from a balcony-box at the opera, I could look down on the pious pilgrims; and verily the P. P.'s were an entertaining party. Some

of them were immensely busy in casting their bundles
and sacks into the hold, watching them with fond
parting glances; and no wonder, since those bags contained all their food, their very life itself, for many
months to come. Others were assiduously getting like
sheep in the way of the sailors, and when rudely pushed
away, endured the push, as I observed, rather like
gentlemen when they *must* endure, than cads, who
rail when railing is of no avail. Others, like additional
sheep, continually went straying ashore, and were
immediately brought back by sailors, who scolded them
vigorously in Provençal French. I had very recently
travelled in Scotland, where the manner in which a
faithful colley retrieves a stray black-face had been to
me a source of frequent delight, but not so delightful
as to witness the similarity of men to animals in
wandering and being caught. The parallel held good
as to colour, for nothing on the face of the earth resembles at a little distance a sheep more than a Bedouin;
and when all were finally packed together close as sardines in a box, and the shades of night drew on, and the
burnus were closely drawn over their heads, nothing was
wanting to complete the illusion. No, not even the
ba-á-ing; since as soon as we sailed, five of the devout
arose, and putting their heads close together, began to
cry the " *La Alláh il Alláh!* " which, as is well known,
is of all human sounds the most like bleating. It is
sheep-ier than monotonous; it is absolutely mutton-ous.

Seated by me on the deck was a passenger who was

almost a man and a brother, so intensely black-brown was his face, which had been further improved in bygone years by a thorough peppering with small-pox, every pit of which—and they were crowded close—had left a mark like No. 4 shot. Moreover, there was a deep scar in the middle of each cheek, the twin-likeness of which puzzled me, until I learned that they had been caused by dervishes, who run skewers or spits into promising children, in order to thereby secure their salvation. At a later date, when intimacy had ripened, I asked this Muslim gentleman if he really thought that such spitting in the faces of the young tended to elevate their minds. He pondered the question deeply, and replied, very gravely—

"How much?" This, in his peculiar dialect, signified "Why?"

I answered—"Because I have always heard, that when a cook spits anything, it begins to go round *doing* good. Did it work that way in your family?"

He answered with something that had Allah in it, of course, and fell into a deep state of smoke over my question.

But I am anticipating events, and hurrying along entirely too fast. Let me present to the reader a little more distinctly a man who shall have a line to himself, I promise you; yea, though there should be only one line in the book, and one book in my life. And that man, without whom the voyage might have been dull indeed, was—

MOHAMET.

In full, Mohamet Wahab, or Abt-el-Wahab. It was
about a week before any of the passengers discovered
that Mohamet was the Egyptian pilot of our vessel;
but as the fact had been made known that he was a
wealthy landed proprietor in Alexandria, and as his
conduct was marked by the most scrupulous and gentlemanly propriety, it was reported that he was an oriental
of the first class, but travelling second class from
motives of mistaken economy, or a laudable desire to
see the world. He was of medium height, taciturn of
manner yet affable, and arrayed in full Levantine-
Egyptian style, in enormously full silk trousers, or
rather in a single trouser, difficult to comprehend and
impossible to describe, yet which vividly suggested
to my mind an ancient legend of a certain damsel who
once put both legs into a pillow-case, or at least was
told to do so. I once hinted to Mohamet that it would
be impossible to run in this garment; to which he
solemnly replied, " Him no wanty run—no bono molti
tumby downo me."

And here I may as well state, that the language or
languages spoken by Mohamet constituted the most
wonderful and bewildering medium of thought I ever
listened to in all my life. At the tower of Babel he
would have been head-man. Those of my readers who
found it impossible to follow me through the German-
English of Hans Breitmann, and abused me accordingly,

had better skip this Mohamet chapter forthwith, and go
on to the next, for there is trouble ahead for them.
Mohamet spoke, in fact, from two to four, and from four
to six languages in one; and his talk was like a stately
edifice, of which the foundation was Italian, the walls
English, the staircases and floors French, while at the
summit was a gay and fanciful Arabesque of his native
tongue, which gave a character to the whole. But the
building was very shaky and ruinous, and the least storm
of a difficulty in the subject of conversation would bring
the stones down in frightful confusion. Mohamet generally spoke all these languages at once, according to the
laws of a conglomerated grammar, the only rule of
which was never to form any sentences twice alike. I
think it must have been by some special inspiration
that I was gifted to understand this Pentecost in a
petticoat; for though there were plenty of people on
board who understood Mohamet's continental languages
and Arabic far better than I, none of them could make
anything out of him save in the tongue of the Koran.
When the captain, who was experienced in Lingua
Franca, wished to comprehend Mohamet, he brought
him to me. I omitted to state that he also professed
Neapolitan and Spanish; but it was idle and wicked
of him to affect ignorance of Maltese, since it was a
fundamental law of his nature that he should converse
perfectly in that dreadful dialect.

It was this person whom I, seeing that he was going
with us, addressed as follows:—

" Monsieur va a Alexandrie ? "

To which he replied—" Oui, signore."

" Parlate Italiano ? "

" Si, master."

" You have been in Europe ? "

" Many time I. Travaliato molto—travel plentee good
'ecl. Venti cinque—how you say him English—twant-
five time a Marseilia die year. France, oui, large a
many time. Englan' too, 'bundance much, *aiya, bass.*"

Before leaving England, I had been in the habit of
carefully observing and accurately noting the speech of
the Rommany or Gipsies, and the practice enabled me
to record Mohamet's remarks with something like exact-
ness. Commenting on the pilgrims, he said—

" She go Mek'ha—bono ver' fine. See Kaaba—house
much too very splendids—ver' good. You know 'bout
Mek'ha—*si ?— liséz*—rid booko—*tāib—kraiz ketir*
(very pretty). *I been Mek'ha ?*—yes—me goned I, six
years ago. I go viaggio him travel moch dreadfuls—
Wahid nucf one an' a half dem Hajis die dead. Suppose her allér Mek'ha, him ritornare all dead some."

I asked him if he had ever heard of any Christians
having visited Mecca.

" No Christin mans ever get come dere—Muslim she
non permetter it, he."

Then I informed him that Captain Burton and Burck-
hardt—those two busy B's of travel—had gone thither;
and Mohamet Abt-el-Wahab was so visibly " riled " at
this piece of news, that I was sorry I told him about it.

"Spose him Muslim catchit she, she tearit all to pieces. *Aiya,*—killem!"

The charming scene which this reflection brought before his eyes seemed to restore his equanimity; for after puffing gravely for a minute, he inquired—

"Him Christin — Frank-mans — he got all sem 'ligion?"

I told him that there were great differences of religion between Europeans—that some were Catholics, who held there were three Gods in One, and the Pope was His Prophet; others were Protestants, who believed that the Triune God had sent one of the Three as a Prophet; and that, finally, there were the Hukamá or Philosophers, who declared there was no God, and that anybody was His prophet, especially themselves. Mohamet had been scores of times in Europe, but this was all new to him, and he said—

"Mash allah! What! you no all believe in Pop?"

I replied that I had great faith in ginger-pop, but in none other.

As I said this, a tall, lank, snuffy, disagreeable Italian priest walked by us up and down the deck. On him Mohamet gazed with an appearance of intense disgust.

"You not likit him *padre*—my not likit him padre I. Her padre he makit storm come, bad weathér—molto cattivo—*battál*—bad voyage like devils. Me hatit padre I,—hit no wash herself—small-dirty—*Yahud* (Jew) dirty all sem, lave pas—him no *táib.* You got some 'ligion you? What make do—how much?"

I explained that my religion enjoined it on me to abstain from bad butter, fat pork, and late suppers, and to wash all over once a day. And he said—

"You got good 'ligion—buono—all sem Muslim. Muslim wash good 'eel. This Ramadan* now—I no eatit I, all day—him Hajis no eatit. By an' by sun she descendre—you see people-mans watch for him. Then all begin cook like hell-devil—eatit, mangiar, smoke all de night—how much. '*I drink wine?*' yes; me drink litt' wine, I. Prophet he no mean *no* wine-drinky; it mean litt' drinky, pretty-small some. *Aiya*—Ramadan be good, makit santé good—*sempre buono per la sanità.* Ramadan *fini* by-by—Christmas come; all sem one Franki Christmas. You, likit Christmas—me likit Christmas, much, I. Very beautiful—*kwaiz ketir*—bells—'Gypsian man, she give some guns, fusil, canón, *bandūk*— boom, boom!—much nass (nice)—bang! bum!—feu d'artifice—fireworks—peoples glad—me glad, I—much merry; gioia *ketir*."

Speaking of the delights of Cairo, Mohamet on another occasion held forth in these words—

"You likit girly—*bint?*—me likit *bint*, I. Cairo *bint* very good-pretty—*kwaiz ketir.* Sing! you likit 'Gypsian sing-music? You go garden, Esbekiah—you hear one much fine sing-girl; him name Bulbul. You know Bulbul—Almah, *kwaiz.* One piastre to hear sing. Ghazie, she one dance-girly, great beautifuls—nass, nass (nice). Si paga *telata* (three) shillin' for see

---

* Ramadan, the Mahometan Lent, an annual fast of forty days.

dance *fil bayt* (in a house).   Thirteen shillin' for
tutto insieme, all togedder.   That nuf ; you not *paga piu.*"

The steamer held her course over the beautiful blue
sea, and day faded into late afternoon—the *sarisham* of
India—and the crimson-purple poured like a dream-
bath for the coming queen of night over the sky.
Turning south from Marseilles, we pass Titan piles
of grotesque rocks, so grimly inaccessible and so
cruelly barren, that it seems as if Nature had been
cheated by some small-minded spirit of evil who was
behind the times long ere time begun.   Here our
boat broke some machinery and anchored for the
night.   As yet the pilgrims had been incredibly
quiet.   Wrapped in their white burnus, packed simply
as closely as possible, they lay on their mats on deck,
every inch of which was entirely covered with them,
excepting a small pass-way.   In this manner, seldom
moving, apparently asleep, they passed the time.   Going
to Mecca, and knowing that perhaps half their number
would die before returning, the pilgrims had evidently
brought the whole of their oriental philosophy to bear
upon "the situation."   So they made a merit of uncom-
plaining suffering, whether they froze or starved ; and
for Bedouins from the burning desert, who travelled in
Ramadan, and were exposed at the end of November to
rain and hail all night long, at times there was abundance of both.   "Deuce take the fellows !" said our old
doctor ; "one can't find out if they are ill.   Sometimes
they die in the night, and never say a word ; and one

never finds it out till somebody observes the next day
that they lie three or four hours without stirring."

But as the sun drew nearer and nearer to his golden
shadow-bride in the sea—coquetting and loitering, and
yet quivering with passion and desire, while both grew
redder and redder in the face—the pilgrims began to
manifest a yearning of a different nature, and to stir
and bustle in unwonted manner. All were watching the
sun like Gebers,—waiting the blessed instant when the
disappearance of his light · should allow them to light
the better-beloved fires of their little stoves, and set the
pot a-boiling. Then Ali pronounced it as his opinion,
by Allah, that it couldn't take more than five minutes to
see that copper-faced old humbug under water—(I should
mention, by the way, that the sun *is* a sham in Arabic)
—while Hassan vowed that four minutes ought to polish
it off effectually. Said the Fortunate began to open his
bag of *kūs-kūs*, and Ibrahim appealed to Mohamet, who
wore a watch, to let him know for the love of Islam what
o'clock it was.

Downer and downer goes the sun—it touches water—
it wiggles into it—it is waist-deep—and now (like a
bad egg floating in a tub, put there by some thrifty
housewife to test its quality) only its "butt" is above
the line,—its tail vanishes. Hurrah!—Allah achbar!
—Bismillah!—*E pluribus unum!*

How they go to grub, these hungry Hajis! and
what messes they make of oil, and meal, and tallow, and
Allah knows what! I saw one who, into a dish for six,

put four heaping handfuls of red pepper, and never winked. *Kūs-kūs* is their stand-by;—what rice is to a Carolinian or a Hindoo—oysters to a Virginian—clams to a Rhode-Islander—canvas-backs to a Marylander—soft-shell crabs to a Jerseyman—terrapin or grass-butter to a Philadelphian—an unfailing and constant source of conversation, the joy of his life, his consolation in the darkest sorrow, his comfort till death. I went among them and begged a handful of *kūs-kūs.* It seemed to be coarse macaroni in hard grains, as if made by rubbing a paste of "wheat and Indian" through a sieve. I should say that it would be desirable to hens, and an object to any man out of shot wishing to fire a charge into game, or to make game of a stranger. As the Bedouins are a highly economical race, I have no doubt that they construct the article, as Frenchmen do all their words, with a double meaning or intent—the one proper, the other otherwise.

So far as I could ascertain, the one object of life with the pilgrims appeared to be religion. Abstaining from grosser food during the day, they indulged in a steady theological banquet of *Allah mal Mahomed,* taking it hot and cold, minced, fried, pickled, stewed, broiled, scalloped, and on the shell. Several of them had nice little illuminated red-and-black-letter Korans, and these they devoured about breakfast-time with as much delight as true Christians take in the morning newspaper. They had brought with them a minstrel, a handsome, troubadour-faced, graceful man, who peformed daily at eleven

A.M. on a darabuka, or long bottomless crockery pot, headed with parchment, which he thrummed with incredible monotony. At this drum-head he held a daily trial of the ears of the unbelievers. First he sang a verse of a hymn, and then drummed one, and this formed the lunch of the faithful, who often grunted with delight at the feast. Sometimes he varied the performance with shrill feats of the pig-whistle order, on a cane-angle six-hole fife.

And here it occurs to me that the pig-whistle pipe is strictly a religious instrument, since the organs used in Christian churches were described by the Puritans as godless boxes of whistles—and because, moreover, the term " Pig and Whistle " comes from the Saxon *Pige πaeskal*, meaning "Hail to the Virgin." However this may be, it is certain that I alone of the Kaffirs or unbelievers took any pleasure in the performance. After listening several times to the humming, drumming, and tum-tumming, a pleasing sense of something like " bumble-bees," mixed up with banjoes and wild thyme blows, and going to sleep in honeysuckles with little country churches twining like Fiske's woodbine round their windows, stole over me. This amounted at first to a fascination, and I would sit gazing at Ibn-el-Shaitan, or whatever his name was,—the minstrel,—until my admiration was noted with mutual admiration by the pilgrims, and I became known as one who, though a Kaffir, had, however, true taste in sacred music. After the minstrel had sung

yj   B

and drummed himself weary, there was a collection of
coppers taken up; and one day I threw half a franc into
the pot, and, moreover, induced several Americans to do
the same.   This was received with an outburst of amazed
joy by the faithful, who, I verily believe, thought we
were well on our way to conversion.

Sometimes at night, as I lay in my cabin, amid the
roaring of winds, creaking of ropes, dashing of waves,
and heavehoing of sailors, I could hear without inter-
mission the hymn of the minstrel at every lull of the
harsher noises, and his " tum-a-tummy, tum-a-tummy,
tum, tum, tum!"   Then there would come a heavy swell,
a rush of many feet clattering above, and as these
sounds faded, and the ship slid down in the long roll,
there would arise the wailing *Allah il Allah* and the tum-
tummy, tum-tummy, tum, tum, tum;—till, while I was
struggling with dim recollections of the distant banjo
played all night long in the engine-room of an Ohio steamboat; just audible, then as now, in my berth; I fell asleep.

But though they did nothing but talk, discuss, argue,
sing, drum, eat, and drink, religion from morning to
night, and so on (including the sedulous passing of a
black paving-stone one to the other), I am sorry to say
that the Hajis were dreadfully deficient in morality,
picking one another's pockets, and stealing each other's
garments, with an assiduity only equalled by their
devotion.   There was not a day on which one of them
did not come in dire distress to the captain, declaring
that all he had to depend on to get to Mecca had been

stolen from him during his sleep, or something of the
sort. One would bewail five hundred francs, another
his shoes. But as they robbed one another all round, and
as the poor sponged on the rich, I have no doubt that it
all came square in the end.

I mention these little peccadilloes of the pilgrims without regret, because I have frequently met with a kind of
would-be-liberal, irrationalistic folk, who think it shows
breadth, height, and grandeur of mind to praise up the
Mahometan religion as simple, single, and true, and
who affect to wish that Christians were more like
the Muslim. For my own part, I can only declare that
until Mahometan bigotry and out-of-door prayers im-
prove the morals of the Muslim, I shall be well satisfied with quiet, retiring Christianity as it is. For my
pilgrims were, I regret to say, dreadfully, weakly,
madly, idiotically vain of their faith. "God," they
said, "had given the Franks science and worldly knowledge, but He has given us the true religion;" and on
the strength of this gift they ladled out for themselves
the fullest measure of arrogance and superiority to all
Christians. I afterwards learned that on the Nile-boats the
miserable Egyptian sailors would cry to the dragoman,
"Have you fed your pigs yet?"—meaning the Christian
ladies and gentlemen who fed them on their leavings;
while the pilgrims, I was well assured, regarded us as
scum. It is not wonderful that people whose religion
exalts them in their own conceit above everybody and
everything should not be ashamed to pray publicly.

For my own part, I think that Christ's exhortation to pray in private indicates a delicacy and depth of feeling such as is to be found in no other religion. It is all very well to say, " Do not be ashamed of your religion ! " But the truth is, that deep love or earnest feeling is, and ought to be, shamefaced; and that is not the truest and tenderest phase of piety which impels a man to kneel and bump his forehead as indifferently before a thousand people as if he were alone.

Mohamet being more liberal, was far more sensible. His religious fancies partook rather of a romantic character. One night, while approaching Alexandria, the star shower of November 1872 occurred. While the rest of us were busy counting the number of meteors to a second, Mohamet remained unmoved. There was nothing mysterious in it to him—he knew all about it; and his explanation was as follows :—

" Sometime him Afreet (evil spirit) come up, *alzar,* 'gainst Allâh. Many many Afreet. Then him Malakin (angels) shootit some arrow they—kill devil, *molto, beaucoup*—and *las estrellas,* him stars wat you see, she de arrows Malakin shoot at Afreet devils. *Aiya!* "

I was pleased with the idea that meteors were arrows shot by the angels who defend the throne of Allah against the rebellious Afreets, and asked him if devils were common about those parts. To which he returned a prompt assent, declaring that in the month of March there was a time of seven days and eight nights during which the Afreets had permission from Allah to go

yachting about the Levant. And they availed themselves, it would appear, of this leave, in a manner which
would certainly have never occurred to any but a
Mahometan devil, since they all went in a solid fleet
with the yards locked, so that at a distance it appeared
precisely like an island overgrown with trees. While
this devils' cruise lasted, ·there was always a terrible
storm, and the Afreet ships were in the middle of it. It
occurred to me, that as the Afreet chose the season of
the Equinoctial for their pleasure-party, this was not
unlikely.

I asked Mohamet if he had ever seen the devils'
fleet, to which he solemnly replied —

"I no see him I—my father he see him—yas, one
time. Storm—yes, *molto.*"

It is hardly credible that a man could have been
scores of times in Europe and not have met with Eau-de-
Cologne. Yet such was truly the case with Mohamet.
One day I produced a bottle of it, and poured some on
his handkerchief. Like all orientals, he was passion-
ately fond of perfumes, and he "went on" over this like
puss in a bed of catnip. It made a deep impression on
him—it must have been very deep, since, though a very
gentlemanly person, it drove him next morning to speak
as follows:—

"You got some dat *anau kalāuna* (Eau-de-Cologne)
—how you call?—you givit me yesterday. I likit I—
much ness (nice). Quella buonissima!—I smell her
on mouchoir all night. Oh, goods gods !—she smellit

much beautifuls. Suppose you got one *small* bott' fulls
—*no?* Si non avete una pickle bottilia—not have some
another one bott'l—suppose you put some all scm for
Mohamet in him small bottle—litt'l bott'—not takec
much from you."

It was a modest request, and the next day I gave him
a small "bott'l" full of the *atar*. Great was the joy of
Mohamet, nor was his gratitude less than his joy, since
he promptly produced a flaçon of otto of roses, worth a
hundred of my gift, which he urged me to accept. I
would not take it: I was charmed to think that a man
existed—even a man in a pillow-case—who did not know
Cologne.

We had head-wind, a high sea, and the miserable little
steamer was two or three days behind her time. Whereupon Mohamet delivered himself of his grief as follows :—

"You got small boy? *No?* Yes, me got one wife
I, *una,* ó due fancialli—litt'l Achmet, *so* high,—litt'l
girly—*sa nom* Aziza, *so* high.   Wednesday com—litt'
Achmet he look out winder,—What, Mohamet him father-
mans no com-it—bad! Thursday—Aziza, she regard
alla finestra—she no sees he father!—bad.   Friday him
wife she look,—What, Mohamet *non cè qui!*—no come !
—too great bads !—vente no buono—*yumkin* (perhaps)
me arrivera Saturday."

So he lit a fresh cigarette, and looked over the top-
rail at the beautiful Monte Christo, which was dimmering
in the distance, and consoled himself with the reflection
that, as it was destined to be so, so it must be, and nobody

could alter it, and it couldn't be otherwise—which is a great comfort at all times to everybody. And just then, as the captain came up, I asked him if anybody lived on the island.

And he told me a darksome and dreamy legend of the deep, which thrilled my soul in the ghostly eventide, —how there were indeed two who dwelt on that lonely isle of the Southern Sea—a mystical swell from Albion's distant shore, and one fair spirit,—the mariner called her Une Belle Cocotte, which meaneth Little Paper Bird in ye Norman tongue,—from the fairy land of Mabille, I know not how true it may be ; I tell the tale as 'twas told to me. Such is the gossip of the Mediterranean.

Then I asked the mariner for other stories of strange lands. And pointing in the direction of Sicily, he said—

" There lies an island, where I once went ashore, and found a cavern and a venerable friar. The friar didn't . live in the cavern, however,—he only kept no end of good wine there, while his home was in a house. And this *bon curé* gave me sheep and fruits as if it were para- dise and two barrels of wine, and wouldn't take a sou from me. Now, having a large stock of sardines in cans on board, I asked him if he thought he would like a few, and he allowed that he would. So I gave him a large ' collection, and he was delighted.

" Some weeks afterwards I again touched at this little paradise of simplicity and good taste. What was my amazement at meeting a procession of beautiful peasant

girls, and observing hanging around the neck of each
what I at first took to be a gold coin, but which closer
examination indicated was the brass *etiquette* or adver-
tisement-label cut from a sardine-box ! I interrogated
the virgins as to these ornaments. 'Kissing them
devoutly, they told me they were the blessed and consecrated medals of St Sardinio, given to them by their
holy pastor. They couldn't read—so it made no difference.''

He looked at me for the rejoinder. I replied—

" That puts me in mind of a little story. When the
Chinese Tae-ping rebellion broke out, it was carried
over in a quiet way to California, and all the Celestials
in the land of gold were divided about half and half into
Imperialists and Rebels. For a long time the laws kept
them quiet, but at last they could stand it no longer,
and marched forth, a thousand strong on each side, to
fight it out ; and as there were no white men in the
business, the authorities let them alone. So they fired
crackers, and bellowed, and made up faces, and shot
arrows, and rushed at one another, and the contending
armies swayed in the tide of battle, and there was an
awful muss. At last, towards evening, somebody by
some accident aimed his matchlock correctly, and killed
somebody else, a Rebel, taking his entire life, whereupon his entire party, being defeated, took to their heels,
followed by the triumphant Imperialists. Some Americans, who had watched the fray from afar, drew near to
examine the corpse, and saw as they approached that it

was clad in what appeared to be a magnificent suit of
gold-plate armour. But nearer examination revealed
the fact that the plates were, like the medals of your
story, only the labels cut from sardine-boxes, with a
nail-hole punched in each, and tied together with grocery
twine."

I don't wonder that the ship suffered from head-winds.
In fact, when I recall the awful yarns that captain spun,
and the anti-yarns with which we retorted, the marvel
is that she didn't founder, and let us all down into something rich and strange. When a Frenchman does anything, he generally does it well, and our captain having
made yarns his specialty, told them with a sweetness, a
grace, and an elegance that utterly defied remonstrance.
I have been on a clam-bake with three Yankee skippers,
and once I shared for thirty-five days a cabin with a
captain who had been a whaler for forty years ; and he
was a whaler! and great at " whalers." But I never met
with any one who could hold a mould or dip to ˙our
French commander. It was all in his manner. I believe that if he had told me over again all the adventures of Samson, Sinbad, and Münchausen rolled into
one, as his own biography, it would have taken me a
week to really disbelieve him. To an Anglo-Saxon or
American spinner of yarns one can always retort with a
sweet grin—" Aw!—a 'say—come now !—that won't do,
you know—haw, haw !—very clever, I dare say." But
no man living could have had the wooden-headedness to
reply to the captain in this wise ; his manner made it

impossible. Take him for all in all, he was a great man, and need have been at no trouble to open his oysters, since the natives would have gaped with such amazement at his yarns, that he could have peppered and lemoned them, and whipped them out on his fork, long before they could have half recovered from their astonishment.

There was among the pilgrims a giant black—a saint —an immense party—who had long since passed on six feet, and done first-class on several extra inches. As the Muslim have not yet discovered that a man is less a man for being black, this ebony Arab held his head up morally, as he did of course physically, very much above the rest, and was quite a miracle of gravity, to which a natural grimness added not a little. One day he puzzled me. While conversing with a friend at a distance, I saw him, as if in explanation of something, put the back of his wrist to his chin, and, straightening his hand, point the fingers at his *vis-à-vis*, and wave the hand, glaring wildly.

Then placing the backs of his wrists on either hip, considerably *en arrière*, he waved the hands up and down, accompanying the motion with a swaying of the head from side to side. I became deeply interested.

Changing with great rapidity, the saint now placed one hand projecting straight before him and pointing dead ahead. On the back of this, the left hand, he put his right elbow, and bending the right hand like the left downward, suddenly elevated both, and for some time waved the two in exact time up and down, accompanying this with a cheerful clicking sound, meant to exhilarate the spirits, and inspire in the minds of beholders patience under adversities, and golden hopes of bliss in a happy future.

Then he very suddenly—in fact, with wonderful rapidity—kicked one foot high in air, and rising and falling on his left leg, with each rise and fall threw his right upwards.

Finally, he kicked each foot up to a level with his chin, first one, then the other, and, as it ascended, clapped the palms of his immense hands together with an awful detonation under the rising thigh. A slap of the hand *sur son séant* terminated the performance.

A light suddenly flashed upon my mind; I saw it all. In his progress from the desert to the steamboat *via* Algiers and Marseilles, the saint had, doubtless, been induced to visit some of those haunts by the sea, dedicated to charming sins and dainty vices, known as gardens, but which, as the only plant one sees there is the weed, may be more properly called se-gar-dens. Here the untutored child of Islam had beheld the *can-can*. It had sunk deeply into his soul. This was clear enough from the perfect copy I had seen him make of it. It was a queer business for a saint; but then, saints in the East are constructed upon different principles from those in the West, as will appear in one of my future chapters.

There was among the pilgrims a young fellow of twenty, who wore a good-humoured expression of countenance, and who, in fact, sometimes smiled. His name

was Ali, and the captain said he was a rascal. I think
that Ali was the only one of the entire two hundred
whom I ever saw smile. Saints never smile, of course,
but Ali was young in the business, and had not learned
all the dodges. So he " smole " whenever he wanted
any. One day I took out my sketch-book and told him
to hold still while I drew him. He replied by covering
his countenance in his burnus, and peeping out with one
eye like a little girl. Then Mohamet went at him in
Arabic, and ordered him not to be a fool. Whereupon
Ali coyly peered around the corner of the cloak, and
burst into an irrepressible titter, and then covered himself all over as if he were afraid of ghosts. More grave,
gruff reproof from Mohamet, and all of Master Ali's
beauteous mug now beamed forth like a full moon on
me. I worked for a few seconds at the sketch, when
Ali, apparently dying of oppressive modesty, burst into
a snigger and concealed his face in his hands. " Confound the fool ! " I said, " why can't he keep still ? "
With an air of singular gravity Mohamet replied, " He
believit you thinkit him pretty." But finding that his
coquetry was lost, Master Ali really kept quiet until
I had his likeness. This picture caused great wonder
among the pilgrims, and afterwards, whenever I appeared,
there would be shouts for " *Libro !* " and " *El kitab !* "
or " the book," which was returned to me with the
remark, " Bono ! *trés* buono ! "

None of the pilgrims, however, appeared to fancy having their portraits taken. because the Prophet had pro-

hibited that sort of thing. But Mohamet, as a man who affected superior enlightenment, and had "seen pictures," held himself quite above such bigotry, and informed me that he had been photographed with his family. "But," I remonstrated, "is it not a sin according to your religion to have pictures?" "No," replied Mohamet; "to *have-it* de pittura no wrong—only wrongs to *make-it* de painture." "Yet if you pay a man to make a picture, you certainly sin." To which he solemnly replied, "Man no make-it photograph—*Sun* mak 'um photograph—man only helpy littee."

I took Mohamet's portrait; but unfortunately he was civilised, and consequently critical. Therefore, when he had examined my sketch, he handed it back with the brief remark, "Him much bad—*velly* bad!" Everybody else called it a good likeness, but Mohamet wasn't going to sink his character for culture, and identify himself with the ignorant and admiring pilgrims in that way. He knew too much entirely to regard a few black marks with a lead-pencil as a work of art. So he graciously intimated that if I would "paintee reddy blue" out of my water-colour box, it might turn out a performance of merit worthy his admiration—otherwise, not.

I once heard a lady in America speak in raptures of her son's skill as an artist. "He made a picture of an old fellow with nothing but a lead-pencil and a piece of paper—that was all he had; and he did it so natural, anybody could see at a glance what it was meant for!" Mohamet's æsthetic culture was exactly on this plan.

The materials formed, according to his estimate, the most important part of the real value of a picture. During the childlike Middle Ages, people used to stipulate that there should be so many crowns' worth of ultra-marine, so much gold, and so much vermilion, used on their portraits; and I am confident that this is done at the present day by the Greek artists in Cairo. It is a sensible system, and has many advantages; not the least being this, that the purchaser sees his way clear to getting the full worth of his money.

CHAPTER II.

SOME of the seven plagues of Egypt inflicted of old are
played out, but their places have been filled with good,
steady, permanent, new ones, warranted to wash and to
wear, of the fast-colour, never-run-away kind. Moreover,
the modern differ from the old in this, that under the
Mosaic dispensation the plagues only afflicted the natives, while the new kind consist principally of the
natives themselves, and are applied solely to distressing
foreigners. It is a curious fact, illustrating these
changes, that in old times the natives of Egypt, in the
form of mummies, were considered soothing and cura-
tive by apothecaries in all complaints, while the same
article in the raw or live state at the present day is too
often the most irritating object on the face of the earth.

The eighth plague of Egypt is the custom-house at
Alexandria—in which I include all the customary inflictions on those who land, and the cusses who inflict them.
No sooner had our steamer anchored off the town than
it was surrounded by boats, and boarded, crowded, and
crammed, by swarms of blackguards of every class and

colour, of twenty different nations, all yelling and roaring like so many devils. There was no order among them whatever, and many of the passengers were really terrified by the ferocity of the creatures, which within five minutes manifested itself by two sharp fights.

These interesting beings were agents for boats, for hotels, or else they were porters, beggars, or touters for jobs. They had a *reis* or superintendent, whose business it was to keep them in order, and this he performed by sitting in an elevated position, and yelling more madly and uselessly than the rest. I am strictly opposed on principle to corporal punishment, but if any corporal would have given that *reis* a good full-weight battering, he should have seen the colour of my money, and tasted of my hospitality.

I asked a well-dressed man if there was no special agent for the Hotel d'Europe present. He replied that he was that very identical agent. I thought it a delightful piece of luck that I should have just happened to hit on the right man. So did he. Innocent that I was!—before I left the country I found out that any man in that party, among all those Greeks, Maltese, Neapolitani, Corfioti, Swindlini, and Liarini, would have sworn for a sixpence that he was the only agent for any hotel on the face of the earth. But once engaged, Humbug No. I. went to work, and, after more howling, our luggage was put into a boat, and with it we went to the custom-house.

Now, I had only four francs in silver in my pocket,

and the agent advised me, if I would save myself a long
and wearisome search, to pay the douaniers. It was
the old story—the same in Germany and England—
though nowhere so atrociously or rapaciously conducted
as in New York. Therefore, when an apparent custom-house official—who was nothing of the sort—came
bustling up, speaking as one having authority, and
telling me to get out my keys and point out my trunks,
and especially when he applied for his baksheesh, I supposed that all was right, and gave him three out of my
four francs. When lo! presto! up started a little dark,
old, owly, goblin, night-ghoul of a creature—a thing with
bright eyes, and a white turban, and a cold, clawy little
hand; and Humbug No. II. informed me that *this* was
the searcher, and warmly recommended me to give *him*
something also, or else he might make it warm for me.
And he *did.* I don't believe that hideous little owl was
a man at all. I believe he was a mummy galvanised.
He never spoke, but wherever I moved, the whole of his
bony, little, cold, claw burrowed into the palm of *my*
hand, and his bright eyes met mine. I gave him my
franc, but he treated it as *nichts;* and as I had no more
to give, he went through two of my trunks in style. I
have been searched on the Russian frontier, in the good
old times of '47, but it was crumbs to this! At last
he let me go. I didn't mind the searching much; it
was his horrible silence, his devilish eye, and his hideous
little, cold claw revolving continually before my eyes
and resting in my hand.

c

In company with an American gentleman long resident in Egypt, we got into a carriage, and, with Humbug No. I. on the box, drove to the hotel. But we had more experiences to endure before we got clear of the custom-house. There is another *reis* there, whose duty it is to speak English, and aid travellers, and keep off official beggars. This one, Humbug No. III., speaks English, but only to beg; and he now appeared leading the army of custom-house subs, and, with tremendous pertinacity, insisted on, I think it was, half a dollar. Him my American friend addressed in a style of blowing-up which was a caution to ears as yet unaccustomed to the oriental way of doing things, and we drove off in a tempest of howls.

Scarcely clear of the custom-house, an Egyptian of the lower class, a fellow with a ready confident smile and incredible assurance, hailed our coachman to stop, and jumping up on the step, seized my friend's hand and shook it warmly. Supposing him to be some old but forgotten acquaintance, the Colonel asked him in Arabic how he did. To which Humbug No. IV. replied in a gushing strain, ending with a request for *baksheesh.* But on looking intently at him, the Colonel burst out, "Why, I never saw the scoundrel before in my life. I wish I had my cane!" But No. IV. in an instant made himself as scarce as hen's teeth, and with a joyous yell at having fooled the Howaga and got off safely, effected his *feliciter evasit* (or cut-his-lucky) up the nearest lane. I must confess that my first thirty minutes' experience of Egypt was not in favour of the natives.

Other sharpers prey upon the green stranger new to the country, but No. IV. made it his " biz " to fall upon the old hands. He had observed at the custom-house who spoke Arabic, and rushing off by a short cut round the corner, intercepted carriages and resolutely went in. Most men returning to a strange country love to be greeted by humble friends who remember them; they don't object to speak the language before their new-come companions. All this opens the heart and purse-strings. No. IV. had observed all this, and traded upon it. He had studied the human heart. It was ingenious, very, but it set me to thinking. Verily, I had come into a country where the darkies are up to sharp practice.

CHAPTER III.

THE Hotel d'Europe in Iskenderīyeh, called by
Europeans Alexandria, seemed, when we entered it, to
keep itself. There were a few beings who looked like
cooks straying about. They answered my questions in
that civillanous manner which seems to say, " Well, you
may ask this once ; but, mind, let it be the *last* time !"
Finally, somebody—I rather think it was a boarder—
remembered to have seen a room somewhere upstairs,
and suggested our trying for it. We went there. It
was guarded by a mahogany-coloured young man, with
large eyes, coming out of a long shirt which went down
to his knees, below which a pair of bare legs terminated
in feet which sailed about in what looked like little
yellow Chinese junks, with the sharp-pointed bows rising
up in the air. On his head he wore a round red cap
wound about with a large white turban. The cap pro-
jected from the turban, and looked like a red egg in a
nest of cotton. There are birds which lay red eggs, and

steal the cotton for nests, from the plantations in Tennessee, so that my simile is a very good one.   In his ears
the dark young man wore shiny gold rings of antique
pattern, and when I spoke to him, he bowed and smote
his breast, and mouth, and forehead; which being inter-
preted means, "I gather the dirt from the ground—I
eat it before you—I put it on my head!"   This was at
any rate polite, to say the least, civil, and it looked
attentive.   This young man was the chambermaid, but
his real name was Ali.   There are only twenty names in
all Islam, and the principal one is Ali—pronounced
Awly or Owly.   Most of the chambermaids are called
Owlies—from a way they have of mousing about in the
dark holes and corners of the corridors.   They smoke
cigarettes while making up the beds, and say their
prayers in your bedroom,—probably for you, conjecturing that you may have forgotten it.   But they make
the rooms up admirably.

I asked the dark young man for water and for *l'eau* and
l'acqua, and to each he shook his head non-understand-
ingly.   Then I ventured to tap my exceedingly small
barrel of Arabic, and drew forth "'*Gib li moya!*"
"Bring me water."   To my amazement and awe, he not
only understood me, but replied, "*Taridó suchna?*"   "Do
you want it hot?"—and I understood him.

Egypt is inhabited by opium-eaters and musk-eaters,
—as they pronounce the word in New Jersey; and the
white nets gathered around the beds suddenly reminded us of this vivid insect, to which we had been so

long strange. The musquito is a bonny bird, who sings
as he flies; unfortunately he always takes his "ṭ"
with his singing,—as they do in some musical circles in
Berlin, and with kettle-drumming in England. Like a
satirical poet, he stings as he sings, and then prints his
lyrics on living vellum.

The Egyptian musquito, or *Namus*, is a poor drivel-
ling creature, not to be mentioned with his cousin the
American article. His bite is annoying, but if you
absolutely refuse to touch it, rub it, or notice it, it slinks
away without further pain—like a vulgar fellow's insult.
As for intelligence, they are far behind the Yankee insect. The reader has doubtless heard of the two Irish-
men who, when abed in New York, were so much
annoyed by musquitoes that they covered their heads
with the sheets. After a while one peeped out, and
beheld a firefly, which had just entered the room, roam-
ing about. "Ye may as well give it up, Phelim," he
cried; "here's wan av' thim sakin' yees wid a lantern!" It is needless to say that it would never occur
to an Egyptian musquito to employ fireflies as *saises* or
torch-bearers. They are mean as vocalists; and when
you catch them under the covering, they weep like
frightened little babes. I have heard American musquitoes thus entrapped absolutely scream, shriek, and swear
audibly, so that the neighbours could hear them. This
is a positive fact!

We had a good dinner at the *table d'hôte*, and I
found a dear old friend in the *okras* stewed with

NO CROWS IN ALEXANDRIA.

chicken. In Egypt the okra is called *bamié*. In the
bazaars they sell little green okras half an inch long,
dried, in strings. For a long time I believed they were
beads of faded *verde antiques*, and thought of buying
some as presents for ladies in England. Now that I
am here, I am sorry I did not; it might have induced
them to import the vegetable, and perhaps get as far as
gumbo-soup. For dessert we had the commoner berries
of the country, such as mandarin oranges, bananas, fresh
dates, and figs. The fact that these were really natives
impressed me wonderfully; and I could not help silently
naming them Hassan, Abder Raman, Muley, Giid, and
Said, as their yellow faces turned pleasantly towards me
under the gaslight.

While in this city,— or on it,—I may as well mention a
very curious fact, for which I was subsequently indebted
to a highly-cultivated well-educated Mahometan friend,
a gentleman of rank. *No crow ever enters Alexandria*,
the reason being, that a certain magician in the olden
time once made a talisman with this object, and buried
it somewhere in 'Skenderíyeh. Should it ever be discovered and disturbed, the spell will be broken, and the
birds will enter, and the radicals of Alexandria will have
the inexpressible grief of often seeing one crow over
another—as of old in England during the days of
Wilkes. (By the way, I thought of this yestere'en, when
I was in the drawing-room of the house which Wilkes
once had for his shell.)

This is a very wonderful story about the crows, but I

have no doubt whatever of its truth, especially since I remember that I once read an old book which stated that Virgil the poet once made a talisman which kept flies and things out of Naples, until some scallawag or *raurien* broke it.   And to confirm this again, my friend tells me that there are no end of people in Egypt who have charms which prevent flies, fleas, spiders, and all such reptiles, from so much as lighting on their persons—yea, which cause them to drop dead when they touch them.   It is a great pity that all the Arabs have not obtained them.   But I must declare that I have not as yet observed that the people here possess many charms.

I wished to get out of Alexandria and into Cairo as soon as possible,—a course to which Humbug No. L— who was, by the way, only a roving drag of a man, or dragoman, was utterly opposed.   He represented forcibly, firmly, and ably the disgrace which I would incur by not remaining a long time in Alexandria and exploring its antiquities under his guidance.   I replied by asking him at what time the train left for Cairo. He seemed inclined to swear there was no railroad between the cities, but contented himself with declaring it did not leave till evening.   I called a waiter, who said that a train left in half-an-hour.   I told No. L to get my luggage within that time to the station.

At the station, the ticket-taker could not of course make change in my favour.   I think that No. I. drove a bargain with him, and beat him down.   After I had got

my first-class tickets, I found there were three first-class
cars or carriages,—one great man monopolising one,
two great men another, a third great man the third. I
could not enter any of these. "The second class were,
however, very comfortable." Then I stood fifteen
minutes in the hot sunshine. I summoned the superintendent. He came, and assumed grand airs and irritation. "If I had first-class tickets, I must *wait* till
another carriage could be brought—these were taken."
Then I gave him my mind, and laid it on strongly. I
was startled at my success; he backed ours at once,
and humiliated. I had heard that this was the way to
do it in Egypt—and it *did*. Humbly he opened one of
the reserved carriages and let us in.

I spoke of the dragoman's bargaining or "bantering"
with the clerk for the railway tickets. They do such
things in some places. When I was in Rome, many
years ago, a friend of mine beat a post-office clerk
down two-and-sixpence on one letter. That same
winter, after I left, a gentleman asked at the post if
there were any letters for him. There was one. "How
much for it?" "One *scudo*" (five francs). "That's too
much," said the gentleman; "I'll give half a *scudo*."
"Won't you make it seven *paoli?*" asked the clerk.
"No, I won't." "Well, then, you may have it at
your own price. I've read it, and it's nothing but a
love-letter."

If I have already once or twice dwelt on such little
weaknesses and petty impositions as half amused, half

vexed me on entering and leaving Alexandria, you
need not fear, reader, that I shall make my capital of
them. It is an easy way to make a book, goodness knows,
to jeer and sneer and everlastingly fillip and quiz and
be-little everything, particularly in the East. But there
are some great and good things in Egypt—the wondrous
land struggling upwards to light—and I trust that ere
we part we shall look at them.

The journey from Alexandria to Cairo is very agreeable the first time. It is wonderfully startling to see
camels in long strings, and palm-trees, and those curious mud-swallow nests of little villages. It is also
interesting too, in the larger towns, to trace as distinctly
as possible the lines of massive antique Egyptian temples even in mud huts, while the wretchedest mosques
and most beggarly Santon-tombs, whether made of the
soil on which they stand or stone, are in every touch
and turn Saracenic. Long before the first old Egyptian
temple was built—at a date probably a few thousand
years anterior to that which was once assigned to the
creation—the humble Egyptian *fellah* intuitively formed
his mud hut in these long horizontal lines, with the
out-curving eaves, and with the dark door cut into the
side, like that of a tomb. Mere need and the material
instinctively suggested these forms; and when the massive temples of after-days were erected, they imitated
the cave within and the mud hut without.

The countenance of the ancient Egyptians is preserved
at the present day in thousands of living faces, and

sometimes the type reappears with marvellous fidelity. Once, during the day, a young girl of very fair complexion walked by the train at a station, crying, "Moya!" "Water!" and no one who had seen her could have doubted that her ancestors had seen King Pharaoh. In the museum at Boulac there are two statues of the earliest period of Egyptian art, and yet they are superior to anything which that art ever produced, excepting, perhaps, the admirable Shekh-el-Beled. They represent a king and queen, who were also brother and sister, *soror et conjux;* and there is a fierce energy, a compound of animalism, strong will, and practical common sense, visible in the expression of both, but particularly in the king, which reveals, as if you had known him all your life, what manner of man he was. Now, I have seen no end of natives, who, in all but the royal *grit* and energy, looked precisely like this pair. As for the Shekh-el-Beled, the village chief, a wooden statue in the same museum, he has more than the features of many a modern Egyptian—he has the indescribable air and style of one. The Cophts claim to be the pure descendants of the old stock; but there is some unaccountable mystery in the matter. I saw a great deal of the Cophts while in Egypt, and studied them closely, but their long comely faces and straight noses are much more Hindu or Indo-European than Egyptian. Dr Morton of Philadelphia, whom I knew very well, thought, from an almost exhaustive study of Egyptian skulls, that the *fellahs* or peasants

of Egypt were more entitled than the Cophts to be considered the original article ; and since one Copht on an
average is worth half-a-dozen ordinary Egyptians, and
is much better looking, I should think they would be
delighted to be proved of another stock, even at the
expense of not being autochthonal or aboriginal, or, as
my friend Major ——, of St Louis, always *would* call it
—abregoynal. A recent writer on Egypt, while declaring that the Cophts resemble the ancient inhabitants of
the country, further illustrates the matter by saying
that the slightly aquiline nose and long eye of the
Cophts are the same as those in the profiles of the
tombs, and " also like the earliest Byzantine pictures."
But the faces of the Byzantine pictures are strangely
unlike the old Egyptian.

The two great men who filled our carriage were a
couple of Levantine railroad subs. They did not like
my intrusion, so did not speak to me, but talked Italian
to each other, and with a great deal of the coloured
clement which came to the windows to worship them.
Sometimes the yellow pine or snuff-and-butter worshippers could not manage Italian. Then they spoke Arabic.
I subsequently observed that in Egypt, Jews, if they
can, pass themselves for Greeks, Greeks for Italians,
and Italians for French. The French all pass themselves
for Parisian. A hotelkeeper in Heidelberg once told
me that, of ten thousand and odd Frenchmen who had,
during forty years, registered their names on his books,
all without exception came from Paris. Should this

meet the eye of any American who signs himself from
New York, on the strength of having staid there over-
night on his way to Paris, I hope he will lay the hint
to heart. The last number of the *Anglo-American* contains the names of half-a-dozen as veritable Jerseymen
as every drank apple-jack, and they had all converted
themselves to New Yorkers, under a mistaken idea that
this would civilise them. It is wiser and more stylish
to follow the example of Epaminondas Buggs of Kansas.
Buggs had four hundred dollars' worth of wilderness,
and one day he found that three Indian families and a
Dutch pedlar had camped on it for the night. He
christened the camp Buggsberg, and when on a foreign
climb, he signs from that place. It is very effec-
tive in Germany, which is the country that Buggs
most affects. You, my American readers, all own land.
If not, you may as well lay this book down ; for I write
for no man who does not put on a clean shirt at least
once a week, and own a thousand acres of North Caro-
lina land, or its equivalent, let us say, in talent, or
beauty, or cheek, or something. Therefore, act like
Buggs.

I saw several scarecrows in the fields, and they were
doubly interesting because clad in oriental costume.
One of the better class wore not only the long blue *diri*
of the *fellahs*, but also a red tarbush and turban. He
looked as if he had been to Mecca—perhaps he had. I
afterwards saw in Cairo a white donkey which had been
to Mecca. A beautiful young Frenchwoman was riding

it. The tail of the donkey and the head of the lady had both been dyed of a golden yellow—the donkey with henna—and they matched miraculously. Both had Kohl-black eyes. Speaking of scarecrows, I may as well mention that nowhere in the world are they so well made as in America, owing to the superior "mind" of the birds of that country. A Yankee once devoted six weeks to making a scarecrow, and finally succeeded in producing the most unearthly horror ever beheld. It scared all the crows in that part of the country white, and they availed themselves of the change to pass themselves off for pigeons, and lead virtuous lives ever after, while one very wicked old crow, in a penitent mood, brought back all the corn which he had stolen for three years past. This is positively a fact! They require very active moral medicine for crows in New England, because the birds are so intelligent. Miss W——, of Boston, tells me that, having put up a mere ordinary scarecrow in their field, they found, some time after, a bird's nest in either pocket. I was glad to see the Egyptian scarecrows, because they indicate a progressive spirit in religious matters, and the beginning of higher art. It is well known that Mahomet forbade his followers to imitate the human form, either in drawing or sculpture. Scarecrows are an infringement on the latter (as Mr ——'s statues abundantly prove). At the day of judgment, Allah will request their constructors to finish the job by putting life into them. As they cannot, they will "catch it." It is a lucky thing for Mr

——, of the Royal Academy, that nothing of the kind is expected from *him*—not even by the public.

They are more orthodox in Upper Egypt—or were, until Mr R. W. Emerson went there: I do not know how it has been since. Instead of sticking the ragged suits on a pole, they put a boy into them. Then they construct of earth and coarse wickerwork a small pile six feet high, and put the boy on it with a large whip and instructions to crack. When he sees a crow he cracks accordingly. As it always takes two people in this country to come to a conclusion on anything, the cracker generally has a younger assistant seated by him, who acts as secretary and consulting attorney. On a still morning, the reports from this committee on crows may be heard a mile.

At Cairo, there was the same insane riot and rowdy revelry of screeching impudent cullud passons rushing madly about, their blue-and-white shirt-tails waving in the wind, all roaring and grabbing at once. A more aggravating set of wretches than the common city natives of this country does not, cannot, never did exist. The tenderest-hearted missionary would like to kill a few occasionally per diem. Moses was the meekest man on the face of the earth, and yet he slew an Egyptian one day in an easy off-hand way, and the Bible says nothing against it. I used to be puzzled at this till I came to Egypt, but within twenty-four hours I understood it.

I wanted to go to Shepheard's Hotel, and a sensible, civil, taciturn little German made his appearance. He was the *bonâ fide* agent for that excellent hotel, and, under his care, we got there with less annoyance and at less expense than I supposed possible. It is perilous to say a word for or against a hotel. Dobbs abuses the " Spread Eagle" as he found it, and lo ! in six weeks, a new head-waiter or cook or proprietor comes in, and makes everything rosy for the next " special." Bobbs praises the " Victoria," and its head forthwith gets a call to a first-class mission in the best hotel in Florence, or is, perhaps, made a plenipo at the " Magnifique" in Paris, and the " Victoria " goes down. *Nil stabile.*

Men speak of the fair as things went with them there. I was three months at Shepheard's, and never more comfortable in any hotel in my life. This was due 'to Herr Zech, and especially to a glorious and jolly Herr Gross, who has the most extraordinary and inexplicable mania for making everybody comfortable of any Herr Wirth that ever existed. Other landlords do this with a special object, but I am satisfied that with Gross it is a mental affliction—the poor man can't help it. I believe it is due to their names. *Gross* in German means " great," and *Zech*, a " spree." " *Fuimus semel in una Zecha*," says the monk in the *Epistolæ Virorum Obscurorum.* A Zecher is a boon companion.

> " In ganz Europia, Ihr Herren Zecher !
> Ist solch' ein Wirth nicht mehr."

The Shepheard of Cairo has very little in common with the Shepherd of the Pickwick Club. A century ago it was a harem, and then it became a hotel—passing, like most elderly " houses," as Germans call jolly fellows, from the service of Venus in youth to that of Bacchus in a hearty old age. It is large and cool and comfortable, and it surrounds one beautiful garden, while it is surrounded by two or three more'; just like Roberto, my dear lady reader, who, while embracing one of the roses in the ballet, is himself embraced by others. In those gardens I did not discover a single English out-of-door plant. . There are bananas and mimosas, Indian figs, cactuses, and, behind the house, a great grove of date-palm trees. It always gave me a high-toned conservatory feeling to walk in those gardens among such genteel vegetables—a sort of Chatsworthy sensation.

One day Herr Vasel pointed out to Mr Emerson in this garden a banyan-tree. No one whose mind is imbued with poetry and philosophy can behold this legendary tree unmoved. I did not; for I immediately jumped up and picked a leaf, which I gave to the Sage of Concord. At dinner our fruit was always served on banyan leaves. With a banyan leaf, five orange-wood toothpicks, and an olive, you can construct a startling imitation of the Egyptian locust.

This is interesting to Darwinians, since, like the

mantis, or walking-leaf, it indicates the miraculous
affinity between vegetable and animal life.

I have said that on one side of the hotel is a great
grove of date-palms. At present it belongs to a lady
relative of the Viceroy. In it is a *sakhyia* or water-wheel,
turned by oxen or donkeys—a strange creaking affair,
everlastingly groaning and wheezing in a weird semi-
human manner. The earthenware pots with which it
is fringed have, at a little distance, an unearthly resemblance to human heads in red tarbushes. Once I
really started at seeing one of them grinning at me in
the elfin light of sunset. There is a strange version of
an old Greek legend connected with these *sakhyias*,
which I give as it was told to me by my friend the Bey—
the same gentleman who communicated about the crows
in Alexandria and the talisman.

" You have heard of Alexander the Great, or Iskander.
According to Greek history, he was the son of Philippus,
but according to the Arabs, it was not *that* Alexander
who was called the Great, but one who sprung from the
race of Hamya or the Hamaritic. He was not only a
conqueror, but also a prophet. He was called Iskander
zul Karnein, or the conqueror of the two horns. These
two horns really mean the East and the West, or all—
signifying that he should subdue all the world. But
the common people understood it that he had two real
horns on his head.

" Now, though his horns signified universal dominion,
Iskander was ashamed of them ; and as they were small

affairs, he hid them under his hair. But he could not
hide them from his barber, so he confided the knowledge
to that person as a secret of life and death. Of course
the barber was bursting and perishing to tell it to somebody ; but he had the sense to know that *secret à trois,
secret de nul,* and that if three people knew it, it would
not be long before he would be interviewed by the hang-
man. Still, as he was absolutely dying of the terrible
knowledge, something had to be done. So one night he
stole cautiously out on the Nile, and whispered to the
pots of a *sakhyia,* ' *Iskander zul karnein !* '—' Alexander
has horns.' And from that day every *sakhyia* repeats in
its long groaning, heaving, wheezing tones, *Is—kan—
der—zul—kar—nein !* " This is a positive fact.

It is needless to tell you that this is only the old
story of King Midas with his ass's ears, and the barber
and the reeds. But it has wonderfully improved in the
Arab version. There is an indescribable delicacy of
drollery in the idea of a great man—one of those to
whom history allows the capital G—being ashamed of
that which gives him infinite power—the two horns of
illimitable empire—hiding them under his hair, and
putting poor Snip on his life not to mention it. In
Saracenic legends, as in Saracenic architecture, this crush-
ing and fusing of older forms and ideas together into
something new is common enough. But it always results in something coherent and fair.

If one thinks deeply enough *into* it, he will find, however, that Midas had no more reason to be ashamed of

his ears than Iskander of his horns.   Apollo, who, like
most great musical emperors, was a tyrannical snob,
had a trial of skill with Marsyas, and appointed Midas
as umpire.   Midas, who didn't *see* the music of the
future, ump'ed in favour of the old-fashioned school, as
he had a perfect right to do if he preferred it, or as he
had no right to do otherwise if he believed what he said.
Whereupon Apollo, like a no-gentleman, yelped at the
decision which he had agreed to abide by, pitifully cried
that he didn't believe in arbitration, because it wasn't
given in his favour, and made a donkey of the man who
had already shown himself a Don Quixote in defending
his guest.   If the world had been made up of men as
honest as himself, Midas should have shown his ears in
triumph as proofs of honesty and courage.

My dear reader, when you have agreed to abide by a
decision, not only do so honestly, like a man, but without grumbling, for it is as dishonest to grumble as to
demur.   And by the same rule, my dear fellow, whenever
a good friend tells you a plain truth, meaning it kindly,
grin and bear it.   It is only when he means it meanly
that you have a right to complain.

CHAPTER IV.

THE first thing that astonishes the stranger in Egypt, especially if he comes from England, is the weather. He may have read and heard about it a thousand times, you know, but then a fellow can't always be remembering what he has read; so he comes down in the morning, and finds such awful jolly sunshine and such stunning zephyrs, that he cannot help remarking, "I say, *what a fine day!*" But when it is the same the next day and the next, he begins to be haunted with a pleasant puzzled feeling, as if there were something wrong on the right side of the reckoning, or *vice versa*, as Jones said when his landlady, for his two-dollars-a-week board, began to give him roast-turkey stuffed with oysters, terrapins, and mince-pie every day. After a week he ceases to say anything about fine weather, and about the same time he observes that only the newly arrived do so.

As for the Egyptian natives, they, not having any changes in the weather to talk about when they meet,

have substituted compliments, and what the Chinese
call handsome talkee. I suggested this one day to
two friends, one a Syrian, the other an Egyptian. They
cordially agreed to the theory, and just to show me
how they could do it, without the least trouble in the
world, went at one another for half-an-hour without
stopping. How the consonants flew! *Salâm ailekum!
Allah yikün mai'ak! Mai' salâmé! Allah yusellimak!
Neharak said! Mubarak!* I am not interested in the
sale of the article, but if the reader expects to go much
among the natives, I advise him to get himself a good
stout *Salâm ailekum* (or "Peace be with you") for daily
wear, three or four *Saba'hak bil-ch'er's* (or "Good morn-
ings"), one *Lélatak mubaraka* ("Thy night be blest"), and
a first-rate warranted to wear *Ezzayak?* (or "How do you
do?"). It is not difficult to count in Arabic—the average
of young ladies and commercial travellers generally master
all the mystery in half-an-hour; and if one adds to this
the words *Kam dee?*—"How much (is) that?" and
Filoos kétir—"Too much money"—he will be as fully
qualified to bargain in the bazaars, and much more likely
to get bargains, than if he had a drag o' a man, or an
interpreter, or interrupter, of any kind, at his elbow,
working for a commission.

The Englishman in Egypt need not fear poverty,
since, as he invariably brings an umbrella with him, he
always has something laid by for a rainy day. If there
is an astonished creature at an unexpected long holiday
in the world, it must be that umbrella when it has been

a week in Cairo. Mine was amazed—that I know.
Passing from Ireland to Scotland and the English Lakes
in 1872, I had from July to the end of November become
so accustomed to rain that I hardly knew a fine day
when I saw it, and did not believe in it when I did. As
for Scotland, an occasional gleam of the sun·in that
picturesque country produced on my eyes and mind the
sensation of a Drummond light or colophonium or fireworks in a theatre—a feeling of amazement mingled
with the hope that they wouldn't do it again.

I do not deny that we had half-a-dozen little dribbling
showers in Cairo while I was there, but "they say"
that three days of English heavy wet would bring half
the town down.   At long intervals there falls—not
every year, however—a tolerable rain, and then the un-
paved streets of the Egyptian quarters become incredible
quagmires, and the most reckless and devoted servants
have to be sent marketing or shopping on donkeys,
while walking is about as easy as it is for flies to
dance on birdlime.

One day I was with an English friend prowling about
on the outskirts of the desert, when a few drops fell.
There was a trumpery or temporary Arab hut at hand, in
which we took refuge, invited by the Arab, his wife, and
child. What occurred I have set down as the germ of a
musical entertainment, which any person who has access
to a tamborine, the head of a barrel, or a one-stringed
banjo, can amply endow with a real Egyptian accompaniment.

OPERETTA.—"THE STRANGER IN EGYPT."

SCENE.—*The Desert.—Arab hut.—A rain of fifty or sixty drops. Enter strangers with guns.*

Arab (basso). Baksheesh, ya Howaga!
Stranger (tenor). Let us sit down in the hut!
Arab. Come in! Baksheesh!

Wife (soprano). Baksheesh, ya Howaga! Bak—sheeeee—sh!
Child (treble). Bat—sees', howada!
Stranger (recitative). Confound you! Can't you wait till I get out of the house?
Arab (fortissimo). Baksheesh!
Wife (diminuendo). Baksheesh!
Child (diminuendo). Bat'sees!
Tutti coro tremendo crescendo. BAKSHEESH!

[*Strangers give the Arab money.*

Arab. Baksheesh for Madama!
Wife. Baksheesh for Madama!
Child. Bat'sees for 'dam-a!
Coro. BAK—SHEESH!   [*Exeunt Strangers.*

I never in my life heard anything which, in the regularity of chime, rhythm, or repetition, approached a musical "entertainment" so closely as this did—only that it didn't entertain us. While we sat on the mat, we heard but that one word "Baksheesh!" accurately intoned by the whole family. It may just possibly interest somebody to know that *baksheesh*, meaning "a present," has for its root the word *bacht* or *bak*, which means luck or fortune, and that this word *bak* is used by English Gipsies, just as it is by Egyptians, to beg with, as I well know, since, at the very last horse-race

which I attended, old Dame Chockamengro said to me,
"Mi rya, del mandy a shekóri for bák!"—"My master,
give me a sixpence for luck." And I gave it with good-
will, as I generally do to a Gipsy, and never did cheerfully
to an Egyptian. Give a Gipsy a sixpence, and he will
thank you politely, investing it immediately in a quart,
and, if you look thirsty, it is ten to one but he will be-
nevolently · offer you a pull at the pewter. Give an
Egyptian the same, and instead of thanking or drinking,
he will salt it down, and promptly beg for more.

Before Shepheard's Hotel there is a stone platform
and steps, six feet above the level of the street, and before this natives are all day long exhibiting something,
peddling, begging, and offering their services. On the
opposite side of the way, donkey-boys with their donkeys
yell and squabble till nightfall, and hack-carriages wait
their call in a line along the street. When a stranger calls
from the hotel step to a particular boy to bring a certain
donkey, the entire multitude of blackguards make a dead
rush at him, howling, screaming, and thrusting themselves between him and the one which he wants. After
he is mounted on a donkey, the other drivers will continue in an idiotic-insane way to implore or command
him to dismount and take theirs, until he has departed.

You can seat yourself very comfortably on the step-
platform and watch all this. The objects offered for
sale are various. I have seen Nubian fans and spears,
sabres, colocynth apples, scorpions, cigars, shawls, pea-
nuts, scarabæi, pumpkin seeds, old coins, transparent

playing-cards, rosaries, sugar-plums, slippers, and singing-birds, all within a few minutes. The first party who came to me was a brown youth in a long blue shirt and grey tarbūsh. His ware was a small ornamented brass vase, with a very little hole in the top. He held it up to me, roaring "*Antico !*" I told him that I had no money small enough to go in it. He reiterated, "*Antico !*" I asked him what *antico* meant. He was very much puzzled, aud finally said it was what all him Howaga (foreign gentlemen) like.

And here I may pause to mention the fact that, not only in Egypt, but in Italy, the lower class, having heard many beautiful objects praised as *antico*, believe that it means beautiful or nice, and have no idea that it signifies old. Once near Naples, many years ago, a little boy came running to a friend of mine, Mr Mosely, of Richmond, Virginia, with a fresh cotton-pod, which he conjectured might be a curiosity to the stranger, and roaring, " Ecco, signore ! è molto antico "—" It is very ancient." And only a few days after, when seated on the very spot where I looked at the boy with the vase, I saw a young American lady choosing a carriage, and heard another youth scream to her, " Madama, take *dis* carriage ! dis one very *antico*." Now, as it was manifestly the newest carriage in the lot, it was evident that the youth had got the wrong word by the tail.

The boy with the brass vase, finding that I was in no urgent need of brazen ware, offered to let me have a donkey for five francs. I asked him how much for the

saddle and bridle? He explained that he did not propose to sell the entire animal for his natural life for
five francs, but to hire him for this sum per diem.
He further demonstrated that this price was necessary,
since "him donkey dinner costit one franc, she; breakfast, one franc—where my to get my money?" And I
replied gravely, "Little boy, get it from people who
are more ignorant than I."

The next object was also a boy—a very rascally boy,
with Gipsy eyes. His profession was snakes. He bore
a large cobra-capello in his hand, and looked like a
serpent himself. Our dear old friend Elsie Venner (by
the way, I have the book at this instant, wrapped up in
the skin of an immense rattlesnake, killed by a college
friend in Georgia) would have been enraptured with
him. I always did love that girl, and I am a bit of a
sapa-engro myself. So I had Snaix up, and took him
into the garden. He demonstrated to my satisfaction
that his emblems of eternity were harmless as old hens,
so I handled them. He produced a great number from
the bag, where he seemed to keep as many as might be
desired in a condensed or expansive state. He brought
out three large cobras, two horned vipers, and two asps.
The cobras are puss-like in their habits, and like pet-
ting. Having satisfied myself that they could not fang
anybody, I brought the snakes, anguine and human,
by special request, into the drawing-room of a friend,
where ladies examined them with interest. The exhi-
bitor having shown his pets affectionately, and kissed

them, then offered to eat one alive if we would pay him a rupee.   We declined and he insisted: had I not ordered him to be gone, I believe that he would have devoured one out of gratitude or on speculation.

I did quite a business with that snake boy, for I was interested in the study of his ware, and I was profitable to him.   One evening I gave him a piastre to show a friend of mine the Cleopatra asp. He bolted with the money — vanishing like an aspirate (as he was) — and didn't exhibit. After that I dealt no more at his shop.   He seemed to be very much amazed at this, and required a strong hint to retire. The last time I saw him was in a rush and jam in a crowd in the Muskee, when I was riding a donkey, and about as likely to stop as a cat with a tree ahead and ten dogs after her. A dozen darkies were yelling at me, " Es-say !—es-sa-ay—nass donkey, master—take donkey !" and among them the serpentarian cried, "Have some snakes to-day—very nice snakes to-day, Sah !" as if they had been crumpets or something edible.   Perhaps his habit of feeding on them alive influenced his manner of advertising them.   I mention the incident of his spoiling what was getting to be a good business for the sake of three farthings, and cheating one who had been kind to him, as characteristic of his race.   They are all childish and irrational in matters of morality, great or small. The shopman who has cheated you, and been detected and punished, really thinks that you will deal with him again as if nothing had happened, and greets

you with a familiar grin the next time, like an old
friend; for the fellow has literally no conception that there
is a man on the face of the earth who doesn't admire
cheating as a fine art, or would not do anything for
gain. Even the Levantine Christians in Cairo believe
that if they can begin the day by telling any kind of
a lie, and getting somebody to believe it, they will be
lucky till nightfall. By the way, people who are fond
of paradoxes delight in saying that these Levantine or
oriental Christians are the greatest scoundrels in the
country. It is not true. I have known several unexceptionably honest and gentlemanly men among Syrian
Christians from Damascus; and I am sure that the
much-abused Cophts are altogether superior to the
ordinary natives.

The next attraction on the verandah was Said the
juggler. I always had a fondness for jugglers. I saw
Robert Houdin in his heyday, and was taught thimble-
rig by Signor Blitz, who was the first to perform in
Europe, half a century ago, the great spinning-plate
trick; at least, the London *Telegraph* or some journal said
so only yesterday. So I looked at Said with interest.
His tricks were of the commonest kind of old-fashioned
hankypanky,—one, two, three, or no balls under cups,
ribbon-pulling and fire-blowing, with poor trembling
Bunny in a box. But he did them rather cleverly; and
as the rogue generally selected after dinner, when the
old gentlemen were comfortably fed and amiably winey,
for his grand *coup*, it is amazing how successful he was.

How the old boys would *haw-haw!* at the ingenious
pulling a cigar from a donkey-boy's nose (this was their
favourite performance); and how earnestly several of
them assured me that he was "a clever performer, sir;
by gad, sir, I never saw his equal!" By the way, I
am quite convinced that hankypanky men all the world
over have a peculiar expression in common, a family
likeness, and this is nowhere so perfect as in the East.
It is of course the droll caricature Mephistopheles—a
mixture of mystery and mirth, with a very perceptible
flavour of genuine rascality at bottom—but it cannot be
fully appreciated until one has seen many of the craft
in many lands. One thing I rather liked in Saïd, as in
other Egyptians who were in the juggler and jocular
vein. He did not, like his stupid hankypancake brethren of the West, perform a trick, and then grin at
his auditors for approbation, as is done by that type of
idiocy a he ballet-dancer when he has made a seventeen-
spin piroutte. No; Saïd always gave full credit to his
master the devil and all his imps, to whom, as we fully
understood, he had sold his soul in consideration of their
aid in his tricks. Therefore, before performing the appalling and thrilling feat of causing eggs to vanish in a
bag, he would cry to the prince of the powers of the air,
"*Afreet, hinna!*"—"Hither, O devil!" And when he had
made a coin vanish, as it were, on high, he would watch
its ideal flight into fairyland with a strange mysterious
smile, and a sudden grave glance and a turn of the ear,
as though he could truly say—

> " I see a hand you cannot see,
> Which beckons me away ;
> I hear a voice you cannot hear,
> Which says I must not stay."

There is a great deal of the Rommany or Gipsy element
among the jugglers of Europe, as there is indeed wherever
the "slangs" or exhibition affairs show themselves. The
word was *smánga* in India; the Gipsies made it into
slang, and applied it to all kinds of cant and theatrical
language. Hankypanky, the current "professional"
word for legerdemain, is also Rommany, *hanku bozu*
being its Hindu parent. *Apropos* of Gipsies and jugglers in Egypt, it came to pass one day that I rode over
with an English friend and my special donkey-driver,
Mohamet, to the great weekly fair or market of Boulac
to see some Gipsies. There, too, was a juggler, vastly
the master of Said in his art. He of Boulac had two
boys as assistants, and pretended to perform his spells
by studying in a volume of magic, which inspection with
a good glass enabled me to perceive was an old account-
book, coarsely daubed over on every page with figures of
what appeared to be red devils, yellow frying-pans, pie-
bald codfish, green extracts from Euclid, pink monkeys,
fireworks, poll-parrots, and other diabolical devices; a
very cursory examination of which convinced me that
this man's soul was unquestionably in the same perilous
condition as Said's. Having pretended by art-magic to
put the hasp of a large padlock through a boy's cheeks,
and having fastened it behind his head, the master implored the devil (after taking up a collection) to aid him

to undo it. But Sheitan refused his aid, and the boy
screamed that he was dying. In fact, after divers well-
acted agonies, he did die. The master declared it was a
great pity, but, since he was dead, he begged the spectators to contribute something to bury him. So he was
laid out and covered. This done, the master suddenly
recollected that there was in some out-of-the-way corner
of his book a powerful spell for raising the dead, but
it was unfortunately a very expensive one, and would
require a fresh collection. This came in very slowly.
It was like the "tuppence more an' hup goes the
donkey" in England. To prove that there was still life
and hope, the magician read to the stiff corpse from the
picture of the blue sheep an incantation which caused
the boy to speak. He was in hell, and his description
of it was much like that of Epistemon's in "Rabelais."
I regret to say that it was more immoral. It must be a
bad place to send a young boy to. The master turned
to the pig and two shoes; this charm enabled him to
raise one arm of the boy. It remained stiff, as did his
whole body, no matter in what curious form it was
twisted. At last a reference to the purple owl brought
him back with a start to life. I regret to say that he
did this with a most unseemly gesture, indicating, as I
feared, that his late visit to the lower regions had by
no means made him a better boy.

I saw other jugglers, one with a very saucy girl for
an assistant. None of them were remarkable as legerde-
maniacs; but all were amusing, from their amount of

acting and Punch-play. They have either more imagination and dramatic fancy than their brethren among
us, or else a very wide field of singular tradition. There
seems to be a great deal of Europe in the Middle Ages
among them; in fact, there is an immense amount of it
current everywhere in Egypt. *Tabarin* and *Le Sieur des
Accords*, and all kinds of merry, roguish, long-forgotten
voices of the gay French olden time, rang again in my
heart when I heard the mountebank of an older type
than Doctor Dulcamara harangue his audience. There
were minstrels, too, playing on the old *vielle* or fiddle,
which they hold exactly as one sees them held in illuminated manuscripts, not up to the chin, but with strings
outward, resting on the knee.

The first harp-playing ever heard in this world was
the twang of the bowstring of some primeval warrior of
the Miocene period; which accounts, by the way, for the
fondness which poets have for pulling the long bow, and
its affinity with the lyre. And even in the days of the
rose-red city, half as old as Time, they had got no further
than making a harp with one string, a sort of large hol-
low bow. You may see pictures of them in the tombs.
Through all changes that one-stringed harp has held its
own; and at the present day there are many men running about Egypt with them, twanging tunes all in one
note at small coffee-houses, and singing metrical romances
all about one man; the whole as old as the hills; just as
they did in Europe in the thirteenth century. If you
would know more about them, consult that Lane of

E

which it cannot be said there is no turning, since there are very few who go to Egypt who do not read his book, and turn its leaves industriously.

I saw one day, on the road near Boulac, an exhibition of a type so ancient, that it is possibly coeval with the one-stringed bow.   There were two or three itinerant musicians blowing and drumming, and about two hundred auditors, nearly all girls and women.   In the centre a young man was acting with another, a boy dressed as a girl.   The performance was immoral to a degree unknown, undreamed of anywhere in Europe for a thousand years or more in dramatic shows, and had it been only this, I should not have spoken of it.   But what was my amazement to recognise in the male actor the identical figure of the old Greek and Etruscan vases, with his fox-tail and Lampsacene symbol.   There could be no doubt of it ; the very attitudes, the whole expression, was of the antique Singer of Sin, that mysterious laughing type which is found in old graves, be they of primeval Italy or Central America.   Monsieur Champfleury may bewail the loss of the *Atellanæ*, or those old Greek farces which were perhaps never written out, and of which such trifling evidence remains on old pateræ and canthars ; and all classical scholars may wish that they could get a specimen of the real old Fescennine or Thespian play.   For my own part, I have no doubt that they both exist in these plays of the roadside. *Selámak !*

CHAPTER V.

THE great guns of genius and the high-cockalorums of
history, from Herodotus down to the authoress of " Egypt
Unveiled," have so thoroughly raked all the facts of this
be-travelled country, that he is indeed lucky among us
small tourists in a great hurry who can pick up on its
well-scorched sandy plains the least novelty or antique.
It is, therefore, with great modesty that I offer my
only original observation, which is this—that the voices
of the feathered creation in Egypt are, on an average,
about twice as loud as those of the same animals in
other parts of the world. More than this, their sleep-
lessness is in proportion to their strength of voice, and
they are in voice, and manifest it, as long as they wake.
In this land the bird of dawning singeth all night long,
and keeps up Christmas solid all the year round. As
for the Egyptian doves, they don't coo—they roar ; so
that Shakespeare (who, as his plays prove, lived a long

time in this country) knew perfectly well what he was about when he talked about roaring you gently as the sucking-dove. *Apropos,* there is a story current both in Germany and Scotland to the effect that the dove once owned a cow, and the crow offered to show her how to build a nest if she would give her the beast. But the crow cheated the poor dove, giving her very insufficient information; and, therefore, to this day the dove builds a bad nest, and sits alone in the greenwood, and murmurs " coo," or " kuh "—meaning cow." And, in their Arabic manner, the Egyptian peasants tell nearly the same story. By the way, this possession of a cow by a dove fully accounts for the origin of pigeon's milk.

Keeping company with the crow has never benefited the dove much, either pecuniarily or morally, if we may rely on what is intimated by the assertion that " Dere 's some tings niggas kin do better 'n wite folks; as de crow said when he gib de pigeon lessons in stealin corn." The pigeon is a great institution in Egypt. Mahomet had pet doves or pigeons, and this has specially endeared them to his people; but they were bred of old in the East, as now, as a bird sacred to fertility, and cherished long before the days of Mahomet. On the Nile there are literally pigeon-towns, where only the floor is inhabited by human beings. The upper portion, which is strangely constructed, is a mass of parapets and towers —the whole well whitewashed and abundantly supplied with projecting boughs for roosts; and here hundreds or

thousands of happy doves egg one another on to rivalry
in raising large families.

Should this book ever fall into the hands of any
gentleman going up the Nile with a gun and the usual
three hundred smuggled cartridges, let me indicate to
him the fact that the very poor *fellahs* do not "raise"
these pigeons for him to either shoot or steal; and, the
assurances of dragomans, sailors, and river-consuls to
the contrary, the birds are not fair game for everybody.
Great complaint has been made of late years that Englishmen and Americans doing the Nile also do great
mischief by killing pigeons, which they have no more
right to than to rob their neighbours' henroosts at home.
Most travellers in Egypt have a great deal of pity for
the wretched poverty of the peasants : if there is any
sincerity in this, let them show it by not pilfering their
pigeons. I have not much hope that this "wale" of
mine will make any impression on such hardened sinners
as old pigeon-shooting sports, most of whom would as soon
shoot at the *fellah* himself as anything, if it were only
"highly fashionable" and "the thing." But there may
be ladies on board the *dahabéah*, and to them I make
my appeal, as poor Lady Duff Gordon did to all Nile
travellers. It is a mean thing to distress the poor, and
all the glamour and license of sport and game, my dear
fellow, cannot make it otherwise. I say all this out of
sheer magnanimity ; for, so far as I am concerned, I
should have been delighted if not a pigeon could be seen
in Egypt. They overdo the thing entirely in giving them

to you twice a day: an Eastern dinner requires pigeons
as regularly as an Englishman's demands potatoes. He
who wrote *toujours perdrix* meant *toujours pigéons.*
Then you get so jolly tired of 'em you know—ha!—and
they say that fellows get salivated, or something of the
sort, who eat 'em all the time. I once read a story that
some learned Medicos in England offered a thousand
pounds to any man who would subsist one month on
nothing but pigeons. Only think! nothing but pigeons!
Numbers of brave young men had tried and failed and
died. There came to London a fine young French
savant and scholar, who was in love with an English
doctor's daughter. He did not succeed in getting rich,
he was starving to death, when the young lady suggested
he should try for the pigeon prize. And the *Græculus
esuriens*, who had a tremendous digestion, did try, and
won it. With the thousand pounds he soon became, if
not rich, at least *riche*, and married the lady who put
him up to pigeoning.

I came by my only great original observation on birds'
voices in Egypt—which I dare say some reviewer will
find among the Herodities, or in Bonifacius his *Historia
Ludicra*, or ―― ―― (fill this blank with Mr ――'s
last catalogue)—by being kept awake many a night by
the roaring of doves, caw-squawling of crows, crowing of
cocks, and the most incredible gobbling of turkeys that
it ever pleased the god of early rising to afflict a land
withal. Among these the cocks were specially uproar-
ious. Heaven only knows why they should be, for they

are not remarkable for size.   This reminds me that a certain gentleman at Shepheard's was lost in wonder one
morning at the small size of the eggs.   After he had conjectured all sorts of reasons, I suggested to him that it
might be owing to the diminutive dimensions of the
hens ; for in Egypt these birds are so remarkably small,
that their "hen-fruit," as it is elegantly termed in
America, is a great credit to them whenever you find it
larger than walnuts.   The Yankee turkey-hen who, fired
by a noble desire to show how she *could* spread herself,
attempted to sit on one hundred and fifty eggs at once,
might have succeeded had she tried the experiment in
Egypt.

Since I wrote that last line, I have recalled—which
means that the deuce put into my head—an incident
which I had better have forgotten, yet which for my
life I cannot suppress, it is so charmingly *apropos*.
There was a very nice young lady—not at all of
the fast kind, but a mild Anglo-Saxon gentle girl—
to whom an elderly gentleman or lady commented
one morning at breakfast on the small size of the
Egyptian eggs.   To which she replied, in the slow, undulating tones of high fashion—"Dear me! do you
think so?   Why I shouldn't be astonished if they were
only half as large.   I'm sure if *I* were a hen, in this
debilitating climate, I shouldn't have the energy to——"
(But no, reader, I cannot continue.   Strange, as Sterne
said of something else in the hen line, that I shrink
with intuitive shiver from writing or even boldly think-

ing what was calmly uttered in the most self-possessed
manner, and quite aloud, before twenty people. Talk
about vice being bold! Bah! There's more check and
courage in pure unconscious innocence than all the
brazen sinners in this world possess. *Selámak!*)

I have been told in Egypt that the hens of this country,
like the native women their mistresses, are much more
gifted at bearing than rearing offspring; and that the
feathered dames have no gift at all as regards hatching.
Nobody in Nile-land will brood long over anything.
The consequence is that all eggs are sent to a public
oven to be scientifically warmed into life. I never visited
these laying-in hospitals in Egypt, but I once saw one
in the United States. It went by steam, and was called
an Eccalobeion. The newspapers called it a Great Moral
Exhibition—I hope they will say the same of this book.
The man who ran the machine gave me a little pamphlet
on hatching eggs artificially. All that I can remember
of it is that the last line said it lifted the mind from
Nature up to Nature's God. I was a very small boy at the
time, but I do not think it had quite this effect on me;
for I remember thinking, when I saw several quarts of
young chickens running about, that, if it were only right,
I would like to steal one. I was reminded of this show
the other day when I looked into Mr Cremer's window
in Regent Street, and saw several scores of shilling chicks
going home for the Easter holidays with slates and
alphabets. I have heard also in the United States from
a native of New England, that he once filled a barrel

with a thousand eggs and set an old hen on the bung-hole. After the appointed time he knocked off the head of the barrel, and found himself knee-deep in what he called " dear little chickens." I was a mere boy at the time, or he had not dared to tell me this. He said, in conclusion, that that hen of his had also made all the eggs, and was indeed an undaunted layer. I told him that he was indeed an undaunted liar, and ran. I was running in a good cause; so the Lord prospered me, and I got over the fence about two rods in advance of him. He lived, it is true, to be an old man; but, as the Rommany Windsor Froggy told me the other day of a wretch who once cheated him at chuck-farthing, " he never came to no good."

In the olden time in the East, especially in Algiers, the Muslim used to compel prisoners and captives to sit on eggs, and if they broke one they got a terrible whipping. The yoke was anything but easy, or a trifle to them—poor fellows ! The Egyptians, I am told, did, and perhaps do, the same. This was considered a great indignity, but I suppose that is because it was on compulsion. It is aristocratic and nice if you like to do it. I once read in a highly respectable agricultural magazine of a highly respectable lady, moving in the first circles, who carried a highly respectable hen's egg about in her bosom until it hatched, and she was very proud of it, and sent it to an Ohio fair and got a prize. If that egg had got smashed, I suppose she would still have carried it about as an *amulet,* as I once saw the word

written on a bill of fare in Frankfort-on-the-Maine.   I
told Kätchen, who wrote the *Speisczettln*, that she had
spelled it wrong; but she got out her cook-book, and
there, under the head of *Eier*, was *Amulet* as sure as eggs.

The cocks or roosters of Egypt are what would be
called "gallus" or gallows birds in New York. Whatever the lower class in New York admires it calls *gallus*
or *sassy*. *Sassy* is not, however, a vulgar word. It is
oriental, and means bold and cheeky. They spell it
Sahási, and pronounce it exactly as young ladies of
colour do when they call one another "sassy niggers."
Cocks keep harems in Egypt, just as in America, from
which I infer that they are also of oriental origin, and
have very bad habits. They are birds of a very dissipated
turn, as is evident from the unquestionable fact that they
first invented the disreputable amusement of cock-fight-
ing, not even waiting till man put on the gaffs. Cocks
will drink anything strong, if you give it to them. A
French physician not long since tried the experiment of
feeding them on wine and brandy, which they devoured
freely, some of them polishing off a whole bottle of claret
each in a day. Those which were nurtured on brandy lived
only four months, but the claret cocks survived nearly
a year. The only perceptible result was that their combs
and wattles became of a deep carbuncly red, and grew
to be three or four times as large as is usual. This
corresponds, it is thought, to the effect produced upon
the red noses of certain other "old cocks" by the same
cause. The fact that brandy with bitters and sugar is

called cock-tails appears to strengthen my theory that
they have a great deal in common with human sinners.
The cock is the first thing stirring early in the barn-
yard, and a cock-tail the first thing stirred up in a
bar-room before breakfast. Somebody once sent to the
farmer's column of a rural newspaper in America a
statement that brandy mixed with the food of hens
would make them lay. To which the editor appended as
comment that he had no doubt of its truth, since he had
often seen it make old cocks "lay" in the gutter. This
was very ungrammatical, but it confirms what I have
said: great truths always meet with confirmations
from every quarter. Egyptian cocks are very bold. Mr
Vasel, whom I knew in Cairo, once had one which ate
scorpions. I have met in some old book of magic or
astrology the symbol of a cock eating a scorpion, and it
had a very deep meaning. But I do not think that the
bird in question meant anything very particular by it,
beyond disposing of the "scorp" to his own advantage.

From what I have said of the intemperate habits of
the cock, one would suppose that, of all flying creatures,
it is best entitled to be called a rum or rummy bird.
The Egyptians, however, apply the term (*farcha rúmi*)
to the turkey. Their turkeys have immense wattles, and
magnificently handsome heads and necks, into which a
beautiful turquoise or *bleu de Nil* colour has been freely
infused. In Cairo, they bring also magnificently handsome prices, and are generally tough; but up the river,
at Siout and further on, they sold us very tender and

fat gobblers for two or three francs. The turkeys are excellent on the Nile, even in very hot weather. Cannot those of England and America be induced to go and do likewise? In America, they are very tough during the summer, as may be inferred from the following anecdote. Once there was a gentleman in America condemned to death. He had the three hot months allowed him to live, and for every day during these months he ordered roast-turkey. When this was reported to a man of taste, he replied that he had now no further doubt as to the guilt of the unfortunate gentleman, and that any one who would eat roast-turkey on the 4th of July would be capable of any crime.

They keep two pelicans at Shepheard's Hotel in Cairo, while they only have one at the "Langham" in London. The two, however, at Shepheard's, though large, are very lazy, while the one at the "Langham" is small, but very useful and active. The woodcock in Egypt—or what I ate for such—were miserable creatures; while, *per contra*, the best Woodcock I ever met in my life was at the same hotel in London. This shows the difference between the two countries. The pelican is also very much used by insurance companies both in England and America, because, as people tell, it surpasses all living creatures in filling out a bill. But the true reason why they employ it is as follows:—Many believe that insurance companies keep pelicans because this bird bleeds itself freely to feed its customers—I mean, its little pels. Nay, not so. There was an old party once,

an Egyptian in Egypt, named Horus Apollo, who told
another story. The pelican, according to him, lays its
eggs on the ground, and the natives make a ring around
them of dry buffalo chips, and set fire to the fuel.
Pelican, to save her eggs, tries to extinguish the fire
by flapping it out with her wings, and in so doing burns
the feathers off, so that she is easily caught. This may
mean that they will perish in raising the wind to save
their nest-eggs. The pelican is the crest of Louisiana;
and once, when a certain gentleman was running for
Congress in that State, I called him in a newspaper
article a Pelicandidate. Bold and reckless scurrility has
no limits in the United States.

Before leaving the subject of Egyptian poultry, I
would mention something that has just occurred to my
mind. The cock, it is well known, indicates the hours
by his crowing, and if he is regular game and good blood,
he does this with unfailing regularity. The Egyptian or
Arab cocks crow louder than any I ever knew, and do
more time-keeping; while the Arabs, as is well known,
first invented regular time-keepers to note the hours by
machinery. This reminds me of a dream I once had.
In my vision, there came to me a man who held a long
discourse on horology, and told me, among other things,
that before men had clocks they always knew the time
by the crowing of roosters. "I see," I exclaimed;
"now they ask what o'clock it is—then they inquired
what o'cock it was." The reader will please to remember that this was only a dream.

Apropos of cocks crowing regularly and of their alas !
too frequent affinity with crime, I am reminded that once
I used to have a pretty regular visitor in a Rommany, or
Gipsy, who was in the habit of dropping into my back
study. In the vicinity was a cock which crowed very
regularly at three o'clock P.M., and about this time I generally gave the Rom a pint of ale. Whenever I forgot or
delayed the ceremony, my visitor would gently hint that
the cock had not crowed in time that day. This is another illustration of the dissipated habits of those birds.

Ere I conclude, let me clarify one thing which I daresay has often puzzled you. What did Moses mean by
saying that " all fowls that creep, going upon all four,
shall be an abomination unto you ? " This puzzled me
till I met in the *Liber Prodigiorum* of Julius Obsequens,
published at Bâsle in 1552, the picture of a four-legged
cock, of which he had an authentic account. It appears
that they had this kind in the old times, but of late
years the race has given out. Yet every step only takes
me deeper into the iniquity· of these creatures. That
they were connected with chicken-hazard we all know ;
this shows that they were noted at all-fours. Verily
there is no end to the depravity of the rooster !

CHAPTER VI.

To have been to Mecca gives a man quite a character in
Egypt.   People say that if your best friend has made
the pilgrimage once, move out of the house in which
you have hitherto dwelt together; if he has effected it
twice, don't remain in the same street with him ; and if
he achieves it a third time, leave the town.   There are
several old Latin and German proverbs which speak in
the same complimentary manner of people who went to
Rome during the Middle Ages.   One declares that the
first time a man goes to Rome he sees a scamp; the
second time he takes one thither; the third journey he
brings one home.   It is rather remarkable that the pilgrims, or Hadjees or Hajis, as they call them, should
bring back such a reputation, considering the company
they travel in.   For it is on the card, sharp and rigorous,
that not less than seventy thousand of them must depart
annually for Mecca, and if the number falls short, it is

made up by invisible angels, who go in place of the missing men. Now, as the number of pilgrims diminishes considerably every year, it is evident that that of angels must augment, which certainly ought to be conducive to the morals of the Hajis, if there is anything in a man's being known by the company he keeps.

There are three ways of getting to Mecca—by riding, going afoot, or by proxy. If you are lazy, and can afford it, you hire a poor neighbour to go there. For the details of the journey and its dangers you may read Captain Burton's book on the subject, which is indeed well worth a perusal. Most people would prefer reading it to going there in person, since, all things considered, 'tis as hard a road to travel, as lies anywhere on the other side of Jordan.

The great annual sight in Cairo is the marching forth of the pilgrims, though Mr Lane says that it is a small affair now compared to what it was in the olden time. Forty years ago it had simmered down to a diminutive residuum; but I can still say of it what I said (from Lever) to Mrs ——— when she complained (the hussey!) that she had lost her good looks and "gone off,"—"I do not know what you may have been once, ma'am, but to judge by the remains, it must have been something very remarkable." And yet, on the other hand, I cannot cry out with the ever-kind-hearted, ever-admiring Lady Duff Gordon, that " no words can describe the departure of the holy Mahmal and the pilgrims from Mecca; " and I am quite certain that I did not " sit for hours in a

Bedawee tent in a sort of dream," as she did, finding in
it "the most beautiful sight of man and beast and
colour and movement—in a glorious spot among domes
and minarets and "— all such sweet Hamelin piping
of fairyland. *That* I did not see, though I daresay it
was like it in the grand old days of the Memlooks, or
Mamelukes, who rode forth in gorgeous robes of crimson,
gold, and azure, glittering with gems, displaying splendid
arms, preceded by bands of inspired dervishes devouring
live snakes, and all the roar and clang of brave music,
horse-tail banners, and minstrels' songs, the drumming
of darabukas, the piping of *nais, rumtum tum de tiddle,*
the sweet twangling of *l'uds,* the yelling of little boys,
et cætera!

What I saw was, *fideliter, videlicet.* The grand feature
at the head of the pilgrim caravan is the Mahmal. This
is simply a splendid canopy or cover for a camel. It has
a pyramidal top surmounted by the ball and crescent, of
silver gilt. It consists of a frame of wood covered with
richly worked brocade, gold and crimson, green and
black, with tassels and silver balls, as you may find in
detail in Lane's " Modern Egyptians." It contains two
copies of the Koran in silver-gilt cases. And this is
borne by a very fine large camel, " which is generally
indulged with an exemption from every kind of labour
during the remainder of its life." After the Mahmal
rode, on another camel, the Shekh-el-Gemel, chief of the
camels, who has charge of the sacred animal and shrine.
He was indeed a beauty, the most astounding specimen

F

of the human wild beast and unmitigated Mahometan savage I ever admired. This attraction was an immensely large powerful creature, looking like some giant Baal-butcher priest of old, naked to the waist, as if prepared for tremendous sacrifice, wanting only his axe, and seeming stark naked as he rode on his camel.

We saw this at the Citadel on December 23, 1872. That morning the whole city of Cairo was in a state of charming holiday delight. Every one, the very poorest, had on new or clean clothes; for at this time every one does his best to look well, and presents of clothing or of ornaments are the rule. It was charming, as we rode in our carriage, to see the women at the windows, the men and children crowded in the streets by hundreds on every bit of wall or on the highest steps of the mosques, rows above rows of smiling dark faces, with snowy turbans and beautifully-variegated *kufiehs* thrown gracefully around their necks. (A *kufieh*, ma'am, is a gay, silk handkerchief, much like a Roman scarf, but with rows of tassels or balls hanging from cords.) I heard that they were dangerously and ferociously pious this day, and likely to insult strangers; but I saw nothing of it—indeed, I should have as soon expected an attack from an infant Sunday-school over its plum-cake and tea. When we grinned they grinned, and we were all good fellows together.

Just below the Citadel, by the Roomeyleh or great square, three thrones, one a very splendid one of white satin, had been prepared under a canopy, and behind and around them were benches and chairs. The white throne was for *Hua Effendina*, His Highness the Khedivé or Viceroy, but he did not make his appearance, being represented on this occasion by the Prince heir-apparent, accompanied by his brothers, Princes Houssein and Hassan, three as handsome and accomplished young gentlemen as any court or club in Europe could show.

It is not often in this life that one sees a grand historical contrast—a moment between the new and the old dramatically represented—but I saw it here, and it was wonderfully perfect. From the camel descended the brawny, naked Savage, with his frightful head of grizzly curling hair, accompanied by two equally un-draped and picturesque associates, and received from the polished Gentleman in European attire a bag of gold, which, according to old custom, is given to defray the expenses of the caravan. Yet a few years more and the Savage, suggestive of wild African Mumbo-Jumbo, and the *Mahmal* and camel, will have vanished, with all that appertains to them; but the Gentleman will remain, and Culture smile at the very little that was lost, and the immense gain that was won in the destruction of the Picturesque.

Ninety-nine out of a hundred tourists, especially the cultivated, wail audibly over the departure of the pic-turesque and antique from Egypt; but my head is not with them, and indeed very little of my heart; it is far more with the intelligent, far-sighted gentleman who rules Egypt, and who has more trouble with this

Arabian Nights' dreamy muddle and with the picturesque than the world knows, and much more than it
is worth.   When I walk through the Mahometan quarters of Cairo, I cannot help thinking what a glorious
new city is destined one day to take the place of this
old agglomerate of material for disease, dirt, and
danger, from which, be it remembered, the curse of
conflagrations and the pestilence has disappeared precisely in proportion as people have plucked out from
it the antique prettiness.   What a place for a Paris!
or, if you do not like Paris as Haussmanised, let me
explain myself by saying that I mean a city of cleanliness, and one cleared of back slums and streets and
ways, like those made by the teredo in ship-timber or
by worms in cheese.   There is no country in Europe
where one could live in such perfect luxury as during
six months in Egypt, were there only a really first-class
city of comfort there.   Already the opera-house and the
palaces, the public garden and many streets around it,
the beautiful drives, and other attractions in Cairo, call
for the admiration and the gratitude of strangers, and
make of it a civilised city; and it seems to me that
these deserve some place for praise among the incessant
peals of admiration for the " artistic bits " and "charming old streets " of the antiquated town.

When the Shekh had taken his gold from the Prince,
seated in state, surrounded by thousands of troops in
their neat white uniforms, amid the inspiriting sounds of
military music, he remounted and rode, followed by the

procession, to that place on the Abbaséen road where
the first halt is made on the pilgrimage. While on the
camel, this worthy man rolls his great bushy head
incessantly from side to side—I have not the remotest
idea why—and this he is said to keep up all the way to
Mecca and back. Every year of his life he has done
this since he inherited the office from his father, who
held it before him. May he be the last!

We took a short cut in our carriage to the first halt-
ing-place, anticipating by two hours the caravan, which
wound its way very slowly through the crowded and
crooked streets. We were not, indeed, in a dream of
domes and minarets—on the contrary, we were particularly
wide awake, with plenty to look at. Pistachio and pea-
nut dealers ran merrily around, singers and beggars went
from carriage to carriage endeavouring to extort from
European ladies something (it was really much more
like the Derby than on the day of the regular races);
and with them went a great stark-naked black man, who
appeared to be somewhat idiotic, but all the more pious
for that—a saint, in fact, whose idiocy by no means
hindered his shrewd attempts to literally black-mail
money from the stylish foreigners who could not endure
his presence. In one place there was a minstrel singing Abu-Zeyd, while beyond the carriages, or up and
down the road, all the gay cavaliers of Cairo might be
seen. I was with an American officer on the Khedive's
service, who obligingly pointed out to me the lions.
"There is —— Bey, there is —— Pacha, there is a son of

the Grand Vizier, that is the chief eunuch of Prince
——." Here, as in the city, there was a delightful *air
de fête*, and the splendid Arab and English horses displayed their spirits in sympathy—the Arabs like graceful savages, and the English steeds like lively gentlemen.

Hearing a drumming, I pierced the crowd, and was
rewarded by an extraordinary sight, which, I am told, is
very unusual now-a-days. It was the famous game of
jereed being played by a number of irregular cavalry
troops, of which at least a regiment was on the ground.
They were wild, strange men, apparently all Turks, or
Arnaouts, or savage Greeks, who were as nearly the
ideal brigand or bushwhacker as the heart could conceive. I had seen nothing like them since I looked at
certain Tennessee Federal companies and rebel guerillas
during the American war. But though the Americans
had made far greater progress towards the indescribable
perfection of rowdy ferocity than anybody else in the
world could have done in the same time, these gentlemen had not only the far greater advantage of having
been born to it, but their fathers were so before them.
There they rested, drawn up in two lines, while four of
their number at the head kept up a mild tum-tumming
each on two little kettledrums, as the combatants rode
wildly up and down.

They were all clad in the ordinary Greek dress of
bag-breeches, dirty shirts, and jaunty vests. Every man
had a carbine, two long pistols, a sword, and a knife ;

but none of the guns or pistols were alike, and all had
flint-locks. One would gallop on his active, cat-like,
hardy little horse at full speed—and they went well at a
tearing pace—pursued by another, who would hurl at him
a light stick four feet long. This he would dodge, and
perhaps in so doing come headlong to the ground ; not
that they were easily dismounted, for I more than once
saw them, when they had dropped their whips, pick them
up from the ground with great ease without quitting the
saddle. It was exciting and reckless fun, and the ease
and promptness with which they pulled up their horses
" short round " when on the run was wonderful. But it
was bad for the horses, there could be no doubt of that;
and so is all the incessant overdriving and mad gallop-
ing about in sands or heavy fields, and exhaustion of the
beasts, as continually practised by all equestrian orientals.
It was a fine sight, however, on a fine day, the weather
such as no one would have changed a degree up or down
if he could, and just as much or as little wind as each
one required—in short, one of those days which occur
about three times *per annum* in England, and are the
rule in Cairo all winter long. This was mixed up with
a gay multitude. There were camels and pretty French
actresses in stylish carriages (for these lambs, however
shorn in salary, always contrive to raise the wind),
Italian *prime donne*, charming Englishwomen (I think I
saw Parepa Rosa there), English lords and English
" legs," American newspaper men, wild Arabs from the
desert, fierce and free ; tourists and donkey-boys, high-

play club men and Greeks, *blasé* old boys with lorgnettes, and black eunuchs, the sun and the shadow, Eros and Anteros, Jews and Gipsies—as jolly a lot of types and antitypes, semblances and parodies, as ever you came across in all your born days.

More music, a rush, a getting back into carriages, and *tan dara da !* the Mahmal and the swell camel and the stupendous savage (boys in America would have called him the " Big Injun "), with his unparalleled wig, and all the lesser pilgers, came on in glory and joy, admired of man, approved by themselves, busy saving their souls with their Sunday-clothes on. With them came the angels—invisible of course—and it was all serene. On to Mecca ! Thirty-seven days through the sands and " bock agin."

I am sorry to say that I was not occupied with deep and wondrous musings as to the mighty power of that grand faith which can bring the stern Bedouin or the grim Tartar thousands of miles from well-nigh unknown lands to worship, *et cætera, ri fol de riddle cum twaddle de guide-bookibus.* Not by much, for I have always held that, of all the works of superstition, the easiest is to set loafers to loafing, to get tramps to tramp, to induce Roms to roam. In fact I only remember one instance when a man who made locomotion his business was unwilling to locomove. One day, long syne, in America, when seated in my " office," I was startled by the entry of a manifest specimen of the loafer class, who announced himself as the Great American Traveller.

"Are you really the Great American Traveller?" I inquired mildly.

" I am."

" Are you quite sure that you are the Great American Traveller?"

And he reaffirmed that he was.

"Then," I replied, pointing to the door, " let me see you travel!"

I think that he must have been the Great American Traveller, for his blasphemies on quitting that room indicated that he had " travelled " considerably. It was not quite fair in me, reader, for it was not altogether original; and perhaps his swearing was excusable, for if anything can make a man swear, it is being caught in an old trap. But to return to our pilgrims. The Mahometan is, for the greater part, a nomad all the world over, and it is only too easy a matter to set even stay-at-home people a-gadding. What I thought of when the procession came was, " How will all this thing work when they shall have made a railway through to Mecca? Will the Mahmal be kept on the sacred camel, and the S. C. be put in a first-class ' car'?" My friend the Bey, by the way, told me that one day he and two young friends once distracted the attention of the guard of a certain line, and adroitly lifted up a little donkey into a first-class carriage and left it there, so that you see this is a Muslim idea originally. Will the big nigger sit *in pluribus naturalis* (as I heard an American say lately), top-side of the carriage, or on the locomo-

tive, and wag even as he now waggeth, from the rising
of the sun unto the going down of that same? Will
they all be entered on the way-book in a hurry, as
" One camel, one f.-c. passenger, two books, one
cloth, G.—free?" (G. standing for Government, f.-c.
first-class.)   Doubtless, doubtless!   For the railroad is
preordained; the trees are now growing which are to
make—or wake—the sleepers.   Wail not over the vanishing picturesque, O beloved! for the picturesque hath ever
vanished since Adam left Eden, and ever existed only
in vanishing forms, as we see the rainbow only in its
departure; but rather look with me at that grand
picturesque of the Infinite, whose beauty lies in the
endless changes of progressive forms.   Not in Gothic
or in Greek, not in Saracenic or Romanesque, in brick-
bats or bric-à-brac, is the true æsthetic loveliness, but
in Man.   And the railway is coming, nothing can stand
before it.   I once saw a German caricature representing a bear and a bull fighting with a locomotive running
them down, and under it a rhyme which declared that—

> " When the railroad is well under way,
>   Neither bull nor bear can cause delay."

Add the camel to the bull and bear, and you will have
the state of the case for the East as plainly as it can be
stated.

I forgot to give a curious little fact, which may throw
some light on the reason why strangers are excluded
from Mecca.   It seems that there is a room there, and
any man who enters it never can by any possibility tell

a lie again as long as he lives. He is in as wretched a case, should he be a Cairene shopman, as ever were the two monks robbed by Robin Hood.

> " ' You shall be sworn,' says bold Robin Hood,
>   ' Upon this holy grass,
>   That you will never tell lies again,
>   Which way soever you pass.' "

Now, it is a sad discredit to Islam, but the word of an Englishman already in the East ranks far above that of a native; and if the Franks, in their adventurous, pushing, travel-loving spirit, should force their way —as they will—into this chamber, they will completely spoil by comparison all that is honest among the Muslim. This would be a nice state of business.

I hope myself that this will speedily be brought about; for in that case all the prying and lying Greeks, *et cætera*, might by some arrangement be forcibly compelled to enter that which would be to them a real chamber of horrors; and last, not least, all my own tribe of bookmakers and authors of these " Six-Days-in-the-East" sort of works, such as I am writing now, will be compelled, willing or nilling, to ladle out the genuine turtle of truth into the plates of the public, wailing for more. So mote it be!

CHAPTER VII.

When a traveller is in Syria, he is a Howadga (*dg* as in
Madge) ; when in Egypt, an Howaga (*ag* as in wag).
But whether he be Howadga or Howaga, he must go and
see such sights as the dervishes dancing or howling,
and report his sensations or non-sense-ations accordingly
to his friends, either in letters or in a book, or in both
together; for who ever wrote home letters from Egypt
but what an army of admiring relatives, especially of the
female persuasion, declared they really *ought* to be
printed, for they would make the *most charming* work
ever written—they are *sure* of it. It is recorded of a
certain American citizen of African descent, that on
being asked if he knew the way to Mr Jones's, he
promptly replied, " Golly, I on'y wish I had as many
dollars as I know de way to Massa Jones's." In like
manner, reader, I only wish I had as many guineas as

my dear friend Miss —— knows that dear X——'s
letters from —— would form the most *delightful*——
But dear X—— has his own ideas on the subject of infringement of guide-book copyright, so that the world
will never get anything from him. Now, I regret to
say that I have had no such encouragement. Not a
page of these pages ever went *per post;* in fact, the
only letter I ever wrote from Egypt of which I can
remember a line was, I fear, quite unfit to print, since
it consisted principally of a litany of curses addressed
to the party who does the letter opening and reading
in the Austrian post-office at Constantinople—the said
party having already with incredible impertinence *aperte
per errare* (or opened by mistake), as he endorsed it,
letters addressed to me.   However, on second thought,
I think I may possibly give that litany, if not in this
book, at least in my great work on the " Wickedness of
Profanity, illustrated by the Oaths of all Nations,"
suggested to me by my particular friend the Bishop
of ——, who has promised to get up all the Hebrew and
Syriac swearing for it.

After writing that last line I had to turn back to the
beginning of this chapter to find out what I was writing
about, having entirely forgotten it, as often happens to
authors (if they would only admit the truth), and, finding something about dervishes, conclude that it was as
likely to have been that as anything—in fact, that
allusion to the bishop makes me certain that some
vague idea as to clergymen was muddling in my mind

all the time and trying to get out. Dervishes are oriental institutions who suffer a great deal—partly from the
duties of their profession, and partly from the frightful
and varied manner in which their name is spelled by
different travellers, all of whom appear to have agreed to
disagree in this little particular. They are divided into
sects which are devoted to piety, dancing, praying,
smoking, juggling, preaching, coffee-drinking, snake-
eating, exhorting, fishing, running spikes into themselves, and similar amusements. Those who whirl are
called *zikk'rs*, which is also the name of their dance.
The name sounds like Shakers, and no wonder, since
these religionists correspond very closely in many respects to the sect which has its head-quarters at
Lebanon, New York, and its tail-quarters out in Ken-
tucky. I think, however, that the Shakers are the
greatest fools of the two. The Shakers sold me some
very nice maple sugar-candy, with walnut kernels in it,
and the *zikk'rs* stood a pipe and coffee, so that as to
refreshments they are about square. Next to the
zikk'rs or dancers come the howlers, who " go " like
steam-engines or menageries when the butcher is drunk
and the meat not up on time. Among both dancers and
howlers are, however, some who take their piety by
jumping up and down, and others by rolling over and
over on the ground, as I have myself witnessed, in
which they answer, " to a dot," to two small sects in
Philadelphia. I once knew a man in that city who was
the " greatest hand " at getting his paper extended, bor-

rowing, shinning, &c., who ever lived. He also exhorted. Once I asked where he held forth, and was told that it was a matter of doubt just then. "He used to be among the Jumpers," said my informant, "but *I* believe he's gone over to the Holy Rollers." Now, reader, it is the blessed truth and no discount, that these people, when under "the influence," behave exactly like dervishes—if not better.

One day I went to see the dancers. Nothing is allowed in this exhibition to shock the feelings of the most fastidious. Clergymen and their wives admitted free—and everybody else. As for me, I had good company, and enjoyed it. It was in a clean, pretty mosque, with a ring in the middle, like a circus, and a semicircle gallery above, with a balcony below for spectators ; not to mention the veiled box for native women, in the darkness of which eyes of light wandered like stars. When I entered, a few musicians were drumming and piping not unpleasantly, and in the centre a dozen or twenty respectable-looking men, in long petticoats, like girls, were making cheeses with astonishing alacrity. They wore oriental vests, and had on their heads those high caps without front-pieces such as are peculiar to Persians. Most of them, owing to their graceful style of leaning their heads against their upraised arms, while the hand hung down over it, their half-closed eyes, and trim mustaches, imperials, and side-whisks, looked quite like *zikk'* dandies. If they had assiduously performed the regular German cotillion instead of plain round dances,

I have no doubt that they would have looked just the same. It is wonderful to see how like causes produce like effects.

The dervish dance is not conducted on the principle of a certain amateur concert of which I once heard, and of which it was said that a jug of beer was awarded to the one who " got done first." At the *zikk'r* show they gave a cup of coffee to the man who held out longest. The four best dancers wore respectively white, purple, blue, and yellow petticoats. If any of my readers should see the same party, and be desirous of betting, I can give them a straight tip. Lay on the old fellow in white. He is the boy for a sure thing. The purple horse is next best. If Old Whitey should chance to be nobbled or off his feed, you may pile the "ponies" on Purple. Blue goes well the first half, but he's a bolter. Yellow has it in him, but he has been badly trained and breaks his pace. All the rest are screws.

After the ball, or the race, or the service was over, a dragoman asked the American ladies—nearly all the audience was American—if they had ever seen a harem. They had not. Would they like to? They would. So he marched them off to a garden gate, and consulted with an unmitigated African who would have made a dark corner in a coal-mine at midnight, and the U. A. produced a bunch of keys and they were admitted. I was not. They reported a large room with half-a-dozen young and old Egyptian women, and a child, sitting on divans on the floor. They giggled and sniggered. The

visitors expressed their delight. The haremites tee-heed
and hee-heed. The room was plain and utterly destitute
of furniture. The women were all smoking. It was not
a scene of oriental splendour or Eastern magnificence.
They left. Somebody was tipped rather handsomely ; I
believe it was the African, and I think he divided with
the proprietor. It is my own private opinion that that
particular harem was built and stocked on speculation,
and is run as a show. I know that it does a good
business.

There is another department of the dervish business
which is carried on, and where the dervishes "carry on,"
—at old Cairo. They were very particular at the door in
making us unboot and put on canoes of the native pattern. This is an oriental custom of extreme antiquity,
as appears from a very ancient poem, which states that

> " Nebuchadnezzar, ye kynge of ye Iewes,
>   Putt on hys slypperes and tooke off hys shooes."

I have no doubt that Neb (which was his real Assyrian
name by the way) did this on entering the temple. I
was reminded of it by the captain, who, when the
dervish required him to kick his leathers off, testily
replied, " Oh, go to grass ! " It was doubtless for the
same remark, under the same circumstances, that the
king was put to grazing. Fortunately the dervish did
not understand English. In fact he smiled. We entered
the mosque. It was a large circular building, with much
of that semi-Gothic clustered ornament, which looks
like broken honeycomb. In one corner of the wall hung

G

a number of barbarous old-fashioned weapons, swords, halberds and clubs. The dervishes were arranged in a nearly complete circle around their chief. They all wore long hair, and many had fine curly locks. Their dresses were various in cut and colour. One man had on, as I remember, a red dress covered with strange figures like animals, of varied hue. They were a wilder and fiercer looking party than the dancing dervishes. The D. D.'s looked like Swells of a pious turn, being really religious Turners. These, however, were Shells—Hard Shells and Screamers. Experience proved that I was right in this religious anticipation.

There were mats in a corner and benches in out-of-the-way places to sit down on, as propriety required, and on these the native visitants, to whom the scene was religious, and for whom the spectacle was really intended, placed themselves. So did the two English gentlemen who were with me. So did I. The rest of the visitors, English and American, stood up by the dervishes, fairly touching them, and interfering with the view, crowding rather closely and talking aloud. I have heard some very ugly stories how these Howlers, when the religious frenzy is on them, attack Europeans who happen to be "convaynient." It occurred to me that if I had been a Howler, I should not have waited to "get religious,"— I should possibly have gone for somebody while still unregenerate. It is not worth while to wait till you are in a state of grace, when there is a proper opportunity to show your science and mill a deserving fellow-sinner.

The dervishes sang and chanted with tremendous
energy, and, as the spirit entered them, let off cries much
like those which are to be heard in camp-meetings and
at revivals. Then they began to bow, keeping the legs
straight. This is not easy to do. Put your back to
the wall and try to pick up a sixpence at your toe-tips.
I believe there are Howlers who can do it with their
mouths. As they bowed all together, they uttered what
I believe was *Allâh!* Recovering their perpendicular,
they bowed and Allâh'd again. They increased the
time,—working magnificently; in about a minute the
whole fifty of them went like one man, and the "jerks"
were superb! Closing my eyes I realised a curious
thing,—that no one could have distinguished by sound
alone any difference between the dervishes and a powerful high-pressure steam-engine. Something like a
dreamy feeling of the olden time stole over me. Me-
thought I was in the sanctum adjacent to the press-
room, while the fourth edition was being worked off.
Once in a while the head dervish or an assistant uttered
shrill cries, and these I thought came from newsboys
out in the street. I opened my eyes, they had got up
to the highest rate, and were running her off at eighteen
thousand an hour,—I mean fifty-two bobs and fifty-two
Allâhs in a minute. I knew this, for one spectator
timed them and joyfully proclaimed it aloud.

Suddenly one of the dervishes, who had distinguished
himself by his zeal, became *mel bûs,* or possessed, and fell
down. Had he been a Methodist or a Roman Catholic, a

disciple of Madame Guyon or any of the five hundred writers whose names are given in Poiret's "De Mysticis," I should have said that he was inspired, or at least have shook my head gravely, and tenderly declared that it was wonderful, and not to be lightly spoken of. It is thus that I feel and think even of convulsionnaires. But as he was only a poor devil of a dervish, and a miserable heathen of a Mahometan, it was plainly enough only an epileptic fit, and we regarded it accordingly. One lanky Yankee youth rushed up, and seizing him by the pulse, produced his watch, and began timing him as if he had been a subject in the veterinary hospital suffering in the cause of science. The lanky youth talked very knowingly. When he had finished his share of the rites and exhibited sufficiently, a dervish rested the head of the possessed on his knee, and gradually chafed him again to consciousness.

There were other transactions which were not less singular. The loud cries, the wild utterances of names of God, or texts, had a strange effect, and when the bowing had ceased, it was increased by a semi-martial music of drums and a kind of flute or trumpet. To this all chanted, and the effect was very good. As the dervishes became excited they uttered sounds of incredible dimensions. It is narrated that once in a coloured Methodist meeting in America, when all hands were crying "Glory," there came such an appalling, hideous roar, such an awful yell, that it "shibbered de windows." "Wh'—wh'—who make dat soun' dar?" cried the

clergyman aghast, among his frightened flock. Out
from the crowd pressed a gigantic negro, seven feet
high, built like Hercules, with a bull-neck, which
emerged from a red flannel shirt, his only upper garment. "Dat was I, bred'ren," cried this promising
convert proudly; "but I 'se only preparin' fur to make
ready fur to begin fur to shout." Scarcely had he
uttered this ere fifty strong hands seized him, and hurled
him headlong through the door into outer darkness.
"Bless de Lor', we don' wan' no sitch converts as *dat !*"
gratefully remarked the clergyman, as he vanished.
Had this unappreciated man only fallen into the hands
of the howling dervishes how different would his lot
have been ! It is for just " sitch converts as dat " that
they are most truly grateful. Nor would his colour
have been the slightest objection. While the drumming
and piping went on, there rolled into the room, with
that extraordinary swaying and swinging step which old
tradition ascribes to fierce military aghas and pachas
(some old actors still preserve it), a remarkable figure.
This was a jet-black man, clad in crimson, with a crimson cloak with flowing sleeves, and red turban, bearing a great sabre. With a very swell air, undulating
chest, and folded arms, he promenaded around the per-
formers, and taking his place in the ring began to spin
—for there were during the entire performance one or
two whirlers at work. I was more than once at the
Howlers, and always observed this coloured military man,

who looked like *ratt*. Now, *ratt* in Rommany signifies both night and blood.

Once when I was at the howlers I accompanied Mr Emerson. I need not say that he did not crowd up to the worshippers. He sat quietly on the bench. I do not think, indeed, that he *enjoyed* the exhibition; I do not think that he likes anything which shows man in a ridiculous light, or lowers him to a brute. He is neither of the vulgar who stare at the odd for the sake of a show, nor of the Mephistophelic who quiz all that they cannot compass, nor even of those who admit Locke as a necessity into metaphysics, with Loke, as another necessity, both into the councils of the gods and their foes.

It must be admitted that the Howlers do the menagerie very successfully. There was one pitch in the performance when it completely vanquished the steam-engine. I really can't imagine, I say, how they do it. You nor I nor no one knows how they do the way the elephant goes. As for the lion, they give the unmitigated roar of the desert without defalcation. Of the tiger we can only speak with unmingled praise—it must be heard to be appreciated; while the laughing hyena commends itself to all our readers as a performance which is both chaste and vigorous. "Take it for all in all, we ne'er shall look upon its like again."

When all was over, one youth with long hair, who had begun to spin, but who did not spin well, could not stop. He had been wound up for twenty minutes,

and was resolved to play his hand out. So he spun
with a sweet smile on his face outside the ring, and came
dancing over towards us with that sputtering sort of
step which a top makes when, in revolving along on a
pavement, it encounters obstacles and jumps. But the
shekh soon stopped his little game, as with a fatherly
smile he put his arm around the young saint and blocked
him off.

Emotions of a calmer colour succeeded the " closure "
of the service. There is a nice café-garden outside the
mosque, and here we were invited to rest and smoke and
receive coffee. I have no doubt that Shekh Shádilee,
the inventor and patron saint of coffee, looks down with
special interest on this establishment. While sitting
here the *rouge et noir* military man reappeared, and
opened his little game by drawing his sabre and executing an ingenious and spirited sword-dance along the
walks. I was much pleased with it, as well as by his
incessant and not unsuccessful efforts to entertain. I
subsequently saw him bumming about the streets of
Cairo, and was told that he was a religious mendicant.
I wish that all the members of his profession—in Italy—
were half as amusing.

I should say, in finishment of this chapter, that one
leaves the dervish performance with mixed emotions, as
if uncertain whether psalms and hymns are awful funny,
or negro melodies and break-downs are pious and serious
inventions. On the whole, I would recommend people
of a susceptible and impressional nature, with refined

spiritual receptivity, not to familiarise themselves with
the dancers and howlers, since, if they do, they will end
by being unable to distinguish between Bones and a
bishop.   The end man will remind you of your latter
end, like a regular Spurgeon, and the champion jig-
dancer will get mixed up in memory with King David.
While at the dervishes, my heart reverted continually to
the Christy Minstrels; and the other evening, at Moore
and Burgess's, I all the while recalled our religious
exercises in Cairo.

CHAPTER VIII.

ONE day Mr Beekman, of New York, asked me if I
would like to see a Copht school. I affirmed, and he
" put me on it." I may not have a better opportunity,
so I avail myself of the present one to thank him for
the various stakes of information which I won out of
this first little moral game which he induced me to bet
on.—N.B. This is metaphorical, not literal.

Mr Beekman introduced me to a young Copht named
Joseph Hanna, which is a girl's name in Europe, but in the
East it stands for John. Hanna is a teacher of English
in the great Cophtic school of Cairo, and, like most cultivated minds striving for higher culture in the smaller
and decayed nations of the East, is most anxious to pro-
mote education and intelligence among his people. He
it was who took me to the school.

Like every building of any pretensions in Cairo, the
school is large, with full-sized apartments, and plenty
of air and light. The boys are not penned into rooms

about seven feet high, where a foul atmosphere keeps the poor little shavers in a state of chronic irritability and feverish " naughtiness." I also trust that they are not punished, as is frequently the case in America, by being kept nearly all day without food or exercise, thereby revenging on the health those misdeeds which half the time would never be committed if parents and teachers had half as much intelligence as they exact from pupils. The windows were open, and through them tarbushed or turbaned and dark men peered curiously at the strangers. The English class was very interesting. We were requested to write a sentence on a black-board, and a bright-eyed, good-looking boy at once parsed it with rapidity and correctness. This is a good chance for a reviewer to say that I couldn't have done it. I don't believe that I could in the same time. I felt glad that I wasn't up at that black-board.

Then Hanna effected. He wrote an English sentence on the board. It sounded rather queerly, and on looking inside it I observed that it was almost as badly written as if it were by Mr ——. I blushed for Hanna, which is more than Mr —— ever did for himself, though he received a precious wigging, only last week, in the columns of the ——. One of my friends, indeed, began to ask Hanna if there wasn't a little error, to which Hanna replied by asking him to please to wait. Then another boy was called up, and that boy was asked *his* opinion of the sentence. His reply was to the effect that it wouldn't hold water, and was full of holes. He was requested to indicate these perforations, and caulk them. He went at it in style, and rubbed out and repaired, and gave reasons for it all, as only the best of good boys could have done.

Some of the younger boys were exercised in reading. Excepting that they got over rather too much ground, and made rather too good time to the minute, as at home, I had nothing to object to. And really, when one reflects that all of this more than creditable, this extraordinary proficiency in the English language is entirely due to the teachings of young men who are themselves Cophts, is it not enough to awake the interest of all intelligent and kind persons in this remarkable race? I say so because it is the fashion to abuse the Cophts, and I believe they have been abused most unjustly and wickedly. It has been usual for a generation for paradox-loving, would-be "liberal" tourists and travellers to affect the renegade more or less, to write up the Mahometans and Turks and heathen, and write down all kinds of Christianity, whether domestic or foreign, especially oriental. Now they may be right as far as Greeks are concerned, for I know very little about Greeks; but when we find a race which is inconceivably preferred, as to honesty, to Greeks and Jews, by their conquerors, as the Cophts are by the Egyptians, there must be something good in them. And when we find that this Copht race is the one generally put in offices of trust requiring talent, in fact, that they are the book-keepers, scribes, secretaries, and treasurers of the Muslim, the inference to be drawn is that the Muslim believe in their integrity. More than this, the Cophts are the most skilful artisans in Egypt; and, all things considered, are an unquestionably hopeful race—let them be looked after.

The best word that even the kindest writer on Egypt seems to have for the Cophts is to call them morose, gloomy, and crabbed. They are all as cross as two sticks, sour as verjuice, savage as meat axes, and look at you like steel traps—so say the books. Now this wasn't my experience. The only out-and-out jolly individual I met in Egypt, a promising youthful Falstaff, a tremendous laugher, was a fat, handsome Copht. Several more moderately hilarious men I also knew, and they were Cophts. The Bey was joyous, and he wasn't a Copht; but he was not Egyptian either. On the other hand, I did not meet with any ill-natured Cophts. Once I thought I saw one at a distance under a black turban; but as I approached he smiled jollily, so that I found it was only a Cophtical delusion.

From the English room we went to the old Cophtic room. The old Cophtic language, as my reader may know, is in the main old Egyptian—the language of the hieroglyphs, with a minor admixture of Greek. It sounds far more pleasantly than Arabic. The written language might be mistaken at a cursory glance for Greek or Russian. Most people are under the impression that the old Cophtic is so entirely dead that two or three of their priests are the only men of their nation who understand it. Such was the case till within some fifteen years, when a Copht archbishop, Kirolos, exerted himself successfully to excite an educational movement among his race, and resuscitate the old language. This was greatly aided by the publication in London of a Cophtic New Testament, with an Arabic translation. The youth whom I saw evidently understood their own ancient tongue well enough. One of them wrote a sentence out and parsed it, all in Cophtic. The idea alone was awful! When an Englishman does not understand a thing, he says it is all Greek to him. A German (more deeply erudite) declares it is *Koptisch*. That is what the boy's performances were to me.

It fills one's soul with dread to think what the boys learn at that school. When I inform the reader that tender children of three or four years begin about where English university men leave off—at Arabic—he may form some idea of their appalling studies. To be a person of the shallowest and most superficial education in Cairo requires a knowledge of Arabic, English, French, and Italian. Most of the donkey-boys can talk these tongues. A man of business adds to them Greek and Armenian; if he have any kind of government dealings he learns Turkish; if he wishes to be considered a gentleman of culture he studies Persian, which has precisely the same effect all over the East as French in England or America.

I was gratified at one little incident in the English room during my next visit to the school, when Hanna gave out for an exercise a brief sketch, or rather mention, of the state of Cophtic culture, in which cordial and

honourable mention was made of the Khedivé, and of
his kind care of this race.   Had this been the only
instance of the popular love for the present enlightened
ruler of Egypt which I ever met, I would not have dwelt
on it.   But it reveals the fact that during my winter in
Egypt, in conversations with people of every class, I
never heard a word regarding him from any one that
was not in his praise.   It may be said that everybody is
on his guard in the East to "speak no evil of the king;"
but I conversed with many who were not afraid to express their thoughts, and would have spared no one in
their confidence.   Complaints of many things and of
many high public functionaries I heard often enough
—rascally great men seem to be about as common there
as with us in America—but the instant the Khedivé was
mentioned, the tone changed.   "Ah, yes! if His Highness only knew of this—or that—you'd see a change."
"If His Highness could be allowed to learn the truth,"
is the consolation of all the people in real or imagined
causes of complaint.   But that His Highness would not
rectify wrongs, or that he does not rectify as many as
he can, never seems to enter anybody's head.   It is a
singular thing to live under a ruler of whom everybody
speaks with sincere praise.   There is no monarch in
Europe of whom this can be said.

The various class-rooms, the dignitaries of the school,
the printing department, were all interesting.   I found
the very intelligent foreman busily engaged in casting
his own type, Arabic, Roman, and Cophtic.   His work

in every department was, however, unexceptionally good.
As he is principally engaged on theological books, I
found that his standard of reference was an Arabic
Bible, a magnificently illuminated vellum volume, six or
seven hundred years old.   But there is a strong smack
not only of the Middle Ages but even of the Romanesque,
or rather Byzantine, in everything Cophtic.   Baron ——,
who with his brother accompanied me on this visit, asked
one of the learned Cophts to write him a sentence of their
ancient language.   This was done with a preliminary
ornamental initial, and the character of the whole was
well given by the Baron when he said that it would have
seemed perfectly in place in a MS. of the tenth century.
I don't believe that Westwood, or Owen Jones, or any
of the blessed brotherhood of illuminators, would have
impugned the Byzantiquity of that document.

We were taken into the church, where I was much
interested by a few curious works of art, ancient and
modern—if there be anything modern in that which is
either purely Saracenic or Byzantine.   One picture interested me much.   It represents a saint, with a gold
back-ground, surrounded by a frame-work of smaller
pictures, each representing an incident from his life.
In its exquisitely naïve and child-like drawing, its
entire expression, and its mechanical method (Mrs
Merrifield's translation of the Mount Athos MS. tells how
that is done), this work represents the infancy of painting to perfection.   The artist who made it is a Greek
living in Cairo, and I am informed he will execute

portraits in this style at a reasonable figure. But I am pleased to be able to state that there is a movement, an advance perceptible in Christian art in Cairo, and that the expression of the beautiful is advancing with giant strides. In Old Cairo I saw two pictures in which the painter unassisted, save by moral consciousness, had got as far as Cimabue, and I honestly believe that neither Mr Ruskin or even Mr Merritt * would have hesitated to ascribe them to that artist. There is indeed every reason to hope that in a few years this promising painter will, either in person or in his pupils, have advanced almost to Perugino, and started on his own account a new dawn of art. Meanwhile I recommend all pre-Raphael lights to go and study in Cairo. I have studied with love, tenderness, and ineffable sympathy every accessible work by Beato Angelico; and I do not hesitate to affirm that for idiotic sweetness there are Greek artists now living who are fully equal to the candid Angelico himself.

We had an interview with Markos, the metropolitan bishop of the Cophtic Church. He was a gentlemanly, agreeable man. The cigars and coffee as a preliminary were also agreeable. In Egypt, owing to the climate, there is something peculiarly refreshing to weary people in a whiff and a drop of the berry. I mentioned this to the bishop, and said that I wished his brother bishops in the West would follow his example to morn-

---

* "Pictures and Art Separated in the Works of the Old Masters." By Henry Merritt. London, 1854.

ing callers. I am happy to say that Bishop Markos
appeared to be highly gratified at this remark. There
are orientals to whom it would appear stingy and barbarous if they knew that there were gentlemen or ladies
who would not ask you to blow a cloud or rattle a spool
as soon as you entered their drawing-rooms. To such I
said nothing; but I felt that I could trust the bishop,
and so told him what a beautiful and touching custom
it was. At this distance I can, however, feel the peril
I was in. I had hardly seen the Metropolitan ere I was
on the way to confession. 'Tis thus converts are made.
I knew a young English lady who conversed with
the ——— once only—and yet she calls him Poor Polly
to this day. The reason was this. Having asked His
——— in French if he spoke English, His ——— replied,
in a plaintive parrot - voice, " Poor ——— no 'peak
Inglis." Is not this perilous?

If the Cophts are a morose, narrow-minded, hide-
bound set of vinegar-cruets, all I can say is they did
not manifest themselves as such to me. The only one
whom I remember· as wearing an expression of discontent, misanthropy, and disgust, not only at foreigners
but the world in general, was an unfortunate youth of
eight summers, whom I suddenly surprised one day on
entering the school, undergoing the wearisome punishment of kneeling on the ground, while his arms were
kept elevated in the air. Such a combination of rage,
suppressed weeping, and entire discontent with his position in life as his face presented, I never beheld.

H

So far as my experiences went, the Cophts were sociable, hospitable, communicative, and cheerful. That they could do more merriment on less solid nutriment, and keep it up longer, than any people I ever met in all my life—or yours either—was fully illustrated one night when, in company with the two English gentlemen already mentioned in this chapter, I went to a highly respectable Copht wedding. We rolled along in a carriage by night, with Hanna, to some part of the town where I had never been before. It was not in the regular Copht quarter, and some parts of it were very irregular and picturesque. Descending, we went on foot, guided by Hanna, through strange ways—sometimes in utter darkness, sometimes into strangely-lighted places, such as the untravelled American can hardly imagine. Then we came to a Gothic archway, through which shone a red light into Doré shadows; and Hanna exchanged signals with somebody, who ran off into the night, like one of Jean Paul's thoughts. Then a slender young man of gentlemanly mien appeared bearing small wax-tapers, several of which he communicated to Hanna, who imparted them to us. The young man also went deep into the night, and Hanna informed us that he was the bridegroom.

Then Hanna ferried us along through some more darkness, conferring at times mysteriously with chance forms, all of which appeared to act in concert with him. At last the game seemed to be getting into a line. Distant sounds of joy were heard; a wave of

wild music came borne on the night-air—it rolled faster
on, and louder. We hurried, and turning the street,
came in full view of the bridal procession—in a sea of
red light.

It was really a wild and wonderful sight, which
requires nothing but the most faithful and literal
description to convince the reader that even the East
can show nothing more picturesque. The resting-point
was the bride. This young lady—they told us she was
very young—was shrouded (as Arab brides invariably
are), rather than veiled, in a thick Cashmere canopy—
that Cashmere which plays such a part in the Arab ballad
of "D'as ya Leylee." I cannot tell how she breathed
through it; and, in fact, they were obliged to bring a
chair more than once for the poor girl to sit down on,
and fan her as well as they could under it. She had a
long flowing white veil-like robe, and wore on her head
a cap which was literally a mass of diamonds. Other
head-dresses are adorned with diamonds—this was made
of them. On her bosom was such a profusion of gold
coin that it seemed as a garment. Behind the bride
walked her female relatives and friends. These ladies
indulged largely in what is called the *zaghareet*, or cry
of joy. The American reader will understand what it is
like when I tell him that it is exactly and precisely the
Indian war-whoop, with all its strange sharpness and
trill. Among them were borne flaring cressets; behind
them came fitful, shrill music. Before the bride on
either side were ranged in procession her male friends

or those of the bridegroom. But it was in a singular
style, for they all marched sideways with their backs to
the houses, facing one another, every one bearing a
lighted taper. So it was of old in the days when there
were five wise and five foolish virgins waiting to take
their part in such a procession.

I am happy to say that our tapers were all right and
lighted. As we were highly honoured guests, they placed
us next the bride. To say that we went at a snail's
pace would be no exaggeration, making allowance for the
difference in size. It was also a crab's pace, for we
advanced sideways. Before the bride were two boys
bearing censers, with which they liberally smoked the
poor girl—they certainly must have incensed her more
than once. And in advance of them walked a very
pretty little boy dressed in the full pontificals of a
Coptic deacon. This was, I suppose, the boy bishop of
the Middle Ages who has so much puzzled antiquarians.
Then there were two young men, who bore those curious
silver flasks called '*khoom* '*khoom*, made in the form of
pomegranates (the ancient symbol of female fertility),
which are used at all weddings in the East. These
pomegranates are also " squirts," and are filled with
rose-water or other delicious perfume. The young men
ran up and down, and jetted it into the faces of the
guests. I found it very agreeable, as did the rest, who
generally cried *Kaman!* or " more!" At the head of
the procession went a good band of music. The airs
it played were mostly of a wild oriental caste, but

sometimes they sounded familiar or half familiar to me; and these, we were informed, I thought, with a little pride, were European. But I like Arab music best for such occasions. It has a strongly-marked character, and is very pleasing.

As we moved on very slowly, our backs to the houses, we passed a literally low drinking-shop, for it was below the level of the pavement; and out of its depths darted a very tipsy fellow-Christian in a turban, who seizing my hand, kissed it eagerly, uttering words which I did not understand. Supposing, as the sailor did when the jugglers' show, in which he was seated, was blown up by a barrel of gunpowder, that this was a part of the regular performance, I said nothing, and maintained my dignity; and, indeed, I had not seen the shop behind me, nor did I notice the condition of my admirer. But the procession appeared to be uncommonly shocked and scandalised, and remonstrated with the jolly toper, who, however, responded to the " procesh," " Why shall I not kiss that good man's hands? is he not a holy saint?" In the East a long beard is greatly reverenced, the higher clergy seeming to be especially blessed in that way; and as mine is of the orthodox size, I had been revered accordingly.

The music, the cries of joy, the glare of torches and tapers, and the blare of trumpets, with the piercing *zaghareet* of the women, and the picturesque dresses of the guests—the whole advancing in a slow, twelve-o'clock-work step —formed the subject for a splendid picture, which was carried out to perfection by the architectural details of the streets through which we passed. These abounded in the old projecting lattice-windows made of turned-work, so characteristic of Cairo, and from these were looking great numbers of Egyptian women, many of them without veils. It is true that most of them were black slaves or servants; but there were many other shades besides anthracite, ranging from rusty-stove to sole-leather, gingerbread, yellow-pine, snuff-and-butter, coffee-and-milk, and old or new ivory, and so on, up to the newly-driven snow itself. All of these tints, with black eyes in them, stared down on us inspired with that fervid curiosity which all the women—bless 'em!—all the world over, take in a wedding. On that subject they are all akin.

And so, with no end of jollity, the procession entered a gate and then a house. The room in which we found ourselves was a strange one. It was about thirty feet by fifty, and was at least forty or fifty feet high. Windows looked into it at different heights from different rooms. It was bare of furniture excepting seats, but a divan surrounded a portion of it; and as we were honoured guests, the fathers of the bride and groom, who were the hosts, requested us to wait until cushions could be brought for us to sit on, which was speedily done. I do not remember ever to have met two gentlemen who combined more gaiety of heart with so much courtesy and refined politeness as these respective fathers-in-law. They asked us as a special favour to them to call for anything we could think of, and lost no time in giving us the best cigarettes I ever smoked, and in providing sherbet (or fruit-syrup water) and coffee.

And then there was a truly singular ceremony; for the bridegroom, who had been absent from the procession, was brought into the room and placed on a high seat, where he was lathered by a barber and shaved as solemnly as possible. I forbore comment and question, supposing that, as the Cophts are a highly intelligent race, it must be all right. But when a nice little boy was seated on his lap, but with his back towards the elder, and the barber proceeded to lather and shave the young shaver also, I could not refrain from expressing my surprise, whereupon I was informed that the child was the younger brother of the bridegroom, and that this was done " to make the young one happy." It was apparently a success, for he was evidently delighted with the honour.

Meanwhile an individual with a basket went about distributing seeds and nuts, which reminded me of the *spargere nuces* of the ancient Roman weddings. I think that pumpkin-seeds were the favourite food on this festive occasion. The Egyptians have pea-nuts, but they prefer pumpkin-seeds. The ancient Romans also had access to pea-nuts, but they placed their hearts on roast peas, which they ate in the circuses and while listening to speeches. I trust I may not be accused of pedantry if I mention that Cicero had a spot like a pea in his face, which accounts for his being an orator. We, the swell guests, were supplied with a saucerful of the kernels

of almonds, ground or pea, pistachio, hazel, and other
nuts.

The company were wondrous jolly, evidently laughing
at anything, gay as larks. But they became jollier still
when a little window twenty or thirty feet from the floor
was opened, and displayed signs of being inhabited.
Somebody hung a little curtain before the window. This
indicated that a female singer was about to vociferate.
In Europe they draw the curtain away on such occasions,
in the East they interpose it. The invisible girl sang,
and the company applauded. They became exuberant,
and continued to be so. I was told that they would
keep continuing until six o'clock in the morning. All
European travellers accuse Cophts of being rare old toss-
pots, steady drinkers, regular rum-buds. I believe that
some of them, especially up the river, *do* occasionally
attack the arraki-bottle and storm the source of joy; but
I would ask, What is the use of being a Christian in a
heathen land if one is to be deprived of all the privileges
of his faith? It may be that the wedding guests of whom
I speak had taken something outside within, to counter-
act the damp, but I don't believe it. I call myself a
judge, and they were all sober as judges. How they
contrived to be so laughy and smiley on pumpkin-seeds
and cold water I cannot conjecture. They gave us some
arraki—I remember drinking the bride's health in it,
which performance, by-the-by, seemed to strike the
Cophts as a great but charming novelty—but they did
not take any themselves. They made the regular breast,

chin, and forehead bow to us when we expressed our compliments; and the more we enjoyed ourselves, the happier they seemed to be.

But soon we were asked if we would not like to witness the marriage ceremony. We would. So we walked slowly upstairs to an upper chamber. There was a table in the middle of the room, and by the wall a small divan only large enough for four people. This divan, as Hanna announced, was for us, because the kind hosts wished to show us all the honour in their power. We were the only persons admitted beyond the nearest relatives and the priests and assistants. Those who believe that Cophts hate strangers, avoid them, and are reserved towards them, would have been of a different opinion had they witnessed the kind, warm-hearted manner in which they kept coming to us to explain this or that, or to ask us if we would take anything, or have a cushion. I noticed this same careful politeness among them in their houses up the river. Our American agent, Waseef, at Siout, is a Copht, and he is a miracle of benevolence, generosity, and hospitality, besides being the only gentleman I ever knew who owned two one-thousand-dollar jackasses. They cost six hundred apiece, but they would come to a thousand in Cairo, with gold at 119.

That marriage ceremony lasted four hours. I am afraid I cannot give a very distinct account of it. The priest read many prayers and Bible chapters in the old Cophtic, and then translated them into Arabic. Sometimes he sang, and sometimes lesser priests led off a chorus of boys, who in turn sang either standing up or altogether sitting down on the floor. There were exhortations and much burning of incense. Then, again, the priest would beat cymbals with the singing; and all the while through the open windows of the room which looked down into the great hall came the song of the 'Awalim and the tumultuous applauses of the wedding guests. I daresay you would have liked it very much.

But now a louder tumult was heard, cries of announcement from men; and amid pealing of music, and a tremendous chorus of *zaghareets* from women, the bride entered as slowly as ever, and as densely veiled. We were informed that the bridegroom had as yet never seen her face, though the very jolly young man in the red scarf, who was opposite to me in the torchlight procession, and who laughed at every word, had told us that he had it on good authority that she was very pretty. But she sat down by the bridegroom, and the ceremonies continued. Finally, the priest covered them both with one veil, and prayed again over the two heads thus brought under one bonnet. It is difficult to sit a long time immovable in one attitude, and sometimes the young heads would unconsciously separate; then the priest would promptly bring them together again, like two stray lambs on a road.

If an ordinary wedding—say "two nods and a five-dollar prayer"—be enough to join two mortals for life, I should say that a Cophtic marriage ceremony ought

to unite them effectually for all eternity. Those who
have investigated the innumerable and intricate ceremonies of this Church find them full of the most curious
symbolism derived from ancient Egyptian and the earliest Christian sources. I am certain that a wonderful book could be written on this subject—perhaps some
German has already done it.

At last they were wedded—I should say " very much
wedded," as the Turkish ambassador at Paris once
gravely said to the French lady who impertinently asked
him if the Sultan his master was married. " *Beaucoup,
madame,*" was his solemn reply. We went downstairs
and there found the company jollier than ever, smoking
and laughing and listening to the singer, as if that
small window were a porthole into paradise. The two
fathers again sat by us, and again gratified us by their
kindness and courtesy. It is not just the thing in the
East to ask for the names of people when you are
enjoying their hospitality; it sounds too much like a
speech of the girl in Omaha who reported that she
" got married to a fellow last week, but had forgotten
what they called him." So I merely said that if I knew
the number of letters in the names of the bride and
groom and their parents, I could predict how the wedding would turn out. This brought out the names.
Fortunately they all showed exactly six letters apiece,
which proves that it will be a lucky wedding. This is a
fact. It is what gipsies call *durkerin* or *dukkerin.* The
parents thanked me very cordially for taking such pains.

The Baron remarked that I had evidently not been among the Rommany for nothing.

Travellers have said that Cophts hate other Christians worse than Muslim.   I don't think that any I met hated us; on the contrary, there was every evidence, on this and many other occasions, to prove that they regarded us sympathetically and kindly as of the same faith. The very manner of their admitting us to the wedding ceremony, and their remarks to us, and their general demeanour, indicated unmistakably that community of feeling and confidence which has nothing in common with any kind of reserve, jealousy, or dislike.   They all speak well of the Khedivé, and I think by this that they are a gentlemanly race; for it is becoming, at least, to speak well of those in authority—or any other man.

We made our adieux at half-past two in the morning. A servant with a lantern guided us homeward, and we retired well pleased with all we had seen.   When it came to be reported, however, that we had been observed travelling in an obscure part of the town secretly by night, in a native wedding procession, bearing tapers, much amazement was expressed; and I believe that we began to earn in a slight degree the reputation of being men of mystery and che'ildren of ker'rime, or at least of being up to ways that were dark and tricks that were vain.   Then we did our own Arabic—such as it was— and used to pass whole days in the barren fastnesses of the Mokáttan Mountains, and the Baron had a gloomy way of riding with the *cortége* of donkey-boys off into the desert—I have known him to do it after dark—and digging up human skulls, which he slung by pairs over his pommel, where they looked like boxing-gloves. As for me, Mohammed, my donkey special, was amazed at being peculiarly employed to introduce me to the fortune-telling, hen-stealing, and tinkering Rhagarin or Gipsies, concerning whom no traveller had ever before cared one copper. Whence it came to pass that we were generally regarded as slightly peculiar, and, I have no doubt, were each set down as people whose talents, like the gentleman's eyes commemorated by Miss O'Flanagan, " were niver put in his hid for the good of his sowl."

CHAPTER IX.

EVERYBODY who goes to the East has his or her say
on dancing and singing girls, and I am going to have
mine.

More than once in Egypt I heard what may be pronounced either an *ah'alema,* or *ile-ma,* or *'almah,* or
'alma, the whole trouble being in the first letter *'a* or
ain, which is pronounced nasally, and is the very sound
which some people, especially Frenchmen, make when
they assent sneeringly to a proposition. *'Alma* in the
plural is *'awalim.* An 'Alma is a singing-girl, but
the word means *learned.* Dear old Lady Duff Gordon
was scornful that there should be Europeans so ignorant as to believe that an 'Alma is merely a "gay
lady," or what the American traveller called a "low-
rate." She informs us that they are learned women,
and evidently believes in their erudition. All I can
say is, that I do not believe any boy would learn much
good from such an *alma mater.* A chanter in English
is reputable, and may work in a cathedral; but a horse-

chanter is not a very reputable individual—in fact the
word is about equivalent to swindler, since it is applied
to fellows who put themselves forward at fairs in the
way of possible horse-purchasers, and sing the praises of
an animal, affecting to be disinterested spectators, when
they in reality share in the profits.   But a chanter, according to dictionary, is a vocal warbler ; and somebody
might declare with indignation that horse-chanters were
noble minstrels who sang of horses.   Moreover—ay,
more than over—there are proofs of it in such poets as
Bayard Taylor, who once minstrelled an Arab's horse,
and the great bard of Camptown races who sang—
ay, more than sang—who *bet* his money on de bob-
tailed nag.

   While I am about it, I will clarify another point unto
you—the difference between certain terms which are obscure unto many. A singing-girl is an 'Alma. A dancing-
girl is a Gazieh or Razich.   It is impossible to give the
exact sound in Roman type of the first letter of this
word, it is neither an *r* nor a *g*. *Razieh* or *gazieh* in
the plural is *ghawázi*.   Bayaderes are not Egyptian.
Europeans call Hindu dancing-girls by this very pretty
name, but the natives call them Nuts.   This is because
their performances are of such an insane character that
they dance as if they were cracked.   When travellers
call an Egyptian dancing-girl an 'Almah, it is as if you
were to call dear Madame Taglioni a Patti.   When they
call a singstress a Ghawázi, it is as if you were to call
Nillson a *corps de ballet*, which would be wrong, since

kings and editors are the only persons who have the privilege of splitting themselves into plurals.

Yet such are the ennobling influences of poetry and song, that even the 'Alma often rises superior in intellect to the herd, and is recognised as intelligent and refined, besides being well paid. As regards their singing, there are three stages to be passed through before the stranger can admire it. I had not been many nights in Cairo before I went with a friend to the Arab *café chantant*, in the Esbekiah Gardens, where, as I was told, good singing could be heard. There was a kiosk or round place for musicians, such as is usual in Europe, but it was jealously shut in with thin curtains, behind which the 'Awalim were singing. The effect on me was that of a combination of old Irish women wailing at a wake, with a strong infusion of caterwauling. The voices were beyond all belief nasal, and what was applauded as skilful trilling, sounded to me like eccentric quavering. When the voice had sustained itself for one or two bars, there was a general roar from the auditors without, over their coffee and pipes, of *kaman !* (*encore !*) or *taib !* (good !) or frantic outcries which I could not understand. All of this was led off by an Egyptian, who seemed to be the fugleman, and was manifestly a member of the troupe. Altogether the 'Awalim did not make a favourable impression. I thought it very solemn. This was the first stage. When I again heard them on other occasions, having looked a little more into Arab music and heard Aida, and thought liberally on the subject, I soon perceived that they surmounted great difficulties of execution, and that it was no easy matter to sing at all as they did.   I now listened with interest, though not with sympathetic liking.   This was the second stage, and I never got beyond it so far as the solos of an 'Alma were concerned, though I did listen to the choruses of the boatmen on the Nile, and especially at the first cataract, with real pleasure.   The third stage is when a man adores the 'Alma, prefers her singing to that of all the *prima donnas* of Europe, and looks down on all who do not adore her likewise, and prefer her " likewiser."   For there are such men.

That there is something in the singing of the 'Awalim to charm is evident from the extraordinary delight with which all classes in Egypt listen to them.   I think that they are more enthusiastic in this respect, and that music enters more thoroughly into the life of this people, than is the case anywhere in Europe.   The boatmen can do nothing without singing, and they sing extremely difficult choruses with instinctive ease.   The skill and grace with which the different voices are introduced or disappear are really charming, and it is to be desired that more of it could be brought into our own popular songs.   The liking or disliking of peculiarities in music is one of the strongest illustrations of the old saying that there is no disputing about tastes, nor can there be when you once know what you really mean by taste.   Carl Engel, in his great book on " Popular Songs," which is quite beyond the comprehension of

I

those promising amateurs who sneer at "tunes," speaks of a Greek who could greatly enjoy airs played with one finger on a piano, but to whom the simplest accompaniment rendered the whole a meaningless jangle. I can remember learning to like Japanese music after I had heard it a few times. Ole Bull, who had studied Chinese music deeply, told me once that it consisted of airs very much like the Scotch.

The great desire of gentlemen who come to Egypt is the dancing-girl. If it were put to the vote, most of them would prefer her to the Pyramids, if not to the Nile. Even the moral and pious, the oldest and coldest, cannot forego this bit of temptation; so they get themselves earnestly assured by their dragoman, or, better still, by some gentleman of acknowledged high character—if possible from Boston—that there is really nothing in the performance which would call a blush, *et cætera*. It is better still if Mr High Character gravely assures them that in fact he found it very stupid, and the Ghawâzi very ugly. All of this is thankfully accepted, for admitting it in full, the dancers are still Improprieties, which is a charm beyond beauty; and however good a man may be, he is seldom willing to admit he did not *see* it, and knows nothing directly about it. Hardened worldlings who frequent the regular ballet are not so deeply disgusted with the Gazieh, nor do they find her so altogether stupid or so invariably ugly.

The dancing-girls are obliged by law to remain at one or two places on the Nile. Formerly they strayed

through the streets of Cairo and other towns, and a
resident assured me that he had seen them perform on
the verandah before Shepheard's Hotel. The result of
the moral restriction has been to confine familiarity with
their feats to the wealthy, since it is still the fashion for
the well-to-do, when they give " fantasias " in their
houses, to send for Ghawázi, who are invariably procured
from somewhere. Thus it was that that eminent moralist,
Mr Bloater, regarded the liquor question. " Can there
be," asked that philanthropist, " a meaner—yes, gentlemen, a more degrading spectacle than to see a man—a
being actually calling himself man—sneaking into a bar-
room, and there tippling a miserable sixpence worth of
brandy? No, gentlemen; if a man *must* get drunk, let him
buy his liquor by the gallon and send it home, and share
it with the wife of his bosom and the babes of his love."

As regards the impropriety of the dancing said to be
performed by the Ghawázi in very select and private
circles, I have nothing to say, except that it should no
more be taken into critical consideration than that of
French ballet-girls under the same circumstances. As
to the grave question of indecency in their public exhi-
bitions, even before men, when no women were present,
I am assured by the most experienced that I had several
very good opportunities of judging what it was. And
my opinion is that, contrasted with the European ballet,
one is just about as good, or as bad, as the other. A
person of intelligence who had never seen either, and
who regarded mere nudity, and the attempt to make the

most of it by languishing postures, as specially wicked,
would, if called to judge, think that the ballet was the
most immoral of the two. A man to whom mere ex-
posure is familiar, as it is to all orientals in daily
life, would perhaps object to suggestive gestures, and
he would accordingly condemn the Ghawâzi. Those
who are accustomed to one or the other very soon
become almost entirely oblivious of the "impropriety," real or intended, and reduce their admiration to the mere abstract *skill* displayed. Innocent
young people seldom perceive anything wrong in either.
The glitter of the dresses, the music, the gaiety of the
dancing, is all that they heed—it is probably as much as
most of us really mind after familiarity has made us indifferent. For it is true that if you only eat the apple
of knowledge until you are tired of it, you will be in
many respects as if you had never tasted thereof.

Most of the dancing of the Ghawâzi is indifferent
enough, especially when European ladies are present,
or gentlemen who manifest no interest whatever in their
performances. It is, however, remarkable that what
skill they do exhibit, even under these circumstances,
is seldom appreciated; for the dullest of them generally
effect merely muscular feats, such as one never sees
in the West, yet which are not directly perceptible.
They all seem to have the power of moving any part of
the body freely, just as certain persons can move their
ears; and it is wonderful how they will continue to
agitate every muscle in the most violent and rapid

manner for hours, quivering from head to foot as if
electrified, without being in the least fatigued, and, what
is incredible, without perspiring.

I only once saw Ghawázi dancing, which was, in the
opinion of native gentlemen, and of Europeans who had
been many years in the country, and had full opportunities of judging, of a really superior and artistic
character. This was at Girgeh. There were two girls,
one quite pretty and young, the other less attractive,
but rather the better dancer. The music consisted of
an orchestra of four or five men and women with the
tair and *darabúka*, two kinds of tamborines, the *nai* or
reed-flute, and the *rabab* or violin. The dancers themselves play invariably, while dancing, on the *sa'g'at* or
brass castanets, which appear to cause no little trouble
by getting untied or displaced. Before the regular
dancing commences, yet while undulating about the
room, the Ghawázi generally sing with constant repetition one or two verses, in which it is not unlikely the
ear most unfamiliar with Arabic will soon distinguish
the word *mahboobe* or "beloved." The following dance-
verses were collected by M. Antoine, of Constantinople,
from different Ghawázi on the Nile, and by him obligingly translated and given to me :—

> "By those black eyes!
> By thy forehead and lips!
> I do love, and beseech thee
> Do not abandon me.

> "The man I love dislikes me.
> In my sorrow I cry

From the bottom of my heart :
Let me a moment enjoy his love,
And afterwards let the world go.

" O Thou ! help me, I cry,
For the man I love,
. The man I love is gone ;
He is gone without return.

" You are a beauty,
Let the people say it.
Your departure is superb ;
He who beholds you
Is maddened by love.

" Day and night why art thou angry ?
By the mere playing of thine eyelids,
Thou driv'st me mad ;
If thou wilt not come,
Send me at least a thought,
I love thee too much,
And great would be my joy in thee."

These dancing-girls were dressed in long skirts, one
over the other, reaching to the ankle, the upper garment being of a whitish-yellow or reddish colour. The
body and arms were clad in a very dark, tightly-fitting
chemise, with white stripes, half an inch broad, about
two inches apart, looking tiger-like. Over this was
worn a very tight jacket of red satin, very short in the
waist, with tight short sleeves. On their heads were
curiously-shaped caps, and their hair hung in long
braids. Around the waist was a silver girdle with high
bosses, and dependent from it in loops was a very
curious and massive ornament or chain, made of eight
or ten triangular silver boxes, and many large silver

beads. A profusion of gold necklaces, coins, and other
ornaments hung from the neck and head. Other Ghawâzi
at different towns wore dresses very different from this.
At one place their garments were of black from head to
foot, with silver stripes, while the braids of hair were
very prettily made, terminating in many silver balls.
At Siout I saw one whose only ornaments were an incredible quantity of gold coins of all sizes.

The first dancing of all Ghawâzi is simply moving
about to the music and undulating the body. Then
waves of motion are made to run from head to foot, and
over these waves pass with incredible rapidity the ripples
and thrills, as you have seen a great billow in a breeze
look like a smaller sea ribbed with a thousand wavelets.
All is done in perfect time with the music. Then the
air changes, and there is a variation in the dance. The
girl stops—she becomes immovable below the waist, and
moves only the body above, rocking and swaying, expressive of suffering from intense passion. At times,
and in time with the music, a convulsion thrills the
waist, arms, and head, and sometimes the muscles. She
becomes quiet; but if you observe closely, the movement,
passion, and exertion are not less intense, and the
breasts continue to move as if vitality remained in them
alone—perhaps only one throbs violently.

There is another change, and the dancer sinks slowly
almost to her knees, as if overpowered with passion,
while the arms sweep in singular but graceful gestures.
Perhaps she " waves " slowly in a walking dance, moving

the lower part of her body forward more and more with a vigorous quivering, and once in ten seconds starting with a convulsion, which gradually becomes more frequent until she apparently yields and expires.

The girl at Girgeh performed a very pretty dance, which was quite a poem. Placing a cup, symbolic of temptation, on the ground, she danced around it in a style which was perfectly Spanish, turning the body and sinking low with great grace and exquisite art. The cup appeared to exercise a terrible fascination, but she was afraid to drain it. Five times, without aid from her arms, she almost lay on the ground with her thirsty lips just dallying with the edge, and then rising, swept in dance, and thrilled, and shivered, and turned, and sank again. The sixth time she had completed a circle, and no longer able to resist, she approached the cup with throbs and pauses, and then, without using her hand, lifted it from the ground with her lips alone, draining it as she rose, and the tragedy of temptation being over, merrily danced about the room in quick step, with her head thrown back, holding the cup all the time in her mouth.

Then the elder girl placed a vase on her head, and danced for a long time a great variety of movements without letting it fall, the same being done in turn by the younger. I did not see, however, as my fellow-travellers did on another occasion, dancing-girls who while dancing made cups run from the head down the side of the face, along the arms and back, as a skilled Hercules in a circus makes cannon-balls travel around him. This is, however, rather juggling than dancing. Sometimes a stick is used in these performances. Sometimes the two girls dance a *duo;* and I have seen this made quite as improper, though not so sickly sentimental, as in any opera-house in Europe, when the *ballerina* falls back into the male object's arms, eyeing him with a leering smile, while she lifts one leg to the gallery.

There are 'Awalim and 'Awalim, and Ghawâzi and Ghawâzi. Some are mere peasant girls who work by day and dance by night; and others are low caste, and dance coarsely, with a male jester taking occasional part in the performances, as I saw at Luxor. I am told that the best are to be seen in Cairo, in the grand harems on great festival occasions. Their style of dancing is the same that prevails, with variations, all over the East; and the great difference between it and that of the West is simply that the one consists principally of expressive movement and pantomime of the body, while the latter is jumping with the legs. There is just the same difference in their dancing and ours that there is in the music; and the oriental is physically quite as difficult as the other.

When I was on the Nile, I gave the Ghawâzi the name " Wavers," as expressive of their movements. Long may they wave !

CHAPTER X.

I DO not know whether it has ever occurred to any of the great philosphoruses who do the Aesthetricks from the reviews down to the refuse of literature, that the street-cries of a nation form the starting-point of its vocal music and poetry. This was seen but as in a glass darkly by the American lady who from the New York cry of *Straw-ber-ries!* made a graceful waltz; but this was not all. The long, shrill trill of many American cries, which come pouring out like musical Missis-sippis, indicates a school and a style of its own. Need I refer to "Hom-mi-ny!" "Tral-la-la-la, lal-la-la" (*ad infinitum*)—"lemon ice-cream—and vanilla too!" with their intonations?

But in the East, in Islam, the street-cry is not only musical and poetical, it is pious and theological. You have heard of the man who cried, "In the name of the Prophet—figs!" Perhaps you thought, as I did, that this was a hoax. Not at all; and really the cries collected by Lane and the author of the "Deutsche Dragoman" and others are so curious, that having paid some attention to the subject, I have resolved to give a few. It is said that a certain Arab being called "a son of a gun" by an Englishman, gravely replied, "I am not a soldier." This indication by relationship is very Arabic. A Spanish dollar is called *Abu midfa*, the father of the pillars; a hunchback is *Abu sandük*, or father of the box; a crab is *Abu kalàmbo* or *Um-el-jenib;* and I am not sure, that if your slipper was missing, you might not get it by borrowing a phrase from Firmilian, and asking for " the sister of my shoe." The stork is *Abu-el-s'ad*, the father of luck; and I should not be astonished if a gun were the father of a pistol, or a pistol the real son of a gun—from which point we started. I may at least observe that Shakespeare, who was really very intelligent, makes Ancient Pistol a son of a gun, if there ever was one. Now, in the street-cries of Cairo, the raisins from Ruhebe are announced as " *Yelli adil ettemr !* "—" O brothers-in-law of dates!" and lupins with the cry, "Oh, how sweet is the little son of the waters!"—" *Ya ma aḥla bunci el-bahr !* "

Fancy yourself in the Muskee of Cairo, its great native street, where all the street-cries are heard. It is a singular semi-oriental place, ever crowded with strange people, and some of their cries are these:—

THE SELLER OF SUGAR-AND-WATER.

Berrid 'ala kalbak ! Refresh thy heart! *It fi el-ḥarára !* Quench the heat !

DONKEY-BOY.

Sar ! I say, Master ! Tek dis donkey, I say !

SELLER OF RAISIN-WATER.

Mu'allal ya walled! It is well clarified, O my son! *Wahayat abúk mu'allal!* By the life of thy father, it is well clarified!

ENGLISHMAN.

I say, Harry, twig the beggars on that camel!

AMERICAN.

Look here! See that girl in the harem-carriage! You can look right through her veil; and she's looking right through it at us!

SELLER OF CHUBAF (a drink made of water and fruits).

Búlak snénak! Take care of your teeth!

MILKMAN.

Sábáchná abjad! Let our morning be white!

CAKE (PRETZEL) SELLER.

Yá rezzak! Ya kerim! Yá fettah! Ya 'alim! O all nourisher! O all good! O determiner! O omniscient Pretzels!

SELLER OF THE BEST PRETZELS.

Sultani yá ka'k! Pretzels for a sultan!

THE NEW CAKES OF HALEB (Aleppo).

Mál haleb, ya na'im! Made at Haleb. Soft to bite!

SELLER OF BERAZIK (wheat butter-cakes).

Allah er-razik! ya berázik! God is the feeder! O berazik! *Akl es-snénu!* Food for swallows! (i.e., young ladies).

PIOUS OLD BLIND BEGGAR (stretching his hands over the head of Syrian shopman and two French customers in an open bazaar).
Selámát! Taibin! Good health to you! Be ye well!

CARRIAGE-DRIVER roars—
Shimálek! Shimálek! (Look out for) your left! your left!

SAIs, or RUNNING-MAN.

Ye-mee-nak! Your right! (i.e., Guard your right side!)

DONKEY-BOY.

Ya bint ! Ya mar ! O girl ! O woman ! *Wughak !* Your face !
Gembak ! Your side !

SERVANT.

Riglak ! Your foot ! *Ka'buk !* Your heel !

LEVANTINE SHOPMAN.

Non è troppo caro, signore. L'ho pagato due volte piu ch'io lo vendo.

PRETTY WOMAN (whose veil has fallen).

Ya nedamti ! ya da'weti ! Oh, my trouble ! Oh, miserable !

UGLY WOMAN (satirically and incredulously).

Wallah ! O Lord !

BEGGAR.

Ana deif Allah wa'n 'nebi ! I am the guest of God and of the Prophet ! *Ara lissa' fatran !* I have not yet breakfasted !

PASSER-BY (in reply).

Allah yeftah 'alék ! God open to thee (the hearts of men) !

ANOTHER (to one sneezing).

Subhan Allah ! El hamd Allah ! Praise God ! Thank God !

ALL PRESENT.

Allah yarhemkum ! God have mercy on you !

THE SNEEZER.

Allah yahdini wahjahdikum ! God guide me and you ! *Agrakum
Allah !* God reward you !

A MAN yawns, and says—

A'ud billah min esh-shaitôn er-regim ! I seek refuge in God from
Satan the accursed !

MUEZZIN (from a Mosque).

*Allah akbar. Ashod ann la ilah ill' Allah. Ashod ann Mohammed
rasul Allah !* God is greatest. I declare that there is no god
but God. I declare that Mohamet is the prophet of God !

Hei 'ala-s-salat. Hei 'ala-l-felah ! Es-salât cher min el-rum. Allâh atbar. La ilaha ill-Allâh ! Come to prayer, come to salvation ! Prayer is better than sleep. God is very great. There is no god but God !

CHORUS OF DONKEY-BOYS.

Velly fine donkey, master ! *Signore, Eccolo qua, bell 'asino ! Ya himar !* Lady, you want go Tunis bazâr ?

ONE TO ANOTHER DRINKING SHERBET.

Henian ! May it do you good !

THE SHERBET-DRINKER.

Allah yehennik ! God give you pleasure !

KIND MUSLIM TO CRUEL DONKEY-BOY.

Ya menhûs ma techâf min Allah bedak temmawit ed-dâbbe ! Wretch ! dost thou not fear God ? Wilt thou kill the animal ?

DONKEY-BOY, in reply.

La, ya Sîdi lâkin nahn nâs fukarâ meskîn ! No, sir ; but we are poor, miserable people !

ONE FRIEND TO ANOTHER.

Allahu a'lam sami 't el wâli ma'zul. Is it true ? I hear that the Governor has been displaced.

FRIEND.

Jestefilu ! Let them do what they like ! Let the pigs roll in their mud !

SELLER OF GARDAKA-CAKES.

'Awaid Allâh el-kerem ! Mercy deserves a rich reward from God !

SELLER OF CHOBS-EL-MARUK (broad wheat-cakes).

Hada ilak ya saïm ! This belongs to thee, O fasting man ! *Y mâ 'arrakûk bil-lel ya ma'rûk !* How they did knead ye in the night, O cakes !

MELON-SEED SELLER.

Ya muselli el-galbân, ya lîbb ! O consoler of the afflicted ! O seeds !

PICKLE-SELLER.

Shâ lillâh ya salichîn ! Something for God, ye religious !

SELLER OF SALAD.

Ed-daim Allah, Allah ed-daim ! God is the Enduring, the Enduring is God ! (This is said because salad soon wilts.) *Mubessir es-séf !* The harbinger of summer !

SELLER OF DRAGUN (Kaiseralat.)

Allah yechûn el-châin ! God is not true to the false ! *Allah kabtlak, ya châin !* God calls thee to a reckoning, O untrue ! (Because this plant deceives the gardener by not coming up where it is planted.)

SELLER OF YOUNG CUCUMBERS.

'Alêk el iwad ya molai ! The recompense, O Lord, is with thee !

LEMON-SELLER.

Allah yehawinhâ ya limûn ! God make them easy to sell, O lemons !

ROSE-SELLER.

El ward kân shôk 'arak ennebi fatah ! The rose was a thorn, she bloomed from the sweat of the Prophet !

HENNA (DYE) SELLER.

Rawâyech el genne yâ tamar henne ! Perfume of Paradise ! flowers of the henna-tree !

CAKE-SELLER.

Shug'l et tôr yâ bindt ! The work of oxen, O maiden !

There are many more street-cries in Cairo, not less curious or pious or difficult to comprehend than these. But enough is as good as a feast, and any obliging shop-man will communicate more to him who would have them. The religious character of many of them suggests as many reflections. I have already observed to the reader that the Muslim calmly puts his religion forward in daily life, prays on the pavement, and intro-

duces piety into conversation without the least suspicion
of cant. In England, efforts in this direction are not
a success. The costermonger who should follow up his
cry of "'Ere's your fresh cowcumbers!" with a biblical
illustration would be considered as blasphemous. And
the texts which are sometimes chalked in the streets of
London would in American cities, at least, be considered
as appalling. Last summer there was a very hot Sun-
day, for England, where it always seems hotter at 70°
Fahrenheit, shade, than in other countries at 90°. Now
there was a long stretch of shadeless pavement, whereon
he who walked felt about as comfortable as the travellers
on Milton's "burning marl." And just on the hottest
part of the walk, and near the door of a cool chapel, was
chalked in enormous letters, *"Are you prepared for hell?"*

As improper to many people are the singular poems
which are occasionally circulated with a view to "popu-
larising" religion. One day while an immense crowd
was waiting to see Her Majesty leave the Palace, a
solemn-looking man went about distributing printed
slips. The one which he gave me contained Rowland
Hill's famous poem in which the Church is compared
to a bank, and the Lord to its directors and president.
Such pious fun works in two ways. When this poem
first became known in America a very graceless gentleman, believing it to be a blasphemous burlesque by some
fellow-sinner, had copies of it printed off and distributed
to his friends as a joke on the "seriously inclined."
When the author of "Erewhon" made a similar parallel,

he veiled his allusions so carefully that one rather intelligent reader among my friends did not see through
them at all.

Bless me! bless me! bless me!—how I digress!
And all I wanted to say was that I believe that the
want of other literary knowledge makes the naturally
lively orientals shape all similes with religion, as
Abraham Lincoln did the gravest matters with anec-
dotes. But the people of the West *have* other knowledge, and apply it; while their religion, which they put
far above it, is not by refined and gentle persons tossed
about in the market-place, or used to season salads.
This is my moral, and I trust, therefore, you will admit
that this little chapter on the street-cries of Cairo is not
without interest or reason.

CHAPTER XL

ALL over the Muslim world or Islam may be seen,
especially in the suburbs of towns, or by river banks,
small cupola-covered buildings, to which, as to the
mosque, pains have been taken to add ornament,
though every other structure near it be of mud
"straight"—or unmingled and plain. These are the
tombs of santons, shekhs, welis, and murabits or
marabûts, all of which words may be translated as
equivalent to saints or holy men. Sometimes these
buildings are of great antiquity, and are said to have
been inhabited by ascetics who never quitted them and
were fed through a hole. In Europe, during that long
carnival of filth, the Middle Ages, in which cardinal
edicts were issued against ladies washing themselves, and
baths were sinful, and soap and towels devices of the
devil, cities were full of these little sties, in which human
pigs wallowed for the daily edification of that class of
the devout to whom the disgusting has far more in common with piety than the beautiful and pure.

Sometimes these tombs stand in the heart of cities, and very much in the way, for, come what may, the religious are shocked at their removal. Not long ago the Sultan gave orders to have a street constructed in Constantinople. The engineer to whom the task was entrusted found that a marabūt's tomb would be directly in the way. He proposed to remove it, but the priests and people rebelled. He " pled " orders. They became furious, so the street was made exactly in the line commanded with the tomb remaining. When it was completed the Sultan rode through it. Great was his anger, I doubt not, when he found the tomb. The engineer was summoned, and he pled " priests." The Sultan's reply was a brief question : " In what time can you have a hundred men here with picks ? " " In ten minutes, your Highness." " Send for them." They appeared, and His Highness remained there till he rode over the spot where the tomb had stood. The present Viceroy of Egypt has a good heart for the same sort of thing—if there be a man living whom I would like to see entirely free to do whatever he pleases, it is he— and his sons I doubt not will be like him.

It is so well established that nobody ever saw a dead jackass, and that Sterne's is an imposture, that when I state that I saw one once in the outskirts of Cairo, of course nobody will believe me. But not only did I see it, but General T—— also,—in fact, he pointed it out. As he also held that a dead ass was a regular impossibility, and could not be, he suggested " mule." But it was an *ass.* Perhaps it was a miracle, and in fact I am sure it was one, for it lay near a saint's tomb, where, as the whole of Islam knows, miracles are as common as flies round honey-jars. And it seems, on due, duer, and due-west reflection, that it was really miraculous, since the very next story which was told me by the Bey was one of a dead jackass and a saint's tomb, albeit I had not mentioned the miracle to himself—in fact, this is the first time I ever told it to anybody. And this is the legend :—

Once upon a time there were two vagabonds named Hassan and Hamet, whose only means of support was a jackass, and a very mean support they found him, as they gained very few piastres per diem by his carrying loads of *ahouna* or *bersim*—corn and clover—from the fields.

So they resolved to drive him to Cairo, where an enterprising young man with a jackass often earns as much as a London cabman. At least, if he does not always earn it, he invariably asks for it, which is quite encouraging, and the next thing to getting it.

When this occurred to them, they could hardly wait till they carried out the heaven-sent idea. They believed it came from Allah, so manifested their pious gratitude by driving and goading the poor donkey with a cruelty which would have appalled a Hampstead Heath ass-driver with horror. I knew one of those men once. He said he knew the French for a jackass, and told me it was *Esel.* He also knew the Rommany for it, and said it was *myla.* There he was right. He denounced fighting as barbarous and unchristian, and said nothing should induce him to follow it as a regular thing. He had lost three knuckles by it, and spake from experience, which *do set* a man right, if anything will.

Hamet hammered and Hassan hastened that ass too much. He couldn't swallow a gallon of beating when he only held a pint. So he upset. They gave him some more stick to make him rise, but he refused to resurge. He kicked a little kick and died.

For the moment neither of his murderers said a word. Orientals always save up their mourning and swearing, as some men do their appetite for dinner, until the fit time. They quietly dug a hole by the roadside and buried him. Then they proceeded to grieve. They had nothing else to do, so poured out the whole of their anticipated fortune in a wealth of woe, and transmuted the jewel of hope into a treasury of pearls. Pearls are tears.

Hassan cried—"O my gazelle! where art thou? Hope of the palm-trees, blossom of the fandango bush, O *Benefseg,* my violet, my pickle—*Auhashtená!* —thou hast made us lonely! O my beautiful!"

Hamet sang—" *Allah yessalimak!* Allah bless thee! *Wallah! astagfir Allah el-azim!* O Lord! I pray for the mercy of God. *Ya Himar-himarya!* O donkey— donkey, oh!"

While they thus sang, weeping rivers, under the palm-trees, behold there came by yet another person,

named Murad, and he seeing the newly-made grave,
and beholding the tears of the survivors, naturally concluded that they had lost a friend. So he began—

"*Inna lillah wa-inna ilahi rági'oon!*   Truly we are of
Allah, yea, verily unto him we return.   *Kéf hál achook?*
How was it with our departed brother?"

Now Hassan was only one-eyed, but he saw with half
an eye that it would be more to their advantage to be
supposed wailing for a friend than for a donkey.   So
he steered his boat according to the Nile.   But if he
was the back of the scimitar, Murad was its edge; and it
occurred to the latter that if the deceased were a saint—or
could be made one—it might also make the fortunes of
all concerned.   So he sat down and beat his breast and
piled dust on his head, and inquired if the departed
were not a holy man?   Also if they were not his disciples?   Also if he was not very distinguished?

"*Walláhi! abadan mafish dseihu fil-dunya!*   By Allah
there was not such another in the world!" cried both
the disciples in a breath.

"Could he work miracles?" inquired Murad.

"Miracles!   He could carry four sacks of corn thirty
miles.   He never wore any clothes.   He never looked
at a woman.   Had he never heard of the great Shekh
Himar?   *Mashallah!*"

Now *himar* means a jackass, but all that Murad reflected was, that if the dead was a Himarite, all the
better.

"*El hamdu lillah!*   Thank Allah!   We have no saint

buried near this village. This will be our prosperity—
yea, as bread unto hunger, and honey upon bread. We
are all holy men, let us make a square thing of it.
Insha'allah! you shall wait on the tomb, and I will
ring in the worshippers with their offerings. You do
the piety and I the biz."

Then they all sat down and howled. There came by
a villager, and another, and anotherer, and another-
est. They cried, "O my lord! my lion! my glory!
my help! my father! my camel! my ass!" It is usual
to cry all of these at a funeral in the East, so that
screaming "my ass!" did not attract suspicion. It is a
comfort to think that there should have been among
these lies one grain of truth!

It all came to pass as Murad had foretold. There
was a fine tomb built, which looked at a distance like a
great pudding on a high plate, and out of this pudding
the three did not fail to pick many plums of prosperity.
Chickens flowed in upon them, and there was a gush of
turkeys. Murad circulated a report that every boat
which left an offering at the tomb of Saint Himar went
up or down the river with an angel whose specialty it
was to keep them off sandbanks. Sometimes they got
sanded or mudded "all same," but this was caused by
somebody on board having an unrepented sin in his
bosom.

They might have gone on happily in the business to
this day, had they only carried out the original agree-
ment of doing things on the square. But Hassan and

Hamet went on the cross with Murad, and "knocked down" on him, which is the New York for cheated. A robbery generally leads to a bobbery, and one day Murad raised the thermometer in the junta.

"*Ibn-el-kelb!*"—"O son of a dog!" he cried to Hamet, who handed him one lean chicken as his portion out of six fine hens which he had caused to come in the day before,—"is this the way you treat me?"

"*In al ginsak, ya ibn-el-sharmute!*"—"Curse your race, you son of a social evil!" was the reply. "Are you a holy man of the temple like us? *In al dagnak, ibn-el-harám!*"—"Curse your beard, O son of a thief!"

"*Ya hinzeer—enti ma 'arass!*"—"O pig and child of sin!" roared Hassan, as he threw a bundle of wax-tapers at Murad, hurting his head. "There is an offering for thee—*telhas teezi!*"

"*Ah ya miletil bazawank, ya maloun!*" yelled Murad, wrought to madness by their conduct, and resolved to be beaten neither in kicking or cursing. Saying this he gave the astonished Hamet an awful peeler on the head with a great stick, which took as great an effect, and then caromed off on Hassan, giving him its twin. And diving to the depths of the gulf of profanity, he brought up this pearl of perdition—"*Ya kafeer—Allah yelbisak borneta!*" Now this means, "O unbeliever! may God put a chimney-pot hat on your head!" which is equivalent to wishing you may become a Christian. (It would be, however, still a pretty severe imprecation if it referred to the hats made by Mr ——, even without any theological meaning.)

This broke up the shop, and the " Co." rushing at Murad, put him out with a " *Ruah lil-Gehennum!* "— which is a forcible commendation to any man, or anybody, in fact, to travel downwards. Murad considered Gehennum or Gehenna in this case to be the village. He rushed thither and split on them. The village arose in its wrath. But when it got to the tomb the holy men were gone. Far down the river in the evening dim there was a boat with sunlight on its sails. A month after there were two new shopmen in Cairo, who had set up with a handsome capital. It is finished!

There is a very famous tomb at Minieh, but the good man who lies in it has no connection with donkeys, for he is buried with his horse. This one is the true king of the crocodiles. Old writers who deal in the marvellous say that the crocodiles have a king and queen among themselves in Crocodilopolis. But this is not true. The Greek Reader says that " *O Neilos esti o potamos ton krokodeilon* "—" The Nile is the river of crocodiles." Therefore he who controls the crocodiles of the Nile must be their true ruler. And it is an established fact that the shekh of the crocodiles who is in the tomb has banned his subjects that none of them is to go down the river below Minieh. *And none of them do.* In fact, since the steamboats have been running, they seldom get so far down as Minieh, and thousands

of travellers have gone for days beyond it, and as far as
the First Cataract, without seeing one.

I would add, that when I was at Minieh I tasted
some rum made there. I had often heard of the Minié
rifle brand, which kills at forty rods. That day I tried
it, yet I still live.

The Bey told me another story, which is connected
with the empty tomb of a certain saint. It is old
Arabic, but the reader cannot fail to be interested in
its resemblance in one point to the strange mediæval
legend of the Tannhäuser.

Once there was a man who was extremely wicked.
He had been a robber. His sins exceeded, as he believed, those of all mankind.

One day he repented. He went to a great marabút—
the holiest man alive. And the greatest sinner said to
the greatest saint—"I have committed all crimes; I
have slain ninety-nine men. Can I be forgiven?"

Then the saint took a dry staff and struck it into the
ground. He said—"When this staff sprouts you will
be forgiven."

The robber in despair left the city. He said to himself, "Assuredly I am the wickedest, and for the
wickedest there can be no forgiveness." So he fled by
night into an ancient tomb.

But in that tomb he found a man, *cum filia mortua*,
and this man was committing a greater crime than the
robber had ever dreamed of. So the robber, in a
virtuous rage, slew him.

That hour the saint saw that the stick had budded
and sprouted leaves. And when the repentant robber
returned he wept with him, and assured him that his
sins were forgiven.

For however wicked a man may be, he is sure to find
a wickeder; and one good deed allied to repentance,
can open to him the door of heaven.

CHAPTER XII.

IT was once said of a certain man that he would tell a story on less provocation than anybody that ever lived. I begin to believe that *that* man was almost I. And it came into my head to say this, because just now, when I was thinking how I had made you readers a promise, a story about keeping promises, and giving a good illustration, came leaping head-over-heels into my mind like a clown through a stage window. I'll be—rewarded if I don't believe that the illustrating story got in before the proposition—as the dog got into the village ahead of the bear!

What I promised you was to write a book about Egypt as it is, considering that I am in a jumbled condition about Egypt as it isn't. And thinking of a good illustration, there came the Bey's story—it comes straight out of Arabic by English—a good mare and sire.

"Sometimes," said the jester to the sultan, "an apology may be worse than the offence."

"Now, by Allah!" replied the sultan, "if you do not give me a good illustration of that—*aktar rasah!*—I'll cut your head off!"

"*Won't* I?" replied the jester.

"Won't *I?*" retorted the sultan, sweeping away.

Now they had each used the same words; but oh! what a tremendous depth of meaning was in the difference of the accents! The jester's meaning intellect, the sultan's force, you observe.

Now the jester was not in the least troubled, but the sultan was very much afraid he should lose the jester. I wish you to note this point keenly,—*why the jester was unconcerned.* It bears closely on what precedes it in this chapter, which, by the way, is the most ingenious piece of subtlety, my dear sir, in the book.

That night the sultan entered his favourite apartment—it was dark. He called for a light; but before it came—Mashed turnips! Mashed potatoes! Mash Allah!—somebody, and that somebody a man, embraced him—kissed him! At that instant light was borne in. The sultan saw that the impudent embracer was the jester.

"Death!" roared the sultan.

"I beg your Splendour's pardon," said the jester. "I took you for somebody else."

"And who else, O slave?"

"For your favourite sultana, O king," was the reply. And the sultan roared with laughter. "By Allah!" he replied, "that apology is worse than the offence."

The jester flourished for a long life. I stood not long

since by the sultan's grave, and an old man who showed it taught me how to spin a yarn with a little lead weight attached to it.

But you don't see as yet why the jester wasn't afraid.

He wasn't afraid, my dear, because the idea of kissing the sultan, and saying he thought it was the sultana, had occurred to him long before. Then he reflected how he could do it without being punished. He had only to tell the sultan that a reason might be more weighty than a cause, or an excuse than an offence. Why, bless you, the sultan was a baby in this trap.

And now you see how it was that a wise man profits, as this jester did, by getting the illustration into his head before the proposition. His dog and mine both came into town before the bear !

" But what was the story of the dog and the bear ? "

Well, if you never heard it, I don't mind telling it to you. But I thought everybody knew that story.

Once there was a man in Minnesota or Maine, or somewhere in that part of the country, who had a dog. He bragged of that dog, he did. There was no beast of the field, or of the forest either, who could hold up against him. And bears ! oh, he was great on bears. That was his particular game. He was a terror to bears —that must be admitted. He was rather sorry for it, too ; he was afraid that Terror was making bears rather too scarce in that region.

One day he met a neighbour. The neighbour said, " That is a great dog of yourn ! "

" He just is," replied the owner. " Hev you perceived him lately ? "

" I saw him about half-an-hour ago," answered the neighbour. " He was havin' a great time with a bear."

" You bet ! " cried the owner. " And which beat ? "

" Well, nary one of 'em was beat. But the dog was beatin' the bear."

" Of course. But why didn't you help him ? "

" 'Cause they were going too fast. It wasn't a fight. It was a race. And your dog was ever so far ahead. He was just gittin' into town when I seen him."

Now can you tell me, supposing that bear really had been destined to catch everything he pursued, and the dog had been so shaped by predestination that nothing could catch him—how it could be settled for them ?

The ancient Greeks knew no better way than to turn them both into stone. But the Arabs, who have a turn for higher mathematics than the Greeks achieved, settle this problem by making them run on lines which are always approaching each other, and yet less gradually. They are continually getting nearer, and yet running more and more into parallels. The bear will catch the dog at the coming of the Cocklicranes, on the very day when the Saxon Heptarchy shall be re-established, and the second edition of —— be issued. And until that day the dog will escape. Now the Cocklicranes may come, and the Saxon Heptarchy might be established. But I am afraid I made a mistake in assuming the third event as a possibility.

For I defy the devil himself to ever induce the public to call for a second edition of Mr ———'s book.

When you propose anything, and then tell a story to illustrate the proposition, it is like the jester with his illustration, or the dog and the bear. Still more is it like setting up one looking-glass or mirror exactly opposite the other on the either side of a room. One mirror reflects the other, and the other that, and so on ; not for ever, for there is a point where the reflection ceases. But no man living can prove where it is.

Now it was with this simile of the mirrors that I began to think up this chapter, and that led me to the dog and the bear, and that to the idea of a story's coming before the reason for telling it, and that to the jester, and that to the introduction. And then came the Holy One of Israel ; blessed be He ; who slew the Malach Hammoves (Angel of Death), who killed the Schochet (butcher), who killed the ox, which drank the water, which quenched the fire, which burnt the stick, which beat the dog, which ate the kid, which my father bought for two pieces of money.

Thus the end was before the beginning, as it ever should be with all story-tellers. You know, I suppose, why all novelists are queer fishes ? It is because, like whitings when served, their tales come out of their heads. And

so it comes to pass that this chapter, take it for all in
all, is the most subtle, wonderful, glorious, ingenious,
stupendous defence of story-telling ever concocted by
mortal man on the face of the earth since the serpent
first induced Eve to peruse the pages of that fascinating
fiction the Apple, afterwards reviewed so severely in
the columns of the Flaming Sword.

CHAPTER XIII.

I BELIEVE I said before that there are only some twenty
names in all Islam, an astonishing proportion being
Mohamets and Owlies. But they have a way of varying
these rations, so as to make them go as far as possible.
Mullah means Reverend, and Abdullah the Servant of
God, but both have the same root. Mohamet or Mahomed becomes Mehemet, Hamet, Mah'moud, and so
forth. Saïd, the Fortunate, is also Sa'ad, Massaoud,
and Sey'eed. Many of my American readers have
heard the coloured people in America say Sa'ady! to
one another for "Thank you!" and perhaps used it themselves. I can remember when our cook, who had been
a slave, taught me to say "Sa'ady" for gingerbread;
and I considered it particularly high-polite in those days,
till cured by maternal objection. It may be new to many
to know that *Sa'adi* means "Luck to you!" and is much
the same as *Selâmek*, the common Mahometan greeting.

Then Abdurrachman, Abderahman, becomes Abdulra-
heem, 'Rachman, 'Raheem, and so on. It often comes
to pass that ignorant little Mahometan boys are not
aware that their fragmentary appellations are really
nicks for larger names, as was the case with a small
Dutch gutter-snipe or mud-lark in New York who had
been caught and caged in a public school. He was
desirous of being a good boy, and of distinguishing
himself—I only hope that *my* youthful readers are in
the same line—and so kept a bright look-out on all the
performances.

Now the schoolmistress began by calling the boys up
and checking off their names. And to one she said—

" What 's your name, little boy? "

" Tom."

" Oh, dear me! No. That 'll never do. Remember your name is Thomas. Now, you other little boy,
what is *your* name? "

" Nickel."

" *Nickel!* oh, no. It must be Nicholas. Now, you
third little boy, what is *your* name? "

The third little boy was the small Dutch gutter-snipe
already mentioned. He had taken the bearings and was
going to sail all right. So with a grin of superior intelligence he replied—

" Jack-ass."

They tell this in a different way. The first boy being
Lemuel, called himself Lem; the second, Samuel, gave
his name as Sam; and the third, who was wide awake,

reported as Jim-uel. From that day forth Jimuel became a fond and friendly term for Jameses in America.

On the Nile the natives have an extraordinary fancy for begging strangers for names. Just as in Cairo a poor man who has lost a son will go and cry in the street that strangers and bypassers may condole with him and help him to bits of comfort, so a woman who is a fruitful vine will hail the boats going down or up the river and ask for a name for her last bunch of grapes. The Bey told me of this curious custom, and added :—
"Last year, going from Damietta, a man cried out to us in the night, 'Name my child.' And my friend replied, 'Mohammed.' But if it had been Shaïtan (or Satan), or Ruah Gehennum (go to—Tophet), it would have been the same thing, for the first name given or the first word uttered in reply must be taken." Anything else would be unlucky, and the child's future prove as wretched as the one wished by a nice young lady in a New England factory to a superintendent. The young lady had struck for higher wages. The super. offered her the old price, and told her imperatively to go to work. *She* answered that she 'd see him at work in Tophet first, pumping thunder at three cents a clap, before she 'd do it. But it often happens that rude people in jest do reply profanely to the request of the parents, whence it comes that along the river you often hear mothers crying to their offspring, " Come here, little Go to—Jericho!" " Go away, Shut-up!—why

do you abuse your brother, Stupid, in that way?"
The name Abu Shadoof, meaning Father of the Water-
wheel, is very commonly given to these requests,
whence it comes that an immense number of little
parents of these aquarian institutions are to be met
with.

The starting-name in Islam is that of the Prophet,
just as John Smith is among us. Mohamet is their
John Smith or José Maria. Then, as Mr Lane tells
us, after Mohamet, or Ahmad, or Achmet, or Mûstapha,
come the names of his relations—Ali, Hussan or Hussein
or Hoseyn; and his friends—Omar, Abu Bekr, Osman,
and Ameer or Amr. There have been many little
family quarrels, taking the form of sects, among the
faithful, referring to these individuals, and great virtue
is attached to their names. Thus it is confidently believed by the followers of Ali that if one walks up
to a lion and says, "Ya Ali!" (O Ali!) the lion
nods his head, like a ticket-taker in the theatre when
he hears " Press," and the man is allowed to " pass."
But if he should say, " Ya Omar!" he is also converted
into a "dead-head," but not of the right sort—for the
lion gobbles him at once.

After this party, the patriarchs and prophets—Ibra-
heem, Isha'ck or Isaac, Ishmaeel, Yacob, Moosa or
Moses, Daood or David, and Suleyman or Solomon—
have their turn. Then come the fancy names, such as
Abd-Allah, " Servant of the Lord; " Abd-er-Rahman,
" Servant of the Compassionate;" Abd-el-Kader, " Ser-

vant of the Powerful." Girls, continues Mr Lane, are
mostly named after the wives or daughters of the
Arabian Prophet, or after others of his family, as Kha-
deega, Ayesha, Amneh, Fat'meh or Fatima, and Zey-
neb. " In Cairo it is the fashion to change these into
Khuddoogeh, 'Eiyoosheh, Ammoóneh, Futtoot'meh, and
Zennoo'beh, . . . which measure implies, in these
cases, a superior degree of dignity." So in America,
Sally becomes Sal*lie*; Mary, Ma*rie*; Polly, Pol*lie*; and, I
suppose, Judy, Ju*die*, and Biddy, Bid*die*. I have heard
this spoken of as a modern invention; but in the ballad
of " Lord Lovel," which is unquestionably ancient, a
man, wishing to speak with highest respect of the
heroine, says—

> " And *some* call her Lady Nan-*cie-cie-cie*,
> And some call her Lady Nan*cie.*"

Here he distinctly intimates by the word " some "
that it was decidedly the *élite* who affected that sort of
name.

Other Mahometan misses are called Maboobeh, or My
booby—a term also applied at times in England and
America to boys. In Arabic it means " My beloved;"
in English it signifies " Now then, stupid!" They
also catch occasionally Mebrookeh ("My blessed!")
This I have also heard in America addressed to young
ladies, sometimes in endearment, more frequently when
they have upset tea-cups, or astonished the natives of
the family. Nefee'seh is likewise a dame name. It

means " Precious," and among the " quality" becomes
Neffoo'seh.

I have penned the foregoing chapter from an over-
whelming sense of duty. There will be among my
readers a few who cannot fail to notice that in Egypt
the natives are not only of a different colour from themselves, but that they also wear different apparel, and it
may possibly strike them that they have different names.
A very observant young lady told me once that she *had*
noticed that their Christian names were different from
ours. I replied meekly that I didn't think they had
any Christian names, but I was told " indeed they had."
I, however, still adhere to my opinion. To resume.
Among these intelligent travellers, those who observe
this difference in names may also be gratified to learn
that these names have meanings, and for such I shall
not have written in vain.

CHAPTER XIV.

IT is generally allowed by most people that Egypt was
the original country and mother of all mysteries, although
Alexander Historicus declares the Egyptians got all they
knew from the Jews by way of Abraham, who set up an
office for fortune-telling in Heliopolis, and gave lessons
in astrology to the chief priests—issuing, I suppose, little
cards on which was inscribed, " Predicts marriage, shows
the face of your future husband, recovers stolen goods,
by the planets.   Gentlemen, one dollar; second storey,
back building.   *N.B.*—Ring at the gate."   This he
learned of Enoch, and, as the learned Jesuit Nicolaus
Caussinus shrewdly remarks, it only stands to reason
that one who knew astrology " could not want all the
sciences, nor a knowledge of those mystical symbols and
enigmas by which all learning was in ancient times con-

verted to darksome lore." In which opinion Alexander
is endorsed by Eusebius of the Spectacles, Eupolemus
and Clement of Alexandria—all of them ragged old
toss-pots and jolly bricks, whose opinion is not to be
lightly regarded. On the other hand, the great and
good Giordano Bruno, my special master, upsets this
theory of Alexander's as easily as you would cannon
chain-shot at billiards, showing that " *Gli Ebrei abbiano
tolti questi misterj da gli Egizj* "—" The Jews got all
these mysteries from the Egyptians," as will appear more
fully in my great chapter on Asses and Donkey-boys—
which chapter if it do not appal you, I hope you may be
delivered over bound into the hands of the—musquitoes.

Among other mysteries still extant in Egypt are the
sweet and secret love-ties between men and female
spirits. I had heard of these wonders, but must frankly
confess I had my doubts as to their truth until I referred
the matter to the Bey, who at once clearly and squarely
assured me they were still as common in this country as
left-handed affairs in England—in fact, he knew himself
of more than one, if not as much as many gentlemen
who maintained a cordial understanding with some
beautiful Melusina. " Did I never hear in my country
of any men being in love with *Jinny?* "

Now my mind at once reverted to Miss Virginia ——,
and Mrs Virginia ——, both familiarly known as Jinny
——, and Jane C——, who wore the same garment of the
soul, and Jinny who is exhorted in the song to get her
hoe-cake done. But I knew that the Bey meant by

Jinny the invisible spirits of the air, so I thrust aside
the temptation of evil to joke or equivoke, and simply
and pleasantly replied, " No."

Now I must inform you that the Bey, although he
would be regarded by my readers merely as a Heathen
Chinee (as I indeed used to call him), so far as religion
goes, he being a turbaned worshipper of Mahound, was,
natheless, an old scholar of Oxenforde, where he had
studied logic, and was accordingly by no means superstitious or lightly given to according faith to frivolous
fancies. Consequently the reader is forewarned and
seriously entreated to believe, even as I believe, in all
the curious things told in this chapter—every one of
which is true on the testimony of men as good as himself, *or you either;* and failing in which faith he may
pack himself forthwith to the dogs, or the d—l, or any
other distinguished politician of whom he may happen
to be a constituent.

And the Bey said that there were assuredly men in
Egypt who had beautiful female spirits for their loves,
and this so frequently, that when any one did not marry
an ordinary woman, his friends understood that he had
found himself a match among the Jinni. In fact, whenever a man led a secluded life, haunting lonely spots,
by springs, fountains, and rivers, in groves, or com-
muning much with the open air on high in ruins, there
could be no doubt of it—a Jin had intoxicated him.

There were many advantages in having a Jin of this
particular brand. They were extremely beautiful—there

could be no deduction from *that*. And many of them
were very generous—in fact, jinnerous—for you may
work it in Arabic with either an *a* or an *e*. They would
call out of the air excellent suppers, pipes, coffee in gold
cups, and then go away and leave you all the valuables.
· This was unquestionable, and it accounted for the property possessed by many men, which, if it did not come
from the clouds or the moon, Allah only knows where
it did come from !

But there were two drawbacks to all these attractions.
Whoever attached himself to one of these beauties must
remain true to her alone for life. And they were terribly jealous, punishing unfaithfulness with death. In
short, they correspond in all respects to our dear little
friend Undine, who, as you remember, was the darlingest
little mixture of spirit-and-water, as Barham hints of the
Lurlei nymph, that ever lived—not forgetting the sugar.
The Egyptian Jinni, be it observed, not unfrequently have
children by their adorers—a perfectly possible thing, as
you may see in the works of St Augustine, lib. iii. cap. 4,
" De Civitate Dei," in the question, " Whether Venus
could have given birth to Anchises by Æneas, or the
daughter of Numitor by Mars," as is treated in full in
that wonderful work " Mons Veneris," by the learned
Henricus Kornmannus.

And I am the more inclined to put faith in what the
Bey told me, since the same learned Kornmannus tells
us that among the Muslim are certain men called
Neffesoglios, born either of the Incubus or Succubus

(the male and female spirits of love); and these Neffesoglios are impiously believed to be born of the Holy Spirit—the Turks honouring them so much that " to be merely touched by them is held to be a wonderful bit of luck." *Quin etiam tangi ab eis singularis felicitatis loco habent.* Yea, even one of their hairs will cure the sick.

And still wider. Does not Johannes Nyderus, in his great book on witches ("In Formicarum," lib. v. cap. 10) show that the race of the Huns was born from the spirits Incubus, and that the whole island of Cyprus was peopled and inhabited *a filiis incuborum*, " by children of *Incubi?* " and yet not merely of the ink you buy either, as I hasten to observe, lest some "intelligent reader " should perceive this point, and hint that they were mere ideal children of the pen, begotten, as one may say, *stylo in pixide*, between sheets of paper. Of which Huns, Bonfinius, whose word none can doubt, tells us that Filimerus, King of the Goths, once banished all the gay ladies from his camps, rightly conjecturing that his scamps would be none the better of them. ("*Meretrices omnes in loca solitaria profligasse ne militum animos et corpora enervarent.*") And the Incubi, seeing these forlorn damsels, came creeping and peeping over the bushes, and giggling through the leaves, while the Ariadnes, noting that they were very handsome ugly fellows for devils, began to do the same, and leer over their fans or fingers, until finally there was as grand an army of flirtations going on in that greenwood and

among the grey rocks as ever you saw at any picnic.
The result of this affair between the starving damsels
and their goblin lovers was the race of Huns, now called
Hungarians ; and it is a curious confirmation of the fact
that the small London punsters of the weaker sort call
them Hungry'uns to this day.

And was not Merlin, the great P.P.—prophet and
poet—"the son of a nun and an invisible spirit "—
ex regis filia Monacha et incubo natus ? And the holy
Augustine tells us that in his time the pretty milk-
maids, and jolly blackberry-picking girls, and black-
eyed Gipsy *juvas*, when in sylvan shades and lonely
glades, were actually so teased and cajoled and be-
bothered by the merry Incubi that they didn't know
which way to turn, " and generally inded by their being
blarneyed intirely "—" *It a molestos fuisse ut concumbere
cum ipsis luxuriamque explere cupierint.*"

And *that* isn't all, neither. I am not done with you
yet. Doesn't Hector Boethius, in his Gothic stories, say
that—not within a mile o' Edinburgh toun, but truly
within four miles of Aberdeen—a certain beautiful spirit
haunted a *bonus episcopus*, "a good bishop," for many
months, slipping into his room every night, and gazing
tenderly and solemnly at him with such great beautiful
eyes, out of a forest of rippling golden hair—"*blanditiisque
in complexum pellicere imo compellere* "—" trying to win
his love with winsome ways," and then gliding away in
dim early dawn, looking over the white shoulder at the
heartless episcopal Adonis? I think I can see the

whole picture : Episcopus in bed, sitting up, praying
fast and wild—the crimson fire and rosy flame—old
carved oak chimney-piece—silver hanging lamp—and
the beautiful spirit in the antique chair, gazing with
glowing eyes like violet stars.

Then there were the Sylphides, Fanny Ellsler and
Taglioni. They were spirits who fell in love with young
men on the stage. I saw them with my own eyes myself, so there can be no "stretch" there. That was long
ago. They were Scotch fairies too, and oh! didn't I
wish that such spirits would haunt me. By the way,
I conversed with Madame Taglioni the very day before
I began this book, and she is still charming.

Then Cæsarius of Cologne tells a wild and wondrous
tale of a certain priest whose daughter was continually
infested by an enamoured spirit. But the priest, not
liking such a son-in law, took his daughter over the
Rhine. A running stream he dared not cross, and the
poor spirit lost his lady-love. But the first time the
priest came back over the river, "the Incubus banged
and thrashed him so that he died within three days."
"*Patrem verò à dæmone sic exagitatum et percussum, ut
intra triduum mortema bierit.*" This was a downright
Deutscher this *Geist*, who probably took a table-leg to
execute his vengeance mit.

Or knowest thou not the deep and fearful song of him
who came from night and dark Etolian woods, and
took the form of Prince Polycritus, and wedded in his
shape the Locrene girl, and fled away and left the wife

to mourn ? And how a strange child was born of this wedding—so strange that the parents were debating in the Forum with the Senate whether it should not be burnt alive, when lo ! to their amazed eyes, Polycritus the spirit appeared, and demanded with fury his child, which being denied, he leaped at the infant and swallowed it all but the head, which he bit off and left lying on the sand—the Etolians being *stupore perculsis*, "rather astonished," which astonishment was increased by the head's prophesying all their murders !

There is also a beautiful story of the fair Hermelina, a charming Succuba, who had, as Franciscus Picus tells us, been the true love for forty years of Benedict Berna, who was sixty-five years of age when Pico knew him, and during all this time Benedict lived alone, and had no other friend on earth save the lovely Hermelina.

> " All other women I forsake,
> And to an elf-queen I me take,
> By dale and eke by down."

And when by chance he went forth *in Forum atque alia loca*, " to the Forum and other places," those who beheld him talking to Hermelina, yet saw nobody, verily believed the old man was out of his mind, which shows how greatly we may be mistaken, and how careful we should be in judging of our neighbours !

There, too, was Pinetus, whom, as we are curtly told, a certain demon deceived for thirty years by giving him her company as a fair woman.

And Jacobus Rufus—yes, there is Jacobus with his

awful story of a girl who preferred the love of a spirit to that of the young gentlemen of Constantine, where she lived—*cum succubo rem habuisse,* "and accepted his attentions "—but who, after the spirit left her—oh, horrors !—began to utter her cries in the form of sticks, pieces of glass, hair-pins, *atque alia ejusmodi*—" and such like." Cheerful !

And in an old chronicle of Cologne it is told that once, when many princes and lords were merrily met in a great and beautiful palace on the Rhine, amid banners and music, with ringing goblets of wine divine, among many fair ladies, lo ! there came a silver bark on the stream, drawn by a swan and golden chain, and in the boat sat a handsome knight, who stayed in Cologne, and married and had a family. But one fine day a goblin snob called for him, and he knew the call and went to the river. There was the " shell boat and silver swan and chain "—*cymba á cygno argentea catena attracta*—and entering it, he left women and babes to mourn—*nec amplius postea esse visum*—" they never beheld him more."

And doth not Alexander ab Alexandro tell us that the fair Alcippe, being loved by an Incubus, brought forth an elephant ? Now I like a man to tell a rouser while he is about it. As is proper, Alexander gives details even to the name of this spirit, which was Marsicus.

No, I'm not going to let you off yet, for my hand is in. Heavens ! what a race of monsters sprang up from the barbarian women of Brazil and their diabolical

adorers ; and does not Johannes de Barros plainly
affirm that all the natives of Pegu and China had
demons for ancestors ? And such an offspring !

> " Ah ! *Sin* was his name,
> And I will not deny
> With regard to the same
> What that name might imply."

Hold on !—don't go ! There's more coming. Another goblin ! Think of the youth Menippus, a scholar
of Demetrius the cynic. One day Menippus packed his
carpet-bag, and with a tin bath-tub started for Cor-
inth. There he saw, at the milliner's shop opposite, the
nicest little girl. That nicest little girl was a gob. She
was a seamstress, and her father had taught her to
sew. He was the same gentleman who once went into
a patch and sowed the tares. This, however, is only a
conjecture of mine : Philostratus, who tells the story,
don't mention it. Menippus proposed marriage. But
there was a certain old Major Apollonius of Tyana, who
knew a thing or two, and he said to Menippus—" Nip,
my boy, don't be in a hurry ; that young lady is one of
the Le Mures—bad family, my dear fellow, a very bad
family. Don't you remember Satanella le Mure who
danced at a little theatre in Athens ? That was her
mother." So Menippus went back on the match, and
the nicest little girl turned into a Snake—at least she
married a man of that name, and showed herself a
" snaky sorceress."

But how was it that Apollonius knew so much about

M

.

the Le Mures? Ah, indeed! Set a—legislator to catch a legislator. Why, Suidas tells us that old Poll himself was the son of an Egyptian incubus by a native girl. Suidas had often seen *her*.

And talking of nymphs who were serpents, and also loved men, there was Melusina, concerning whom I have a whole book. She really married Raimondin the ancestor of the De Lusignan family, which sprung from her. Six days she was a lady, on the seventh she became a serpent, and being caught at it by her husband, wriggled away into the grass and was never seen more.*

And, finally, there was the noble knight Peter von Strauffenberg, *Eques ex Mortenaco*, who for many years lived happily with a beautiful *succuba*. Peter was getting along very well, and took his lager regular, and promised his Liebchen that nodings couldt efer bart dem. But the Emperor Sigismund heard of it, and said to him, " Beder, mine poy, dish von't do. I ton't likes dis dings. Subbose you go mit yourself, Beder, und kit marrit mit some Yungfräulein. Dere ish de Gräfinn Wilhelmina von Schnopplestein. When you ton't marry her, mine tear poy, by Donner, I guts your het off." So Peter, to save his head, got married— *votam fregit, aliamque superinduxit.* But mark the sequel. It was like the story of Undine—on the third day after his marriage Peter died.

* "Raimondin n'eut pas plûtost aperçu cet horrible spectacle, qu'il se repentit de sa curiosité, et connut *Qu'en matière de femme il est souvent dangereux de voir plus qu'elle ne veut qu'on voye.*"—*Histoire de Melusine, Tirté des Chroniques de Poitou.* Paris, 1698.

That is all, and let it be a warning to you. See how it is that, when you tell a story, though it be never so true, yet if you feel ever so little doubtful about it, or, what is worse, suspect that others doubt, what piles of evidence you at once adduce, and how you rake heaven and earth for confirmation! How you begin, as I have done, without waiting for a wink of dissent, to quote all the old yarns you can scrape together! Which is all very pitiful! As the Bey always cried when he saw the ruined temples and mosques—"What a pity! what a pity!" Moral of morals—never tell big stories, even if they *are* true.

CHAPTER XV.

.

EVERYBODY who pretends to intelligence or intellect goes
away from Egypt with an original theory of the Pyramids, so that of late years it has become hard work to
invent a new one. I have heard of a German who was
so hard put to it for an idea on the subject, that he suggested they were great natural crystals, as you may
read in "Meister Karl's Sketch-Book." If you will
take a nitre crystal, you will see that it consists of two
pyramids joined at the base, each having a flight of
steps around it, such as time and ruin have made about
Cheops. Now there is a great deal of nitre in the soil
of Egypt, so that, all things considered, there was a very
fair base for this theory to stand on.

The Pyramids are not as well managed as they might
be, being left to the care of a parcel of rascally Arabs,

under a worthless shekh, whose chief business is to
extract shekels from travellers. During one week I
heard of three perfectly well-authenticated cases of extortion, or attempts amounting to highway robbery, by
these enterprising young men. One lady in the depths
of the Pyramid had been compelled to pay over two
Napoleons. One gentleman had the option offered him
of paying a Napoleon, giving a certificate of good conduct,
or—catching it! The third case was that of the Baron.
They didn't make much though out of him. Listen!

We had all been told—the Baron, his brother, and
I—that we should find it a stiff bit of climb up the
Great Pyramid, especially if we tried to do it without
help from the Arabs. Now, as we were not inexperi-
enced in much stiffer climbing, and had been prowling
about of late in the Mokáttan hills, doing their crags
and jags without much trouble, it did not occur to us
that we could not go up a far easier ascent without assistance. Moreover, there was a very ugly story current
in Cairo that a lady of the highest rank, quite a *knee-
plush-ultra* individual, had caught—O horror!—the *psor-
iasis*, or a dusted jacket—from these Pyramid loafers.
So the Baron wisely determined to go it alone, and alone
he went easily enough with only a big stick for a companion. But about half-way up the enemy half-waylaid
him, demanding a heavy baksheesh, and threatening all
sorts of sorrows for him unless he would comply.

Now the Baron is one of the mildest mannered men
you ever knew, albeit his experience of life has been

greatly varied, and he has lived in countries where there
are more dangerous people than Egyptian vagabonds.
So he gently produced his revolver, and softly said that
if they *would* stop the way he was very much afraid he
must shoot.

Now if there is a being on the face of the earth who
is afraid of a fire-arm it is an Egypto-Arab, especially
when the shooting iron is in the hand of a gentleman.
For the poor devils have been so whacked, mauled, shot
at, cut, thumped, grilled, bastinadoed and carbonadoed
by their betters, that, esteeming themselves as mere
carrion, they can see no especial reason why they should
not be shot at sight, if it pleases the Howaga to do so.
And you will always find that it is just this kind who
are most prone to bullying and extortion when they
think themselves the strongest.

The Baron, as I told you, produced his revolver, and
said, "If you lay a hand on me I will shoot you—
dead."

"You do *dat!*" screamed the Arab. "Suppose you
do dat me go to your consul."

"No," replied the Baron, gravely. "If I do that,
you will go to—the d—l."

So they let him go. Since I have returned to England I hear that an enterprising Scotchman has solicited
of His Highness the Khedivé a concession to show the
Pyramids. I trust he may obtain it. That shop needs
regulating. If he gets in I hope he will construct a
climbable staircase to the summit. I proposed this idea

several times to lovers of the picturesque, and they
squalled—"Oh, no, no! It would destroy all the thing-
gumy—the what d'ye call it?—the romance, you know."
But I don't see it. The surface of the Great Pyramid is
only jagged broken stones projecting like large steps,—the
facing was torn away thousands of years ago by amateur
lovers of what was picturesque in their day, in order to
build pretty palaces and summer houses with. Stones
more or less would not injure the appearance of the pile,
in fact, they would be a partial restitution. And if I
were His Highness, I would farm out all the ruins in
Egypt to an English company, which should charge a
shilling a head to all entering a temple, or a pound for
the lot, with the promise that the temples should be kept
in repair, and, where possible, restored. And I sincerely
trust that the company would be empowered, if such
powers can be extracted out of that terrible imbroglio
called consular jurisdiction, to seize all tourists caught
cutting or writing their idiots' names anywhere, or
knocking off pieces of ruins or statues, and inflict on
them such punishment as is befitting. Burying them
up to the neck in sand, and leaving them there for the
next party to dig out, would not be too mild an infliction
I suppose, or else they might be appropriately branded
with their own names. It is painful to see how unscru-
pulously men will dig and scratch their names even on
statues and bas-reliefs, mad with the petty mania of self.
There was one American who travelled with a hammer
and chisel in his pocket, whose name is carved deeply on

every flat surface in Egypt ("*nomina stultorum semper parietibus insunt*"), and another who, I was told admiringly by an eye-witness, was regularly accompanied in his excursions by a nigger with a paint-pot and brush.

When I went to the Pyramids, it was in a gay party. There is a very pretty little chateau, or summer-house, once erected by the Khedivé with his usual splendid hospitality towards all guests, for the Empress Eugénie. This building is immediately near the Great Pyramid. Its walls within are well frescoed in very good taste with views of Egypt, and here strangers are sometimes permitted to remain, so that we had a comfortable shelter. Then with a friend I ascended the Pyramid. Another friend, who was in authority, and knew how to make the natives understand it, gave them, I suppose, a straight tip to let me alone. Certain it is they *did* neglect me in the kindest manner, to my joy and surprise. My ascending companion regarded the chattering cortége which ran behind and before us in an amiable light, as one might so many monkeys, and being a little under the weather, accepted their aid. He informed me afterwards that they cheered him all the way up with hideous tales of daring travellers who having, contrary to all the laws of God and custom, rashly gone up the Pyramid *alone*, tempted by Satan, had all perished miserably. There was the Russian prince—surely His Excellence had heard of the terrible death of the Russian prince who had indeed attained the top, but was immediately hit by the wrath of Allah—for his feet slipped and he rolled

from the top to the bottom, leaving behind him, at every
bounce, fearful blood-stains—*ug-gh!* There was another
Howaga, he tried to climb without assistance; it made
them creep to think of it, in fact it still haunted their
dreams, how, first calling them and begging their forgiveness, he mildly laid down on the summit and died.
He was just about the size and age of that other Howaga
there who was madly venturing to climb up without their
assistance—God help him!—and came from the same
country. In fact, every one of these gloomy tales ended
with a direct allusion to myself, and the firmly expressed conviction that I had not long to live. The
reader who has never been in the East can have no idea
of the exaggerative and romancing style of these people,
or the serious manner in which, when once started, they
will go on. One day, a dragoman in speaking to a lady
friend of mine of an old gentleman of peculiar appearance who had gone up the Nile with him, said seriously
that the elderly party in question had on a pair of cotton
gloves three hundred years old, with six thousand holes
in them. I attribute this style of narration to the great
age and magnitude of the ruins in the country.

The amount of extravagant, frivolous, and elaborate
writing which has been expended on the Pyramids is
best rebuked by their stern simplicity. The rudest
monument of the earliest and most savage time was
the *cairn*—a heap of stones; and the Pyramids are
nothing but the cairn built with a view to permanence.
They are grand because they are large; they are simple,

not from a cultivated sense of the beautiful in art, but because the age which gave the type to which its descendants adhered from superstitious fear or blind conservatism had got no further and knew no better. They are magnificent as to size; they are "artistic," because the simple types which Nature supplies to the beginnings of architecture in different countries are always graceful; and they are barbarous because there is nothing in them which is not compatible with a barbarous age, and because they manifest a disposition to astonish by mere size and expense.

Well, forty centuries, or rather seventy, of humanity, if you include those who reside around in the neighbourhood, look down from the summit of the Pyramids, where Arabs very appropriately offer you antiques for sale. I thought it queer that one elder offered a number of silver pieces of Phillip III. of Spain, A.D. 1618, which he was willing to dispose of for just about their silver value. But there is a kind of money far more ancient than any made by man which abounds in this Pyramid, and may be had in great amount for the picking up. These coins are the curious nummulites, a kind of flat, round, petrified shell, abounding sometimes by millions and for miles in tertiary fossiliferous limestone. They get their name from the Latin *nummus*, a coin, and are well named, for their resemblance to old, rusty coins dug out of clinging, hardened soil is very remarkable. They are found of all sizes, from a spangle to a half-crown, but sixpennies and shillings seem to have been the average

currency in Cheops. The people about the Pyramids
call them the Sphynx's money; and one day when I was
in the Mokáttan hills I began to collect them, whereupon Mohamet, my donkey-driver, and one or two of
those Arab youths who always improvise· themselves
everywhere out of the ground wherever you go, began
also to cull nummulites with a zeal and fervour only
equalled by the disinterested benevolence they manifested in bestowing them on me. And Mohamet, to
enhance their value or interest, informed me that the
Bedawee, or Bedouins, actually used them for money,
which a very nice young lady who lived in Cairo, and
spoke Arabic, considered doubtful. "That is just like
the Cairenes," was her "opin,"—"always making fun of
the Bedouins. But I can tell you that the Bedouins are
not so green as town-people think." And I am inclined
to think myself that some of them, whether green or not,
have sensible, unaffected natures. I think I saw as
much in the face of one once. I was standing in the
Muskee, looking into a gunsmith's window, when a very
poor but pleasing Arab of the desert, a regular jolly
sand-boy, with a long staff, stopped by me, and gazed
fondly and wistfully on a very fine revolver. Then he
looked at me, and pointing to it asked, "*Bikam di?*"—
"How much would that be?" And not to frighten him
I replied, "*Ithnine vinto*"—"Two Napoleons," though
I am sure it must have cost eight or ten. But I astonished him "all sem," for, with a smile of complete
impossibility, he replied, "*Two Napoleons!* Why that

is more than I am worth in all the world!" and with a jolly nod went his way, not breaking his heart over it either, for he was a brick, "ragged and torn and true."

But to return to the nummulites. How did they get into the rocks? Don't you know? *No.* Do you want to? *Yes.* Well then, listen!

Once during the reign of Suleyman-ibn-Daoud, or Solomon the son of David, it was found that specie disappeared from circulation in a most mysterious manner. The Jews generally know as much about exchanges and the daily rate of gold, and the night rate of silver, and the regular sight-rate of notes and copper, and all the secrets of financial alchemy, as most folks; but this time there was a party at work which was just a peg above the Jews in all their own little peculiar games— and this party was that of the devils or Afreets; for the devils having observed, with their usual intelligence, that nothing sets people to damning themselves and everybody, and everything else, like a drain of specie, set to work acting just as their nearest relations, friends, and children do at the present day (I refer to the gold ring in New York), and engineered for a rise in gold. For the devils were the first bulls—as you see by their horns—and a precious set of dirty devils they were, like their relations!

For a time the devils had a jolly time of it exporting specie and gambling. Gold ran up to thirty-five thousand and three-eighths per cent., and one venerable pot-bellied old devil in spectacles and broad brim put

up on it that it would reach forty within a month. But
Solomon had his eyes upon him and all the party. The
devils drove everything before them until gold did indeed
reach forty. And then there was a squall! Very early
on that famous forty morning, one devil who did business in the Sikka-el-'Het, or Street of the Wall, thought
he would take a few gold pieces out of a bag, just to
gamble with through the day at an ancient game called
Pharaoh, or Faro, after the King of Egypt; for these
devils, not satisfied with playing at their business, used
to have day-games where they dropped in to take a
drink, and also drop a few coins. Now it seemed to the
devil who opened the bag that his money had a very
rusty look. He grabbed it wildly—a loud squall was
heard, and other devils, rushing in, found him with his
horns stuck fast in the wall, and blaspheming himself
into blackberry jam with rage, for he had tried to dash
his brains out, forgetful of his spikes.

And soon there was a great wail heard all along the
Sikka-el-'Het—a sound of devils wailing for their gold,
and would not be comforted, because it was not; for
one and all had found that the gold had turned to stone.
Solomon had blocked their little game for them nicely.
"Rot me!" exclaimed one fat devil, whose education
had been neglected, "if I didn't feel when I opened my
fire-proof as if I was quite putrified myself." He meant
petrified, you know, but it's of no consequence.

So the devils took all their stone money and pitched
it sky-high, and skimmed it into the Nile or over the

sea, which then covered a great part of Egypt, or else made ducks of it, while others, finding some ignorant country people with poultry to sell, passed it off for the new coinage, and so turned it into ducks and drakes. But they were all pretty considerably ruined, and have never recovered from it—in fact, they have been lame ducks themselves to this day, which accounts for Vulcan and the lame devil on two sticks, and your gout and my tight boots, and Polly's limp, and no end of things —*in secula seculorum.* Amen!

That allusion to Vulcan—if you don't mind my going a bit out of the way—reminds me that I forgot to mention, as I intended, in the first chapter, that sailing by Sicily we saw Mount Etna. I have a great respect for Mount Etna. People say that Vulcan still lives there. Sometimes he is seen going in and out of the hill with a short pipe in his mouth, an anvil under one arm and three or four sledge hammers, a couple of pincers, and some tongs in the other hand. There is no use doubting, for this is a fact. This time I'm in earnest. Old Strozzius Cicognara in his "Universal Theatre of Nature" proves it. On the twenty-first day of March 1536, a certain Sicilian merchant met not far from Messina, one evening late, ten great rough-looking customers, *habitu fabrorum,* "dressed like blacksmiths," led by a lame and limping individual. Ah! but *he* was a strapper, and looked as if he could clear out a bar-room of professionals in three minutes. The merchant eyed him closely, and noticed an uncommon likeness to Vulcan.

"Hallo, old chap!" said the merchant, speaking politely and humbly; "where are *you* going at this time of night?"

"To the shop," replied Vulcan (he spoke Latin of antique pattern, saying *Versus ad fabrilem officinam*). And saying this, he pointed up into the awful snow-fields above.

"I should like to know what sort of a job you've got on hand up there *now*," moralised the merchant.

"It's a wery small idea *you've* got," said Mr Vulcan, "my fine feller, of what kind of jobs *I* work at. But it won't be long before you, and no end of duffers like you, find out. Day-day!" Saying this, the whole gang walked right into a cave of red-hot lava, and vanished in the fire. The merchant, all stiff with horror, died the next day, and towards evening the mountain was in full blast of eruption. Mr Vulcan, the saaterengro, was at work. The Messinners thought that the end of the world had come, until it occurred to them to pray to Saint Agatha, and, as old Strozzius says, "this game succeeded beyond all their hopes, and the row was stopped." For, as Paracelsus says, "Verily there be men and creatures which walk and live in the chaos of fire." Surely, certainly, of course, and truly. And women too. Sall Amanda for instance.

It is usual for travellers to look from the summit of Cheops at the Nile, and exhale reflections on the past. It seems to me that the time has come when the steamboats should inspire much more golden-carmine writing

about the future. It may have been a river of mystery,
it unquestionably is one of incredible misery above the
Cataract, and if Africa is ever to be redeemed from
slavery and all wretchedness, it must be by the current
of civilisation, which here as elsewhere always has to
travel up stream. Hurrah for steamboats on the Nile!
One real miracle such as science works is worth a thousand legendary lies. Paulus Diaconus in his blessed life
of Saint Mary of Egypt, says that when she died on the
9th April, Zosimus, who confessed her, came miraculously
in one hour as far as it took him twenty days to travel
afoot returning. If Zozy had gone up the Nile in a
dahabéah and returned in a steamboat—especially about
low-water time—he would have equalled this miracle.
In 1271 the pious Johannes Teutonicus by singing in
Christmas night three masses, one at Halberstadt, one
at Mayence, and the other at Cologne, astonished people
—they would not call it a miracle now. Get out your
railroad timetable—I think that " Bradshaw " makes it
possible—that is to say, if Johannes had only read hunting masses. St Augustine tells a jolly story how one of
his scholars was dreadfully puzzled over a passage in
Cicero, and the said scholar was over the hills and far
away, while a mighty ocean rolled between, where the
stormy winds did blow. But Augustine was a clever
fellow, both English and American clever, so he got up in
his sleep, " that is to say, not I, but my form " (*imo non
ego, sed imago mea*), and appeared to the youthful cove
in a dream, and straightened out the paragraph for him

in no time. But if the good saint had only been adjacent
to a telegraph, he need not have waited till night to perform the miracle.

Descending to a level, we visited the Sphynx—the
oldest type or symbol of wisdom known to man. It was
old beyond age even when the tremendous screecher was
cut, for people never erect such monuments as this to
anything wise that has not been long dead. "It is a
strange thing," says an old writer, "that Wisdom, who
is the most beautiful of all things, should be such a
lover of monsters as to surround herself with a trinity
of them, even as Venus is surrounded by the Graces."
Demosthenes gave his own view of the thing once, says
Plutarch, when, in coming out of the city gate, and drawing a hearty breath of fresh air (they had been making
it warm for him in the Assembly), he stretched out his
hands towards the citadel and exclaimed, "Oh, my
Lady Diana! what horrible beasts are the three in which
you take such delight—the Owl, the Dragon, and the
People!" But the Sphynx and not the people was the
third monster whom the lady loved. In fact, the Sphynx
must have meant the mystery which is above wisdom,
since it was on Minerva's helmet, where she had to *look
up to it.*

They dig up out of the sand at the very base of the
Sphynx to this day wonderfully large and beautiful
petrified specimens of the sea-urchin or echinus, or something like it. The one which an Arab sold me is eight
inches in diameter, and marked with a five-leaved

N

flower, as beautifully as if dotted and lined by the hand
of an illuminator. And it was curious, in its way, to
see among the beautiful tombs living specimens of the
sacred beetle or holy tumble-bug, tumbling and blunder-
ing around in the sand as if wandering about in a wild
way in the spot where they once were worshipped, and
now missed something, as if they had staid out too late,
and come home too late to die. In fact, with their
black shiny robes and shiny heads, these beetles do look
uncommonly like little monks, and remind one of the
last abbot of Heisterbach on the Rhine. The good old
abbot had a serious way of straying off into the neigh-
bouring mountains and losing himself in pious medi-
tations. Once he staid until it was night—poor old
fellow! he was Rip Van Winkled or quite cornered, and
when he got home there was no home to get into, only
some old ruins. Stumbling about and nearly blind,
he came to the tombs of the thirteen brethren, and feeling and counting them, he understood it all. And to
this day he may be seen midnightly bewildered and
puzzled, counting the graves and waiting his turn.
Some time a fourteenth tomb will be there, and then the
poor weary old abbot will creep into it with a hearty sigh
of satisfaction, and go to a good long sleep. And just
so do the poor bewildered scary-beetles go among the
tombs, as if hunting for their own graves. It is a bad
thing to come home late for dinner, or to be Dan
Tuckered out, but, O reader! think of coming home
too late to be buried. Fortunately I have the satisfac-

tion of reflecting that your prayers will never keep you
out in that way o' night—whatever your sins may do!

Our ride home that evening was unquestionably fast,
as we had extra horses,—and cheerful, since I can recall
several curious specimens of minstrelsy which made it
joyous. The Khan told us that when the Italian opera
was first revealed unto the true believers in Stamboul,
they were greatly delighted with it, and on coming out
would make frantic efforts to sing fragments thereof. But
use is second nature, and at the second or third bar the
Muslim vocalists would diverge into the Turkish nasal
dirge with a long *Wa-á-á-áh!* to supply their forgetful-
ness of the Italian words and music, but bringing up all
right in the end.

Tremma Bizanzio—*aou, wow, wow, wow*—eterminatrice,
Sull' te la guerra-a-a-a-a-ai discendera—*aou, aou, aou, wow, wow, wow,*
Qui non compiange—*aou, ou, wow, wow, wow, wow-wah!*—quell' in-
felice,
Ha cuor' de tigre, *aou aou, wow*—o cor non ha, *ou, ou, ou, aou,
wah, wah!*

Here a gentleman, whose name and title I suppress,
and whose religion I do not allude to, began to favour
us with an effort at a popular air, as follows :—

> Cham-pen Charley ismi ném,
> Cham-pen Charley ismi ném,
> Cham-pen Charley ismi nem, mi boya,
> Hua kaman jan mi ana spree.

Then I attempted to give the "Maid of Athens," its
meaning being greatly aided by a singular refrain contributed from the road. For, go as fast as we would,

there was a running chorus from a small army of Arab
children who kept up with us, so that, as they all sang
at a regular interval, we had the following:—

> Maid of Athens, ere we part,
>   *Baksheesh!*
> Give, oh, give me back my heart.
>   *Baksheesh!*   ·

I am indeed far away now as I write, and silent, but
they are still singing, those unceasing children of Egypt,
that quaint old refrain of *baksheesh*, even as they sang
it before King Pharaoh. *Baksheesh!* Time may come
and time may go, but they 'll keep on for ever. You bet
on it. Even as the three musicians who met to play
the Devil's Sonata never stopped, and are still fiddling
away in the vault of some ruined old palace in Venice,
so those children are even at this moment musical with
baksheesh; for *that* is the song which will resound in
Egypt *in secula seculorum.*

> They sang that song 'neath rosier skies
>   All when the world was young ;
> And when the world grows old and dies,
>   That song will still be sung.
>
> I 've heard that word on English soil
>   From the roving Rommanee,
> And still it tracks me by the Nile,
>   And will not let me be !
>
> It is *bak* or *baksheesh* all day long,
>   'Neath palm-trees or in clover ;
> And when they have ended that plaintive song,
>   They begin and sing it over !"

CHAPTER XVI.

IF a thing of beauty is a jaw for ever, as the American
husband said of his handsome, scolding wife, then the
donkey-boys of Cairo are the most jaw-yous and beautiful
creatures on the face of the earth; for the sound of their
voices drieth not up, and wheresoever thou goest they
go, and their ways are thy ways, and thy people their
people—if they can get hold of them; and their number is threescore and one thousand asses, and as many
more as you want (what is mentioned in the next text
not being however so numerous at present in Egypt),
for Egypt is the original fatherland of asses, from which
country they Exodusted all over the world, and then into
New Jersey, where they find it harder to get a living
than they did in the Nile country under the Pharaohs,

or in Spain under the Moors, owing to the superior intelligence of the New Spaniards.

If there is anything I'm square on, it is that when a
highly intelligent man generally passes for a blockhead,
or a genius for a fool, or a wit for a "gump," as often
happens—I daresay now, reader, you have really found
it so—there are always the true principles of greatness
to be found in him. Now I have no doubt that the Ass
is one of these people. The deepest thinkers of antiquity
pondered mightily over this thing, and perceived its
truth, and accordingly elevated the ass to a degree of reverence of which you have no conception; and as Egypt
would be incomplete without a chapter on donkeys, and
as the matter, jesting apart, is replete with curiosity, I
will even undertake to show how it was that certain
races thought so highly of this animal.

Now I suppose you know that there is a great division
between the Shemitic race—which includes the Jews,
Arabs, ancient Phœnicians, and Carthaginians, and all
speaking their family of long-nosed languages—and
the Indo-European—of which lot you are probably a
flourishing member—which came from Central Asia, and
includes in the rough the natives of India and Europe.
Now there are several strongly-marked distinctions between the Shemitic folk and Indo-Europeans, the principal being *that the former always sit down to do a thing
when the latter stand up to it.*

But the great difference between them is that of which
I have spoken—their reverence for asses, yes, their

tender regard for them, and their faith in their integrity, honour, and intelligence. And perhaps they are not so much out of the way, all things being considered. It is generally admitted that the horse is the gentleman among animals; but if you had the twenty most intelligent horses in the world in a field, and one of the dullest of donkeys, it is not a horse, but the ass, who would first find out how to pick the latch of the gate, or let down the bars and lead his people forth out of captivity into Canaan. Asses are abstemious and temperate, but far more gallant than any other animal, and far more intelligent in their gallantry, as Rabelais indicates in his excellent story of the ass who was invited to a party, which, if true, should cover the animal with immortal honour.

The Jews thought so highly of the ass that it was, according to them, the only animal that ever spoke. And it is pretty evident that they believed it was a common thing for donkeys to discourse in Balaam's time. Suppose an ass were to speak to you—and in Hebrew at that—what would your reply be? Why, " Great goodness!" or, "O Moses!" or, "Well, I never!" You would be thunderstruck of course. But how did Balaam answer? Why in the most composed manner possible, as if he had been used to talking with asses all his life. He said, "I am angry because you made fun of me," and proceeded to inform Neddy that if he had a sword he would do for him, just as he would have spoken to any other gentleman under the circumstances. If you had a talking donkey, would you have gone in for killing it? Not if I know you. Wouldn't I see bills on every wall within a week of a Great Moral Exhibition of the Great Moral Donkey—converses fluently—and so forth? That is the way you would have borne your affliction.

" That you should ever be a Balaam and ride a donkey!" exclaimed pretty Mrs ——, meeting Mr —— one day in the Muskee riding along, with Mohamet walking solemnly behind.

" And why shouldn't I be Balaam?" was the reply, " since I have met in my way with an angel."

I observed, by the way, that the talking donkey is still an institution in Egypt. There was a rusty old bummer who used to navigate about Cairo. He was always confoundedly in the way. He accounted for his existence by leading and showing three monkeys and an ass about as large as four tom-cats. When about to perform, he would talk to the little donkey, and it would put its mouth up to his ear and whisper a reply, which the master at once translated into Arabic. The expression of that donkey's eyes when it whispered was something wonderful! If it didn't talk it wasn't for want of intelligence—and if it *did* say all that the old bummer translated for it, Balaam's moke was an ass compared to it, and no mistake; but it confirms the story of Balaam —a little.

Early on the first morning when I arrived in Cairo, I heard in the garden, into which my room opened, the sound of violent blows. Supposing that some native was being corrected, I opened the door-window and stepped out. It *was* a native, but he was whaling a donkey. The quadruped was loaded with packages for a lady boarder, and Hassan was trying to superinduce him to lateralise or dorsalise up to that lady's door. There was no earthly reason why he shouldn't, but he voted for the negative. So the native verberated him till he reverberated. It was a very pretty little Esel—just the thing for an artist—and I was going to be Sterne over it and remonstrate, when all at once I saw him slyly turn his head, unobserved as he thought, and take a sidelong squint at his boss. The little rascal! If ever I saw a look which indicated that a little mischievous cuss wanted to see how far he could go in roguery before he would have to cave, that ass's eyes showed it. Bless you! why, the Egyptian donkeys are as much beyond those of other lands as a peach is ahead of a persimmon, or a real canvas-back superior to a ten-year-old hen stuffed with a No. 3 mackerel. Finally Hassan, finding that blows did not move him, went in for a wrestle, and the ass ditto. The ass rose up on his hind legs, and if that fight could have been done in a circus with a band playing, you would have deemed a dollar cheap that day to see it. But Hassan circumvented him by pulling up the left hind leg, and finally lifting the whole concern, ass and bundles, into position.

The ass was the type of the Jews and Arabs, and the ox of the settled agricultural races, which was the reason, I suppose, why the Hebrews were commanded

not to yoke them together. But there came a day long
after when the ass and the ox met in amity—the only
animals who witnessed the nativity—" *Asinus et bos
fuerunt testes nativitatis Christi* "—as a sign that this
event *should* witness the union of all races in love. And
when Mary fled into Egypt it was on an ass. How
often have I seen at sunset on the Nile—on the long,
dark line of the bank, against the orange sky and
below the palm-trees, all in the same intensely deep
neutral tint—some woman bearing a babe riding on an
ass, followed by a man in long oriental robes holding
a staff—the whole the very living picture, in all perfection, of that Flight, compared to which the Hegira is
coarse and trivial. You may see this any evening by
the Nile, and, to my mind, there is nothing so tenderly
beautiful in all Egypt—or in all the world.

Giordano Bruno, who wrote a stupendous book on
asses, begs all those who associate ass and asinity with
beastliness, ignorance, and folly, to put themselves in
place of the deeply and terribly illuminated Hebrew
cabalists, who penetrated not merely to the third heaven,
but to the profound abyss of the supermundane and
ensophic universe, by the contemplation of the Ten
Sephiroth. But your brain would reel and your eyes
blinden to pass through these dazzling regions of in-
telligences, essences, seraphim—Haioth Haccados, Has-
malin, Elohim, Benelohim !—which even I, guided by
the clue of the tail of the sacred donkey (which is a key
to it all), can hardly follow. Suffice it to say :—

" That from the sensible world are derived the ten spheres, or the *primum mobile*, the starry heaven or firmament, the heaven of Saturn, of Jove, of Mars, of the Sun, of Venus, of Mercury, of the Moon, and of the sublunary chaos, which is divided into four elements. To which, as assistants, are ten moving spirits. And these are Mettatron, the chief, Raziel, Zafriel, Zadkiel, Camael, Rafael, Ariel, Michael, Gabriel, and Samael—under whom are four terrible princes, the first of whom governs fire, and is the Behemoth of Job; the second the air, being called by the cabalists commonly Beelzebub, the prince of flies or flying evil things; the third the water, and is called by Job Leviathan; and the fourth the earth, over which he walks continually, and is called Satan. Now according to the cabalistic revelation *Hocma*, to which correspond the forms or wheels known as cherubim, which influence the eighth sphere, in which lies the virtue and intelligence of Raziel, this Hocma means wisdom, and the symbol of this is the *ass*."

It was a hard pull on you, reader, confess it; and hardly fair in me to take you into such a cloud bramble-land as that. Yet if you did read it (which I in silence doubt dumbnably) you will not be astonished at what Tacitus and others affirm, that the Jews of old were believed to worship in secret an ass in their temple in Jerusalem. "Wall, s'posin they did, what then, hä-ay?" Only what I said at first, that the Shemitic or Arab-Hebrew race has entirely different ideas and feelings as to asses from men of the western world, cherishing no feeling of scorn or sneerfulness against them, and, far from making them symbols of ignorance, adoring them as types of wisdom.

Now it's hardly worth while for you to curse this for a stupid, pudding-headed, pedantic chapter, and a swindle and a sell on your sublime soul, which lives in eternal dread of being *baw'd*—I believe that's the way you pronounce it—by anything above the level of the last town joke. "Best thing aw eveh hea'd in my life, baw Jove!" When you are in Egypt, you will see asses—you will have to ride them—you may observe them. Should you do this, it may profit your soul to reflect how deeply the great and wise and good among mankind have laboured to bring to light the great asinine truth, and remove from man's humblest and yet most spirited servant, the obloquy which has rested upon him. You too may be immortal!

As for the Mústaphas, Hassans and Ibn-el-Sniggle-fritzes who drive the donkeys of Cairo, a more accomplished set of vagabond young niggers cannot be found on the face of the earth. According to Charles Kingsley, who is generally accurate in his estimates, they swarmed in Alexandria in the fourth century like pies in dog-killing time in New York, and it is estimated that they are on the increase. They all speak English; many of them are clever in three or four languages. Occasionally a foreigner takes a decent one for a servant; but in course of time, if he don't become a dragoman, he generally wends his winding way back to donkeyising.

First, as a boy, he tries to save enough to buy an ass; then he gets a better one, then several, and finally sells out and opens a café.

I had one who specially attached himself to me—a grave, sober youth of thirty-five. Mohamet being honest and civil, got through the Baron and myself a handsome *clientèle* of English and American customers, so that he flourished mightily, becoming well-nigh a sort of sub-shekh—which word, by the way, is pronounced neither sheek nor shike, but to rhyme with check—remember! Now the nature of the Cairo donkey-boys at once appeared, and very loudly, in this, that the instant I, or the Baron, or brother, came forth, the whole tribe of assass'uns would make a dead rush for us, each screeching that *he* had Mohamet's donkey, or that he was Mohamet's man, in the extremely slender hope of swindling the original Mohamet before his very face. The remainder, be it observed, beginning to implore Mohamet, in paradise or on earth, to give them a job; the outsiders, meanwhile, who had no chance, shrieking continually and rapidly, " good night, aah ! " " good mornin, masaa ! " " good day ! " " go to dev'l ! " " how dy do ?" " velly fine donkey—hū-ā-ā !—*hauou !* "

The vulgar Arabian in general, and the Cairene donkey-boy in particular, hath a nasal grunt—the *hauou*—which means everything, but which reaches its climax in expressing victory and contempt. Should the London cabmen ever get it, fights will rise. It is insulting, it is vulgar, it is unanswerable, it is funny. Arabic is the worst sounding language in the world, and this is the worst sound in Arabic. They have something like it in Norfolk, Old England, and something much more like it in New England; but they lack the last squeeze-of-the-bottle blackguardism of the Arab sound. He who has heard it never forgets it. One day the Captain saw an Egyptian difficultivating or difficulturing with his donkey. The ass wouldn't go, and the native didn't want to either, but he wished *it* to go. There was a fight and the active employment of the butt end of a date-palm leaf—and a wacket and a wow, and a wiot and a wumpus. Finally the animal succumbed. That was all the Arab required. Sitting down, he calmly surveyed the ass from head to foot, and in withering tones exclaimed *hauou !* Asses all understand the dialect of their Arab masters, in fact, they bray it perfectly, and I have been told what it is they utter. I regret that it will not bear translation. I may, however, say that a lady writer on the East uses the expression with consummate cheek, well knowing that very few readers would understand it. Bless me ! bless me ! what beings we all are ! Haug me if I don't think, with Neal's character, that this world is divided entirely between the found out and the not found out.

The Captain never recovered from that *hauou.* I believe that he told the story every half-hour for a week, in the hope of being able to catch the sound, and thereby vanquish all his enemies. He only got so far perfect, however, as to make you wish you had your revolver when he came to it. The last time I saw him he was

on the Mecca donkey—white with a yellow tail—
Mohamet solemnly following. "Why are you riding
that hard-mouthed brute?" I inquired. "Because,"
replied the Captain, using severe epithets with reference
to Mohamet and his ass, "the brown donkey stumbled
yesterday and let me down in the mud." I looked at
Mohamet, and he replied, with his solemn Allah-achbar
look—"*Him stone in one road!*"

"It was a lie," the Captain said—"there wasn't a
stone within a mile." Very likely. That Mecca donkey,
by the way, puts me in mind of a story. I trust that the
eminently moral magazine from which I took it will
not abuse me as irreverent for telling it. It has been
known to do such things. Once at a camp-meeting the
clergyman observed a person who looked very grave indeed, and thinking that a case of conviction was present,
began to address him. "My friend," said he, "be not
sad. If you are afflicted, God will remove your sorrow.
He can do all things."

"H-h-he c-c-cant," stuttered the grave man. Now
I must mention that the clergyman had an enormous
mouth.

"Oh, my erring brother!" said the pastor, "what is
there that God could not do?"

"W-w-why," gobbled the stammerer, "He c-c-c-c-
couldn't make y-your m-m-mouth big-g-ger, without
set-tet-ing your ears b-back!"

Now that Mecca donkey was so *hard* that his mouth
had been sawed back to his ears, and he was altogether

in the condition of the stammerer of the story. He had emphatically an open countenance, so that if he had only carried the mail he might have passed for a pretty respectable crocodile. And here I think I will let him go. He has been ridden rather hard in this book—that's a fact.

I was wrong in saying that I never saw the Captain again. The really last time I saw him was in a French toy-shop in Cairo not far from the Muskee. He was buying an immense dancing-jack, or marionette, or punchinello, as a present for a king of his acquaintance with whom he was going to take a few days' elephant-shooting in the country. The king would take the dancing-jack and hang it up in the Ju-ju house as the last elegancy in the way of idols. Only that the white cotton cord between punchinello's legs would be supplanted by an invisible horse-hair, and a concealed priest would pull it in answer to awe-struck worshippers. That is the way they do the Winking Madonna in Ju-ju land. The Captain didn't tell me this, but I had heard of it before. I do not like to chaff missionaries. But you must not be astonished at what I tell you about the heathens and heath-cocks of Africa. They have been known to get down lower than worshipping a dancing-jack. I have heard that in Ebonyland, a few years ago, a traveller was shown by them what they regarded as their dearest idols and chiefest charms. They believed they were a kind of Koran, and so far they were not far out, for there was an awful lot of rubbish in them. They did not know what they were, as you will believe me, when I tell you that they were copies of the life of ——, the eminent Self-Made Man—which is probably, next to the Bible, the most extensively disseminated work on the face of the earth. Hearing from somebody that there was a country called Africa, the eminent self-made at once had several large cases filled with his life and forwarded. I have heard hard stories on the heathen and their degradation, but I don't think they ever got down quite so low as this before. However, they sinned ignorantly. If they only had known *what* they were worshipping, wouldn't there have been a row! I think this story is the best argument in favour of converting the heathen I ever heard.

I have already alluded to the fact that in Egypt "ass" is a title of honour. When a man dies, as I said before, his weeping friends call him this and other names aloud. If the eminent self-made, just alluded to, were to come to Egypt, I doubt not that all the natives, and everybody else, would at once concur in calling him an ass; in fact, I think I can remember to have heard this title applied to him invariably, ever since I can remember anything. However, since it is a term of respect in its way, I was not astonished to hear a donkey-boy roar out to a gentleman one day,—" Nice donkey, sah! Velly nice donkey. You like donkey, sah—*donkey like you.*" He meant that a mutual fondness would arise between the gentleman and the donkey, but it sounded like a comparison. Not that it made much difference either way.

o

I have said that Egypt was the fatherland of asses, but certain writers have thought that Judæa was their true home. And, in fact, when we reflect how the Hebrews represented reason under the image of an ass, "turning that which was the subject of ridicule into matter for reverence, and this into adoration, contemplation, admiration, honour, and glory, and this again into matter cabalistic, archetypal, sephirotic, metaphysical, ideal, and divine," we must admit that they thought well of the creature, to say the least. So that it is not remarkable that divers learned old bricks and cherubimical bottle-bruisers, reading all this by the light of the stars, and finding out that by astrology the ass is the animal peculiar to Saturn and the Moon, and that the Jews are also under the same planets, being Saturnine and Lunarian, as Sebastian exclaims in Bruno's "Cabala del Cavallo Pegaséo," they boldly declared the Jews to be the original asses, a view strengthened by their well-known temperance, industry, long-suffering, obstinacy, piety, moroseness, stiff-neckedness, philocrusiness, and other eminent virtues. All of which Bruno declares by another speaker to be assertions partly true, partly near the truth, partly like the truth, and partly contrary to the truth—or untruthful.

Another party held that as the Jews really derived their religion from the Egyptians, they were impostors in claiming to be the original and genuine asses. And there is a bright yellow colour of truth in this statement, if we admit that the golden calf was actually a

golden ass. In fact, I am reluctantly compelled to deny
them this honour, since though they have unquestionably had their full share in disseminating the solemn
doctrines of Asinity or Asinism, they were not the first
to begin them, as Heaven knows they were anything but
the last to carry them out in that part of the world
which lies west of Palestine, and where at the present
day the most bigoted Asinarians chiefly abound. But
if the Jews be robbed by the Egyptians of this distinc-
tion, it may comfort them in their discomfiture to know
that the Egyptians are in turn accused of having acquired all the principles and secrets of genuine Asinism
from the Persians, one of whose kings having been called
an ass by the people of Egypt, and that not in the true
and sacred sense of the word, but in a jeering, chafing,
and chaffing way, gave them a devil of a thrashing.
Having accomplished which, and taken them all prisoners, he compelled them to worship the image of an
ass, and to sacrifice to it their precious bull Apis,
which was an extremely jolly go for the Egyptians.
But they made the best of it, and in order to conceal
the disgrace, boldly took, not the bull by the horns,
but the ass by the ears, and declared that Asinism was
the most perfect and beautiful of all religions; and that
they were sincere in their belief can be doubted by no one
who sees what the mass of the multitude of Egypt worshipped, or how they made of themselves dumb driven
cattle, and got down to worshipping onions—though in
justice to them I must say they never descended to

adore any self-made men, the real extent of whose manu-
facture is money. That was reserved for the more ultra
asses of the West, the reason being that they avoided
swine in every form, having a special detestation of the
ultra fat, sleek kind, and being possessed of a jolly little
commandment which specially forbade them to anoint
or lubricate any such animals in any way. And you
will observe that the three great nations which adored
asses could not go *pigs.* They drew the line somewhere,
as the Rev. Mr —— does in his after-dinner stories.

" Ægyptis igitur, Judæis et Persis execrationi fuit."

" Pigs were detestable to Jews, Egyptians, and Persians." For which reason the Egyptians, in their hiero-
glyphics, represented men who were dead-gone and clean
washed away with vanity, conceit, folly, ostentation, and
other vices by the pig, "*quod ejusmodi sit porci natura,*"
" that being the natur' of the beast," as Horus Apollo
says, and he knew if anybody did—you may bet !

I cannot conclude this chapter on asses in Egypt
without speaking of something cognate for which we are
indebted to Apion Grammaticus, "*et reliqui Ægyptii,*"
" and other Egyptians." I refer to *kephalomanteia* or
divination and fortune-telling by means of an ass's head.
This, according to Apion, was entirely a Jewish idea,
and Tacitus following them, picked up the fancy that
they worshipped an ass-head for God, which was not
altogether a fair statement by any means.

That the ass is a prophet, at least of weather, and

therefore one inspired with wondrous darksome lore, appears from the story told in *Pausilypo sive Tristium Cogitationum et Molestiarum Spongia.* I know you have read it, but no matter, let's hear it again.

"Why do I keep an astrologer?" said King Louis the Eleventh to La Belle Heaulmiére; "Pasque dieu! *biche*—that I may avoid what all women so vehemently desire—the being ruined."

"I would do it for half the money you give him," said La Belle Heaulmiére.

"I daresay thou wouldst," quoth the king in a tone which sent the damsel to the window. "Good morning, child! I ride to hunt."

"Beware of rain, your Majesty."

"Silly child! it will not rain to-day. Has not my astrologer inspected his tablets? Doth he not know the constitutions of the weather? Hath he not promised serenity?"

The damoselle smiled and waved her hand from the window, and went on with her cap-making. In the forest the king was deep in thought.

"By Our Lady of the Silver Shoes!" he meditated, "what did she *really* mean? Can it be that she suspects——?"

Just then the king observed a dark-faced varlet in outlandish dress, who furtively shot before him among the green leaves.

"*Halte la!*" exclaimed the king. "Knave, art thou not Hayraddin Maugrabin the gipsy?"

"Yea, sire," exclaimed the wayfarer.

"They tell me," said the king, "that thy race can read the secrets of the stars and of the soul. Canst thou tell me what now concerns me?"

"Yea," replied the Gipsy in a wild rhyme.

> "He who rydes huntyng
> Over ye playne
> Without an umbrella
> Shoulde gare of ye myne!"

"Glory of God!" said the king, "here is a double crown for thee, my good Hayraddin!"

"*Bengis lel tute for a ratfolly juckal!*"[*] said the Zingaro bowing humbly to the ground.

"What didst thou say, O Bohemian?" inquired the king anxiously.

"They were words in the ancient tongue of Egypt, your Majesty," replied Hayraddin. "Words of blessing which shall make thy life golden. But, your Majesty, beware of rain!"

The Bohemian was deep in the bushes. The king rode on.

There came by a charcoal-man with an ass.

"Thou wilt do well, O king, to return speedily to the city," he cried; "yet a few minutes and the rain will fall by hogsheads."

The king glared gloomily at him. "Thou too!" he

---

[*] "D—l take you for a bloody dog!"

cried. " H 'm !" he muttered—"meseems I have heard my cousin of Burgundy, who speaketh German, say that the demon of the forests goeth about as a *carbonarius*. Women, gipsies, charcoal-men ! 'Tis strange !"

Verily it was, for as the monarch spoke a drop of rain struck him on the nose, and, in the words of the ancient chronicler from whom I take this tale—" *Aer nubibus obduci, cœlum tonare, fulgurare, tantus denique imber decidere, ut fossæ undique aquis stagnarent.*"—" It rained like a thousand of brick to the square yard, it thundered as if the contractor had got the noise for nothing, yea, the ditches ran over and embraced in one vast pond."

The king took refuge in a village, and then went home. The next day was fair. He rode forth in the forest and met the charcoal-man.

"Tell me," said the king, "where didst *thou* learn astrology, and who taught *thee* the pluvial art of imbreous prevision ?"

"O king!" replied the *carbonarius*, "I never yet saluted even the threshold of a school, yet I keep at home mine own astrologer, who never yet deceived me."

"*Thou !*" exclaimed the king in awe,—" *Thou* keep an astrologer, and a better one than I can ! Man, dost thou know what it costs me ?"

"Mine, your Majesty, costs me nothing, for it is only my ass. When it is going to rain he lets down his ears, walks slowly, and rubs his sides against trees and walls, which having observed yesterday, I did warn thee to return."

" Come to court, good fellow," said the king laughing. " I shall dismiss Galeotti, and take thee with thy prophet. It will only be changing a false ass for a true one."

For, as you see, reader, donkeys are prophets inasmuch as they are ass-trologers !

CHAPTER XVII.

HE who in Cairo goes shopping goes hopping—with rage
—until he gets used to it. There is a theory current
that things may be bought here and in Stamboul, and
all over the East, very cheap; and so they may if you
will pay for them half in money and half in time. Bargain all day, and come again to-morrow, and put up
with more mingled servility and insolence than a thing
is worth, and you may bring a shopman or a bazaarian
down to three farthings profit on a trade of five pounds.
Bless you! if such beautiful things are to be had at 15
per cent. less than their value to you, don't you suppose
the shopmen in London would find it out and sell them?
And do you really know what there is for sale in London
and Paris?

The habit in the East of a shopman's asking much more than he expects to get is universal, and a meaner invention never turned up in history. "Never give a man more than half of what he asks," is a rule of pretty general soundness. "Great God, gentlemen!" exclaimed a horse-dealer one day in my hearing, to some friends of mine, as they turned away without a word after asking him the price of an animal and getting his answer; "you don't suppose I expect to get as much as I ask, do you?"

They have a cheerful way in the East of letting strangers take part in your trade. Any blackguard, no matter who, who can put in and chaff you, and praise the article, and make believe he has "chanted" it, generally gets a little present from the shopkeeper. When Mr Shaw was a prisoner in Tartary, his Hindu servant, being fluent with two or three languages, and ready with cheek, actually made a good living by "chanting" in the bazaars. Many of the shopmen in Cairo do not understand English or French, but a vast proportion of street blackguards, broken donkey-boys, and ex-deputy scullions do, and they swarm around the bazaars; consequently as soon as you price anything some volunteer dragoman usually starts up and goes for you. You may feel yourself perfectly capable of conducting the affair yourself; you may cry, "*Imshi ya kelb*"—"Begone, O dog!" or, "*Ruah, yin al abŭk*," which will often send him away, but another will come, and more probably a knot of neighbours will unite to convince you that you

ought to pay to the uttermost farthing. I have known a
great dirty, scrofulous, nasty, coal-black Congo nigger,
with Heaven only knows how many of the plagues of
Egypt on him, in a single ragged shirt, to jump up and
literally snatch or tear an article out of my hands which
I was examining, and begin jabbering away in his
heathen lingo, apparently abusing me for not immediately paying down the price, until reminded by the
familiar "Dog!" that he was taking a liberty. But
what did he care? Where one Frank would dismiss
him, ten would tolerate him. The Muslim mob have no
real respect, in fact, no respect whatever for Franks. A
gentleman who had lived many years among them said
to me that contempt and hatred of Europeans was as
carefully inculcated in their minds as an accomplish-
ment. And many Europeans, and especially Americans,
seem, by undue familiarity, and hail-fellow-well-met
manners, to do all they can to encourage impudence in
them, when perhaps they are not naturally inclined to it.
I never shall forget one old English party—a vacant,
globular gentleman, whose round, glazed eyes suggested
an idiot owl, and whose short, squat figure recalled a
bloated blue-bottle, buried in a high shirt collar, and en-
tombed under a pan-cake tile. One day in a café, hearing strange and unearthly cries from some one seated
out-of-doors in front, I investigated, and found that
they proceeded from the vocal blue-bottle, who, surrounded by a select party of obsequious dragomans and
congenial ass-drivers, was imparting to them, in strange

cawing tones, which rang like an awesome sound from the grave, the ballad, "If I had a donkey vot vouldn't go." I am sorry to say, however, that this kind of familiarity, so incomprehensible to an oriental, and which opens the way to no end of "disagreeablements" and impudence for quieter people who come after, is commoner among a certain class of Americans than with the English. I trust I give no offence by saying this, since its foundation at home was often laid in real kindness of heart, and in a social equality which I should regret to see shaken. But it is true, and there are Americans of the kind who may be known at the Café Anglais in Paris by their confiding to the garçons the deepest secrets of their souls and families, so far as their limited knowledge of the language permits —silly men who cannot conceive the possibility of addressing anybody, high or low, save in a bristly, free-and-easy "funny" way; and it is to be sincerely desired that this kind, who are of all others most morbidly anxious to be "gentleman-*like*," should learn how far they fall short of it by such conduct. That the Egyptian donkey-drivers or lacqueys of all the world *like* this class of loving travellers, esteeming them fondly, is as natural as that they should love a wealthy and affectionate own brother—and that they will even do more for their money is not incredible; and if such travellers would marry their sisters, and bid them dine with them every day at the same table, and lend them their shirts, I daresay they would be even fonder of them than ever, and exalt them above all the world. But unless one has the tongue of an ass, he pays too high a price for his honey when he licks it from thorns.

This excess of benevolence to everybody has, however, its rosy colour, and is rather the rust of a virtue than a real vice, such as arrogance, contempt of the poor, and the regarding them at all times as mere machines and conveniences. If the former be sometimes laughable, the latter is invariably hateful, if not damnable ; and it is better to be steeped to the hair and bone in the one than be ever so lightly stained with the other. Those who are gushingly familiar with garçons are not the less good Christians for it; in fact, they are the very men to whom I should look for many large and golden pumpkins of virtue among the weeds of silliness; while all one could expect among the impenetrable thorns of cruelty would be to find at last a poisonous puff-ball of pride. I have no doubt whatever that the seven young American gentlemen whom I saw one evening in a first-class hotel, making a solemn farewell procession around the room, gravely shaking hands with all the waiters, and tenderly bidding them good-bye, were quite as good men as the delighted lookers-on who smiled to one another. I am sorry to say that the ungrateful garçons laughed as much as anybody. They had, if sincere, broader and better principles than the men who laughed at them, and would, unquestionably, be *far* quicker in giving ability a fair chance to rise above adversity, and would reward and admire it with less cant and self-sanctimoniousness than the other kind display who make a merit of praising talent when they can no longer keep it down with its nose to the dirt, of which illustrious kind of merit England possesses so many bright and shining examples. But there is often a great deal of a certain kind of cant and vanity mingled with American condescending familiarity; sometimes a desire to astonish the brutal natives by showing them what it is to be superior in heart, and sometimes, I fear, a fond desire to get more than other people do for the same money; a kind of policeman-and-cook affection of the cold-mutton kind, which prevails among travellers of all nations all the world over. *In medio tutissimus ibis*, " virtue is ever in the middle," as the father of evil said when he went with a fast young lady on either arm. Is it not best, O reader, to avoid extremes ? There is no great credit in being an apostle when those who come after you have to endure all the martyring, while you have only to eat nice humble pie and delicious dirty pudding, of which you are naturally fond, and of which you do not even know the proper names !

The extraordinarily abusive manner in which high-caste natives in the East generally speak to the low-caste, and the miserable fact that the latter cannot separate this and arrogance from superiority and rank, is the best proof that they wretchedly misunderstand familiarity. "Dog" and " pig" seem to be the usual preface to all remarks wherever one would say " my good man" in England. I may be mistaken in this, and hope to

Heaven I am ; but such observations as I made certainly seemed to establish it. Thus I was assured that in shopping in Constantinople the language of a swell customer over the counter ran generally, *viz.*, " O dog ! how much is this? Son of a Kaffir, I will give thee four cents ! Pig, thou liest ; it cost thee nothing, for thou didst steal it the day thy father was hanged. Son of a social evil, send it to my house. Beast of a thief, *afreet yeehdek !* Devil take you !"

This is not a pleasant style of conversation. But imagine a native, who is accustomed to respect only those who use it, after swindling and grossly insulting a gentleman, hearing for reply from him, as one did, in meek tones, " Why, Mustafa, how you talk ! I really *never* was so treated in all my life !" This means something among civilised people, but to Mustafa it probably sounded, if not like begging his pardon, at least like the address of the old Yankee lady, delivered out of the window to the burglar, " You naughty man, ain't you ashamed of yourself—*go away !* " Well, he went ; and perhaps, after all said and done, it was a model speech—in its way. It *is* a pity that the man was a " burgular."

To be a chanter, intermeddler, and bargain-helper, or number three in a trade, is such a regular business in the East, that the shopkeepers would be unhappy without it. There is something of this in Paris and Italy, where one is often amazed to find people absolutely bent and determined on giving fees and commissions to guides and valets and servants when it has been forbidden, and when they have profited in nothing whatever by them. One day the Baron good-naturedly acted as interpreter for an English stranger in a shop in a transaction for a hat. When it was purchased and the stranger had departed, the shopman asked the Baron if a franc would be enough for him; from which I infer that people of a highly respectable or *distingué* exterior take part in such transactions. When the Baron declined a commission the shopman was amazed. There is in Cairo a regular formula which the chanter utters if a trade has gone on for some time without coming to a conclusion, since he, honest man, must not lose his time. So he says to them, " *Bihayat Allah, ya siyâdnâ, uchlusû elmaslaha 'ailâkedâ. Ettregâkum irdû min shan ha-l-dakn*"—" By the life of God, gentlemen, is the affair to end so, or so? I beg you accept my proposal for the honour of this (my) beard." Why his beard should be honoured, or where it comes in, I do not know. That there is a shave in the business somewhere is apparent enough, but I am too indolent to trace out the devious mystery of his meaning.

The class of travellers who never feel quite happy in the East until they have at least once eaten on the floor with their fingers, and had "pipes and coffee" brought to them gratis in a bazaar, will be grieved to learn that this last interesting custom is dying out, and that, unless one shells out rather handsomely, he might shop for a month and not get drop or whiff. So far as my inquiries go, pipes and coffee are dangerous omens, being only produced when the shopman expects to swindle you heavily, or has already done so, and "'opes to see you again." Like the sherry of a London tradesman, it is generally paid for in the end —not by the master.

There are places in Cairo where one is bawled at, beset, bescrewed, begimleted, and besought to buy in a manner which is, as a curiosity, a great success. In England, in the Middle Ages, when all shops were booths, as they are among the natives in the East to-day, apprentices and masters roared out all the time, "What d'ye lack?" and chaffed and touted for custom in the same manner. In the Turkish, Tunisian, gold-smiths', and arms bazaars they are remarkably beg-garly and racketty, and the traveller who is gifted with the love of chaff may there be happy yet—not "still." That the Egyptians, like many small French shop-keepers, are silly and child-like, preferring chatter to business, and given to carrying out their first foolish impulses, is continually apparent. You stop and look at something which has caught your eye—perhaps a five-franc pipe-bowl—but before you can well make out what it is, Mister Mustafa or Achmet catches up a carpet or a church lantern—if it were a donkey it would be all the same—anything which would bring a higher profit than the pipe-bowl—and pushes it in the way, chattering like an insane ape; while the chanters, who appear as if by magic, begin to crowd the carpet or lantern

P

down on you as if it were the one desire of your life.
You hurry away; you see a glass case full of curiosities
at the next shop; before you can look into it, it is
covered with a swarm of slippers and opera-cloaks, and
the same yellow chorus of Italian and Arab rings and
sings as you run.   You proceed, but before you can look
at the sword hanging by the door of the next den, it is
caught up, or down, and you are implored to say what
you will give—you are sternly asked if your intentions
are honourable before you are well aware of the dear
creature's existence.   It never seems to enter their
small heads that you have any mind or ideas of your
own, but must be shown how to think to buy.   Tell
one—or a small French shopman—that he has driven a
customer away by running at him as soon as he stops
to look, and he will inform you, with an air of importance, that he don't want people hanging round
unless they want to buy something.   He means business, he does, and can't afford to waste time.

Sometimes this spirit of commercial enterprise leads to
rows of rivalry, and even fights.   Street-fights in Cairo
are settled in a very singular way, not by the first blood,
but by the first spit.   It isn't nice, I know, but it's true.
One day in the arms bazaar I asked the price of a large
knife or dagger of a poor, miserable, limp-looking Jew,
with his neck swathed up as if in instinctive dread of a
halter.   The very facsimile of the knife had been offered
me the day before for seven francs (it was one of those
German affairs manufactured by thousands to sell as

oriental curiosities in Cairo). The poor creature asked me, as he had a perfect right to do, sixty or eighty francs for the deadly implement, and then, what he had *no* right to do, followed me along the bazaar, clamorously exacting that I should trade with him. Soon I stopped at another shop, where he interfered with my contemplation of the wares by sticking his knife at me and screeching for an offer. There was a rather full-sized disciple of Islam who ran this establishment, and he, seeing that the Hebrew was spoiling his business, emanated rapidly from the den, and speedily began to develop the electricity for Israel. I don't think I ever heard two men yell so; but the Muslim's voice was a steamwhistle to the penny trumpet of the child of Zion, and his resources in blackguarding were absolutely illimitable. Seizing him by the beard, he danced round him, roaring, " *Achrud! Yahud! Yin-al-deenak! Yin-al-dagnak! Ibn-el-haram! Yinalek! Yachatem il ard bisouritak!* " and other elegant extracts from the works of eminent Arabic moralists and poets (for the translation of which apply to the next donkey-boy), until the entire bazaar was in a row-de-dow. At last the Jew opened his mouth, when the Muslim ended the fight by spitting in it, whereupon the vanquished, without another word, ignominiously fled, knife-in-hand, quite unconscious that there was a looker-on who regarded his antagonist as the most disgraced and disgraceful wretch of the two.

A few days later I saw another row in the Muskee, of so singular and incomprehensible a nature that for a week after I felt bewildered and dreameled whenever I thought of it. I have been trying to study out the principles of that fight for four months now, and am no nearer to it than when I began. If any reader who knows the East will explain it to me, I will owe him something handsome for as long 'as he likes, with the privilege of renewal. And it went as followethly: A man was sitting in his bazaar, on the bunk where they all seem to be tailorising on their cross legs all day, when a soldier all in white came up, and in the gentlest possible manner tried to arrest him. He mildly replied he wouldn't go. Soldier softly took hold of his arm and meekly pulled at it. Shopman amiably resisted. Three friends in turbans came up and tenderly patted soldier on back, as if he were choking with too much law and justice. Shopman dispassionately pulled back. Soldier held on. Shopman placidly fought. Soldier serenely spit in his face. Shopman tranquilly caved in, and submissively walked off. Sum total, equanimity, resignation, endurance, forbearance. All the while another soldier stood at the next booth, so close by the arrester that their elbows touched. He never turned his head to look at the row; nobody looked at it but I and a street-dog, although a hundred folk were within ten rods. Nobody was interested, nobody saw it. I don't understand it. One day in Boulac, as I was taking a pipe in a one-horse café, a soldier came by holding a party by the shirt-tail. "Him tief-mans catchéd' was the explanation of my café landlord, who spoke English with remarkable elegance and purity. But where was the mob following? where were all the little boys and girls? Confound these people! do they take no interest in social problems? And yet they have a penal code, and roasted pea-nuts—excellent pea-nuts. They are partially civilised. What does it mean?

They have unusual and curious ways, these bazaarian heretics, of raising the rent on you. One day I was buying in the perfume bazaar a small bottle of atar of roses. There came up a small jet-black negrolet, eight years of age, with a cheerful grin. This was introduced to me. I was implored to give it a *baksheesh*—it was so good, so beautiful. It had virtues. I refused. The shopman was hurt—the "chanter" was hurt. Delicacy had been "jabbed" somewhere. But they were still polite, and bade me farewell with a forgiving smile. Though I was coarse, they were still good and great. Truly they are fond of money, these people. I have heard that they do not believe in a Trinity, but I doubt it. Ammon was and is the god, in Egypt, of Immorality; and the modern Egyptians adore all together, and all in one, Ammon, Mammon, and Gammon.

Verily their ways are rum—*satis supcrque.* One day in the Tunis bazaar I was buying a *búrnus*, a white cloak with a bag behind, to pull over your head—if you be a lady. When I was a boy there were only a few old women who wore from olden time such things. They used to call them *hoo-ods,* and enterprising boys thought it a game thing to slip behind and drop pebbles, hickory-

nuts, chinquapins, apple-cores, green persimmons, and
juvenile potatoes or senile eggs into them. Youth is
ever joyous, and follows earnestly that one precept of
the virtuous Cato, *Trocho lude,*—" Be sure you play at
marbles." Talking of boys dropping things into tempt-
ing receptacles, I was told the other day, by the author
and artist of "Old Inns," * a touching story. There
was or is in Westminster Abbey the tomb of a king—
I think it was Richard's—Richard Rex, if I am not mistaken—and in it, at a convenient distance, was a slit or
hole like a letter-box. One day the tomb was opened,
and it was a pensive sight to behold what the Youth of
England had dropped as tributes to departed glory
through long centuries. There were quarts of antique
marbles poked in by little Ranulphs and Jhons—tip-
cats of the days of the Tudors—diminutive dolls, once
nursed by pretty Pernels and Josianes, babbling black-
letter baby-talk—top-cords contributed by young Round-
heads—wooden swords by dashing Cavalierlings—about
three hundred ha'pence of all eras and politics—and no
end of those delightful tiny pipes to which the smokers
of England remained faithful for two centuries. Of a
truth, boys will be boys.

"Well, how about that bazaar?" Sure enough—
the Tunis bazaar, wasn't it? Oh, yes! As I was saying, I was buying for a lady a *burnus,* and the shopman,
who stood up on high on the booth in an eloquent and
commanding attitude, preached aloud the doctrine that

* "Old Inns." By Edwin Edwards. London, 1873.

the object would cost three napoleons. I say "preached,"
because he *did* preach. He was gesticular, vigorous,
forcible, racy, lively, impassioned, sparkling, glowing,
lofty, poetic, sublime. He was an Arab Splurgeon,
and his text was Burn-us. I had heard something like
that text before, as you spell it ; but I think the clergymen referred more to burning other people, and not
themselves. Now my knowledge of the tongue is
slender, but I shot enough pigeons out of his flock to
perceive that he was gumming Arabic (for he was tooth-
less) equal to any howling Dervishmaelite ever registered.
But I was firm, and had an immense advantage over him
in not being able to talk his language. I could say,
Wahid vinto—filoos ketir—"One napoleon—too much
money." *Wahid wa nusf vinto*—"One and a half napoleon—too much money." *Yeskoot !—filoos ketir !*—"Shut
up!—too much money!" There was a great crowd—a
mob, in fact—around us, and as he "norated," I closed
every sentence with "And one and a half!" He would
not hear of it—"One and a half." "Three," was his
last word.—"One and a half." "By the life of his
father—O my eye! three."—"One and a half." "*La,
la, la,* LA! No, no, no—once and for ever—three!"
—"*Achir kelám*—the last bid—one and a half." "*Min
shan chatrak,* seeing it's you, three. Any other man
four."—"One and a half." "Three."—"One n'alf"——

Meanwhile a little shrewd-looking old fellow kept
pirouetting round me with a slightly puzzled, slightly
amused expression, and I could observe that the native

bystanders evidently regarded my conduct as incomprehensible.   This little old cock-sparrow was the Co. of
the firm.   At last he came up to me surreptitiously
and whispered in my ear, "Don't you see the bargain's
closed?   Pay the money and take the *búrnus!*"   "But
he says *three*," I answered, "and I won't give but one
and a half."   "Pay your money," he said, smiling.
Three or four bystanders significantly nodded to me, and
coughed expressively or winked, as much as to say,
"Fork over and cut!"   Meanwhile the preacher was
on a grand "tare" of vocal splendour.   One and a half
had gone over the dam to the dogs, and he was running
"Three" in triumph through all its moods, tenses, cases,
packing-boxes, and inflictions.   The money was paid;
but he stood there, the last man by the last ditch, swearing he'd have three or die.   The *búrnus* was rolled up,
but he preached on.   The bundle was carried away,
and the last thing I can remember was seeing him standing on high in the rosy evening light, holding forth *on*
three—and holding out *for* it!

Every Mahometan has a rosary of ninety-nine beads,
called a *soob 'cha*, on which he counts his prayers; a
fact on which I insist, as I have heard it denied by both
Christians and Muslim.   For particulars, see Lane's
"Egyptians."   Turks will say they only play with them,
which they do.   Franks are afraid that Christians got
them from the heathen, which they undoubtedly did.
Hence it comes that bead-making is a business in
Cairo, and there is a whole quarter full of wooden-

bead makers. They make them of beech-wood, roll
them in sandal-oil, and sell them for sandal-wood. It
is a religious trade. Beads put me in mind of a little
story. I had a friend in Cairo, as I now have in
London, who is a wonderful judge of gems, especially
of turquoises. What he don't know about turquoises
isn't worth knowing; what he does would · have
astonished the writer of " Lithiaka," or of " Jewellery
and Precious Stones." I knew them both intimately,
by strange chance. And he has one sensitive point—
he cannot bear to look even at a mean gem, a vulgar,
cheap, soft-diamondy affectation ; and he hates ignorance
in such matters—oh, how he hates it ! Well, one day
prowling with poor Mohamet over in the beadmakers'
quarter, I found a man busy at work manufacturing
cheap rings. They were of brass, gilt; and to supply the
real turquoises for them, he was splitting great blue-glass
beads, and setting them *en cabochon.* Considering that
he only *asked* twopence for one, they certainly were very
cheap and handsome. I am naturally fond of wearing
really elegant jewellery, and so immediately purchased
one of these bargains. That afternoon I wanted my
friend's opinion. I had bought a very fine turquoise ; I
would show it to him. Was five hundred francs too
much for it? I got it from a very honest-looking man.
There it was. My friend took the ring—looked at it.
Such a look ! He was too much disgusted to speak—
too much revolted at me and the ring and all mankind
to vocabulise anything. He believed I had been

swindled. It did look as if a Pennsylvania Dutch infant might have been deceived with it, but he didn't pity me. I was too big a fool to pity—too stupendously green to converse with. " Five hundred francs—*bah!* " And there was a deep damnation in that bah, surely!

Muslim use these sandal beads for prayers. But they have a way of counting them off while they are sitting gossiping about their neighbours. As ladies in the West generally kill off one reputation to one cup of tea, so the faithful average one " character" to a bead. The Mahometans settle them with sandal-wood, the Tabbies with " scandal-water." In the Middle Ages the excommunicated were cut off from wood and water, and to the present day the excommunicators seem to have the privilege of these luxuries. I have seen sandal spelt scandal in some old book, so that there is evidently some root in common to them—probably the real root of all evil. My own theory is, that what grew from that root was the tea-tree—the tree of evil without the good!

It may not be of much consequence whether one spells sandal with a *d* or a *t*, or scandal with a *c* or a *k ;* but there are words in which the transposition of these two letters makes a de'il—or a deal—of a difference, as in *Frank* and *franc*. Most of the Egyptians dislike the former, and adore the latter. I have even heard it asserted that there are Egyptiennes who would not look at a Frank in public, yet not scruple at any sacrifice for *half* a franc under more retired circumstances.

When one studies the Egyptians in their bazaars or workshops, they present so many curious and puzzling phases that if you were to ask me what I expect of them in future, and of their capacity for progressiveness, I should answer that the grounds of the coffee are so muddled that you must mix a fresh pot before I can prophesy; or that there is so much dirt on the national palms that the hands must be washed ere I can chiromance anything. Those who try to educate them find that up to a certain point they have the rather ominous capacity for learning far more quickly than German or Anglo-Saxon youth, but it is feared that they find it more difficult to get beyond a certain point. This, however, has not been fairly tested, and it certainly seems ridiculous that the descendants of such a highly intellectual and imaginative race as the Arabs should not be capable of any degree of culture.

This question of illimitable progress for a dark race, and the determining its existence by the most trifling tests, as many have done for the Egyptians, reminds me of a decidedly appropriate story. It happened in the winter of 1865, after General Thomas had driven General Hood out of Tennessee, that I was in Nashville, where, with a very intimate friend, I occupied the house of a noted rebel; and as there was a large library and piano, with other comforts, we "made out" very *à notre aiseily.* If I am asked if our consciences did not afflict us for such confisticating, I reply with a simple unvarnished fact, which I am sure will be duly appreciated by any professional reviewer who takes this book in hand. In that library my host found a manuscript poem in praise of slavery—dull beyond all belief, dull as dish-water, torpid as clams, dead as door-nails, heavy as lead, flat as a flounder, tame as a sick kitten, slow as sloths, sluggish as slugs, blunt as the edge of a mattress—a pointless, unlively, stolid, stupid, humdrum, grave, Bœotian prosy poem of twenty-five thousand verses, which would infallibly have been published had he not nipped its existence. Think of that, my brethren of the press and pen. I add no more.

In addition to the piano and the library, my friend had the further amusement of setting the poet's slaves free. One of these was a six-footer named James, who fully came up to all that could be expected from what used to be called an "intelligent contraband." In three weeks' time Jim learned to read and write a little, and (what he perhaps prized quite as highly) having a kind master, who paid him for his labour, and gave him fair "outside chances," acquired a real silver watch, which was the joy and comfort and solace of his life. Jim's vocabulary was limited, but he had a large stock of shrewd sense, and contrived to express many creditable ideas in a very ingenious manner.

I was wont to sit of evenings in the office, in a chair, while Jim on a low stool fed the fire with enormous logs —wood-fires of America! when shall I see ye again? And by their light he was certainly a curious picture, as he narrated, for my pleasure, the drollest and quaintest

stories from his old slave-life. I was very anxious at
the time to collect information which would verify the
statement, then so stoutly denied, that the blacks, if free,
would work, since it was on this point that the mere
expediency of emancipation turned. The statements
of the cotton crops have since answered that question.
And Jim, being very impartial, was very useful to me
in this inquiry. One evening, by way of joke, I asked
him—

"James, what is your opinion of the indefinite perfectibility of the coloured race?"

"What dat?—'defnit pertectibility—dun'no, massa."

"Well, do you think they'll go on improving and
getting better, and growing smarter all the time—for
ever and ever?"

"Well, massa, dat 'pends—'pends a good deal on de
culled fokes demselves. Some will an' some won't;
but it can't be 'spected, of course, dat dey'll *all* learn to
write deir names an' git watches."

This was Jim's idea of indefinite perfectibility, or infinite perfection. You need not laugh—he was not the
only man in the world who regarded his own acquire-
ments as the *ne plus ultra*, and measured everybody else
by them. I have no doubt that the Egyptians are all
capable of writing their names and acquiring watches—a
very large proportion of them read Arabic; and they
are, in one respect, superior to any race in Europe—I
mean in an almost innate capacity for decorative art.
But for that I propose a separate chapter.

CHAPTER XVIII.

Once I had a cocoa-nut carved in a rococo pattern, and
a friend called it a rococo-nut. I fancied once that
Egypt must have been overdone with tawdry modern
French and Italian influences in art, and that the rococo-
nut represented the head of every native architect and
artist. So far as Alexandria is concerned, this may be
the case. It seemed to me to lack not only the great
but the graceful. But in Cairo it is far otherwise. The
latter city has, it is true, no modern wonders to boast
of. But its ordinary builders and decorators have remained true and faithful Saracens, out of sheer, enviable,
delightful ignorance of the modern trash currently called
taste; so that one often finds a gateway of a year, which
in every respect, whether of design or execution, is much
like the remains centuries old. Perhaps I err when I
say quite like. This is not so as regards mere mechanical execution or purity; for the native stone-cutter has

grown careless, or else does his work like an amateur of true culture but indifferent skill, presenting in this a marked contrast to the French or English workman, whose cutting and polishing are faultless, but whose designs are any kind of soulless graceful ribbons, vines, or curlicues that the wind may blow to him. As yet the Cairene knows nothing but the mosques, the tombs of the Memlook kings, and similar remains—all of them beautiful, because they all belong to one marked period in history. This period had its distinctive poetry, architecture, language, music, manners, and customs. It had its peculiar pottery and dress, dances and food. Whenever a student of art sees any object belonging to this period, he calls it Saracenic, Moorish, or Hispano-Moorish, according to the period or its sub-divisions. The Ancient Egyptian formed another period, with a distinctive character or style in every little object, in everything formed by human intellect. So with the Hindu, Chinese, Greek, with its Roman following, the Romanesque and Gothic periods. And so it was with the so-called Renaissance, or revival of art and letters in Italy, which also made a period—rather a jumbled and incoherent one, but magnificent in the details of painting, sculpture, and literature. The young reader who would learn to judge of art cannot impress on his mind too deeply the fact that *every great period in history has its corresponding style of art, and that this goes down into the minutest details of life, and is visible in every object.* Simple as this may seem, it has been the hardest thing

in the world to get it into the heads of critics and
scholars. It may sound to some people very much like
telling them that everything which is Dutch is Dutch,
but I doubt very much whether they could fully comprehend even *that* in art matters. You may call it a self-
evident truth that every period has its art, running
through all its buildings and furniture, literature and
crockery, giving the whole a similar character, but as
yet very few have really found it out.

Now it is because so few people have found this out, or
feel it, that there is so little popular criticism or description which conveys a correct idea of, let me say, for example, Saracenic or Moorish art. I have in my memory
a glowing, gushing, wildly enamoured description of the
tombs of the Memlook kings; but it does not give you
the right idea of them. I have before me a handsome
book, beautifully illustrated with the leading lions of
Egypt; but it is incorrect, and why? Because the writer
and the artist admired them in a spirit appropriate
enough to Gothic or Renaissance art, but which did not
and could not penetrate the very different and very peculiar feeling which inspires the Shemitic Muslim. Now
neither of those people had understood that history has
its *differently*-developed periods of architecture, and that
the same gush which does service for York Minster must
be a very poor gush, however brilliant, if it would answer
quite as well for a mosque. Do you begin to see now
that it requires some brains to even understand that what
is Dutch is Dutch?

The Shemitic religion or feeling, whether Hebrew or Mahometan, clung closely to the idea of one God, and that God a distinct self-existing person. As Spinoza said, speaking, I suppose, for the Jews, "People mostly think of Him as a great man." This kept them from personifying nature, as winter or spring; when they did it in Thammuz, the prophets went after them with a hot poker, or as love and beauty (they caught whole showers of hot pokers for this), or fertility (the hot pokers came in a driving hurricane for *that*), or as light, strength, speed, youth, intellect, or anything else. Consequently they made no smaller gods, and no graven images. Moses, like Mahomet, saw distinctly that if people made pictures of men or statues, they would go on making them handsomer and nobler, till they got them into godhood, just as Greeks and Romans had done, just as Hindus and Egyptians partially did; which would make it unhappy for Moses and Mahomet, who wanted no rivals. So the Mahometans made no statues. Nature was a beautiful piece of godwork to them, full of graceful lines and curves and angles, crystals and stars, and nothing more, and they put nothing more than this into their art. But it *was* god-*work* to them—don't forget it—which is more than can be said of the manufacture-pieces of job-work of the present day.

Very different from these Arabs were the Greeks, to whom in beautiful images, and the later Indo-European races, to whom in grotesque incarnations, all nature was full of beings, personalities, shapes of souls, thinking forms.

Q

God was not separate from His works to them—He was
in all, and all was in Him.   Therefore all nature was
one infinite fruitfulness of Saturns, Apollos, Venuses,
satyrs, fairies, saints, giants, goblins, dryads, naiads;
even the dead leaves which flew before the first breeze of
the after-coming storm were little fays or elves; and the
breeze was the wind's bride, and the wind was the wild
huntsman, and everything was everything else; and all
creation was like those pictures which you have seen in
which the light is all made of angels, and these of
smaller angels, and these of angel-ets, all commingled.
As the Edda says, "Hast thou understood—or what?"

Now don't grunt that it is all "stoopid," or say you are
afraid I fire over the heads of most readers, which means
that I fire over yours, O thou of little sense and infinite
laziness!   Read it over again, man, and understand it;
it isn't transcendental, or mystical, or patented, like Mr
———'s pictures—and poetry.

Well, Gothic art was full of graven images—in fact, it
was all graven images—and what they wanted in beauty
and grace they made up in variety, fun, fancy, and sentiment; just as the little lame boy or crippled girlie in
the family generally has more quaintness, and is more
entertaining, and really more lovable and delightful,
than the beauties.   Nay, the goblin-child often has the
largest, deepest, softest eyes—she is the one who first finds
the brownie in the cellar.   And so it was with Teutonic
or Slavonian or Celtic fancy, as compared to Greek.
Gothic art was never so happy as when elves peeped out

of its leaves, and bears and monkeys studied books and
fiddled on the vines, and meek saints melted in glory
on gold or grisaille windows, and all heaven was one
merry Christmas fairyland, where the dear sweet Lord
himself was Christkind, Chriskinkle and Krinkel (as I
was taught to call it), and Santa Claus—children are
not accurate. And this fairy life got so thoroughly into
the art of the Middle Ages, that even when there were
no figures or faces introduced, the designer and carver still
gave an organic living expression to all the lines, and
drew and cut as only those men can whose skill is influenced by vitalised forms. We always feel, like children, that the little men are in there.

Now Saracenic art is as beautiful in its way as
Gothic. But its way to its artists is as the way of the
stars in heaven to the astronomer, as the flowers to the
botanist, as crystals to the mineralogist. Who can
look through a kaleidoscope, though it contain only
angular bits of coloured glass, without pleasure? Children love it, even with the Grimm-Gothic fairy-book
in their laps. Who does not study with pleasure the
lovely forms of frost-work, although there is no suggestion of life in them? It may be objected here that
both Gothic and Moorish work coincide in using kaleido-
scopic and frost-like fancies; but I reply, that even when
they employ almost identically the same forms, there is a
wide, wide difference in expression and manner. How
exquisitely rich and florid, yet graceful, is the porch and
cornice of the tomb of the Baharite Memlook Sultan,

Hassan! how entirely correct in their way, or how corresponding to one graceful, noble idea are all the mosques and tombs! And the style, with its execution, is as original, in fact, as it is exquisite. Arab civilisation had many details in common with the middle-age European —it had enough to quite confuse the careless observer and merely rhapsodic critic, who only tells you what he likes. Heaven help him and his readers! "The worst of these foreign witnesses, my Lord, is that they will not answer plainly yes or no to all questions." Do you, or don't you, like the Saracenic, or Hindu, or Chinese? Many people can answer yes or no to these queries without reserve. They are the same folk whom you can hear asking and answering one another, "Do you like poetry?" "Yes, almost all kinds except blank verse."

But Arab civilisation and art, though they had so much in common with Christian civilisation—even the pointed arch, and much chivalry and hawking and piping—differed in reality from it as widely as from the Greek. The handiwork of decorative artists in Europe and America at the present day is nearly identical as to *motive* with the Arab, the object of the one working being to show his personal skill, and be as "correct" as possible. When this is the deepest feeling in the original design—and it can be no deeper in an inorganic school of decoration—it will be still more apparent when carried out by a literal machine of a workman. In the Middle Ages both designer and workman were more in love with their grotesques, and produced more genial work; but they were not gifted by nature with any better eye for symmetry or colour than the Arab.

Nothing can be more graceful or picturesque than the *róshan* or *meshrebee'yeh* — the projecting lattice-windows of Cairo: I admire them heartily. They are exquisitely fine in details—pretty in every way. But there was something cold in them—something incomplete; and as soon as I looked at one carefully, I found out what it was. It was all the difference between Arabic and Gothic in a nutshell. The exquisitely pretty work was all machine-made—all turned in a lathe and fitted together—a triumph of joiner's work. Had it been Gothic it would have been hand-carved, and thereby one step nearer life. " Man," as Goethe says, " is properly the only object that interests man "—and works of art are the links which connect us. Now I have met with men who would like turned work better than carved work, especially if it could be done very cheaply by steam. I once knew one who preferred a house meanly rough-cast in imitation of stone to the real stone itself. He said it was " more artistic." There are such people. But when that which gratifies you in man's handiwork is *that* (beyond utility) *it is inspired with man's skill and feelings*, it is idiotic nonsense and æsthetic blasphemy to say that machine-made imitations are as good. But do not think I do not admire the Cairene lattices. Orientally they are beautiful, and full of poetry and romance. Ayesha or Fatima casts from them the almond-blossom at the handsome Greek Anastasius passing by ; all the songs of the Romancers and the tales of the "Thousand and One Nights" ring from them—the deepest child-romance of my boyhood and yours—in the days of Haroun al Raschid, with their atar-gúl and yasmin perfume, and peris and genii float around them. This magic of Eastern romance inspires all the crystal and star-like diagram beauty of the mosques, and tombs, and minarets. It is not less fascinating than the Aryan, only it is not the same. With all their spirits, oriental legends and art are properly human ; and with all its people, Gothic art is really mythical—(I wonder if anybody thinks that word means false or untrue here ?) —and fairy-like.

It is pleasant to observe that the sense of decorative art is so deeply implanted in the Arabs that they work beautiful and characteristic designs without patterns. I have watched two men embroidering on one tambour-frame in the Muskee ; they had nothing before them, and nothing drawn or traced—they were simply executing a pattern of exquisite beauty "out of their own heads." There was an old fellow whom I used to haunt ; his specialty was inlaid-work of mother-of-pearl and ebony in little diamonds, squares, and triangles— chairs and stools, boxes, mirrors, and tambourines. It is very easy work—I recommend it to young ladies. He made charming designs, always without premeditation. At Kenneh, on the Nile, they make from clay immense quantities of the porous water-jars called *kúlleh*, so

indispensable in a hot climate, since they keep water
cool without ice. They are turned in an immense
variety of shapes, but though sold at the pottery for
only a halfpenny each, are unexceptionably graceful—
that is, when the workman follows his own impulses or
instinct, without an effort. When we stood, a party of
gentlemen and ladies, around one, and he made efforts
to turn out something *extra*, the results were ugly and
silly. I drew correctly enough from memory the pattern of a simple curious " lateral " jar, which is common
in Egypt, and is made at Siout; but though he must
have seen it very often, his eye, unused to pictures,
could make nothing of it. The foreman was sent for,
and he also gave it up. Now the fact that almost any
peasant in Egypt, as I am informed, can make these
graceful and classically-shaped jars without training,
will appear very significant when I state that once in
a large glass-factory in Pittsburg, Pennsylvania, when
a small glass antique vase of the very simplest possible
pattern was given to the workmen, there were none who
could produce a facsimile of it. They could make what
seemed to them to be perfect imitations, but all were too
squat or too long, or wrong in some way. I often found
by experience that it was quite impossible to have the
simplest patterns reproduced at a pottery in Philadelphia; the workmen had a positive mania for ugliness,
and the principal actually hated the sight of the Greek
and Etruscan or Roman outlines which I gave him.

At Siout there is made a soft red ware, merely ornamental; for I believe it will not hold water, and it washes off in stains, but which is of extraordinary brilliancy and beauty. If I remember rightly, Mr Birch, in his "History of Pottery," states that it is not known whence the Romans procured the clay for their famous Samian ware, which is found in great quantities wherever they went. Was it not made of this Egyptian red clay? of which, by the way, there is an extraordinary story, to the effect that the deposit or bed whence it is taken is only of two acres in extent, and this is annually covered by the inundation of the Nile. But this is all the better, since the river always restores as much red clay as the workmen take away, and never deposits red clay anywhere else. This red ware of Siout—they also make black pottery of equal merit—is in an incredible variety of forms, ornamented in good taste with highly characteristic and really elegant designs. Many real old Egyptian patterns occur on this ware, which is, however, in its general shape, Saracenic. I do not call it Arab or Moorish, because I believe it is also made at Constantinople. What is purely Egyptian are the little monsters of Siout ware, representing crocodiles, monkeys, cats, birds, and many things of unearthly and grotesque form, all resting on a flat surface of three or four inches by two, the under side of which is scored with cross lines like a grater. They are used by Europeans for lighting matches, and by the natives as scrapers for the soles of the feet. This ware is *very* brittle indeed—most smokers have had pipe-bowls of it—but when packed in date-palm crates, each piece well wrapped in soft paper, it may be carried safely enough. In boxes it is sure to break. An immense quantity of this beautiful ware was sent to the great Exhibition in London, and every piece arrived in pieces. I brought a crate of it to London myself safely enough.

There is beautiful and singular jewellery made in established patterns in Cairo, such as the Rigleen or "feet" ear-rings, which are like fans with five knobs or balls at the edge, to each of which a small coin is sometimes attached. Then there is a necklace, called, I think, a *sh'rayer*, or something like it, the pattern of which is given in Lane's "Egyptians." It resembles a row of fish each an inch in length, and is unquestionably an ancient Egyptian ornament, the fish bearing, on close inspection, a much closer resemblance to the *uræus* or hooded snake. Although much of their gold and silver work is coarse, it is proportionably cheap, and the metal of a high standard, strictly established by law— a particular in which Egypt may be creditably imitated, not only by America, but even in London, if there be any truth in the late disgraceful allegations relative to the abuse of the "Hall mark," which should set strangers on their guard when purchasing such ware. In Cairo, one customer, it is true, is often made to pay twice as much as another; and I knew of a Hindu who sold tinsel embroidery to a lady under the solemn assurance it was gold. Great care must be taken against this thing, especially in dealings with the Jews of this city, who have an extremely bad reputation. Many persons are under a very false impression that diamonds are cheap in the East, and these gentry do their best to favour the belief, when in fact there is no part of the world where diamonds are so much in demand, or where they bring such prices. London is, I believe, the best place in which to buy these gems.

I suppose that in time Europeans will set the Cairene artists at work on "European" patterns, and destroy much of their originality. Already in India the leaven is beginning to work. At the last International Exhibition in London I saw that the Mizpeh ornaments and rococo designs and Oxford-Street patterns of England were being imitated by Hindu jewellers. As a very clever lady artist, who had lived in India, said to me, "People see how well they work in their own native way, and say, 'If they could only be educated, what beautiful things they would produce!' So they attempt to educate them, and all the charm disappears."

The proper remedy for this would be an art school in Cairo for the purpose of sustaining and cultivating pure native art, and to teach the workmen the beauty and value of what they already have. Europeans should go to the East to learn art, not to teach it. The extraordinary originality, beauty, and skill which are to be found in Barbary, Egypt, Turkey, and Persia, in embroidery, arms, leather-work, and hammered or engraved metal—and to these a score of other branches might be added—should find a common centre in the most rapidly-advancing country in the East, under the patronage of the most intelligent monarch in the world. I believe that he is "strictly" a vice-roy; but he is a monarch *de facto*, and I trust that the day will come when he will be as fully king in name as he is already one by nature.

The importance of a school for encouraging native Saracenic or Moorish art, as well as of Egyptian independence, will be seen when we reflect on the immense industrial influences which Egypt will inevitably exert in a few years on that vast inner African country which is rapidly coming to life under the advancing railways and telegraphs. Travellers told me—and I met with great numbers, both of Europeans and natives, who had travelled in the far southern Nile lands—that the natives, having a true Shemitic mania for making money, are keen traders and skilful workmen. I saw much silver jewellery from Soudan—all of it original and beautiful, some of it of exquisitely fine workmanship—and was often assured that it was made with only a hammer and a nail. I can well believe this, having observed that the tools used in the goldsmiths' bazaar in Cairo are of singular rudeness. One day I watched a mere boy making very fine gold jewellery with implements such as would hardly be found in the stock of an English tinker. All of these intelligent blacks would be incredibly benefited in time by the influences of an art school in Cairo. Whatever is for the advancement of Egypt is for the good of all civilised nations, and that to a degree of which few people are aware.

CHAPTER XIX.

EVERYBODY wishes to go up the Nile and see the nigh-
lands and N-islands, and have a good, lazy, jolly, foolish, high old time of it. They hope to sail along an
ancient dream-river, for once in a life, with a joyful face
and sparkling eyes, happy as a king, pleased as Punch,
jolly as the day is long; to bask in sunshine, tread on
enchanted ground, be tickled, treated, welcomed, by
dreams of old days; roll on velvet, kick in clover, wallow
in a bed of roses, blessed, in heaven, in paradise. "Oh,
if I could *only* go up the Nile!"

Now I am going to astonish you by telling you that
all of this is true enough, and, for aught I can see, may
be realised to a dot by those who go in good company and
health, with hearts readily attuned to merriment, and
heads not ignorant of the past, and eyes not blind to the
beautiful in art or nature. If ye have these ye may all
depart unto your respective places, and Mr Great-Heart
and Mr Valiant shall play upon the well-tuned cymbal
and harp for joy.

All that you want is to know how to go about it. " If
you only knew what you wanted or what to avoid, you
would save time" ("*Nescis quod optes aut quod fugias, ita
ludit dies*"), as Mimus Publianus observes in his "Dicta."
To be sure your friend Sordidus A. Varus, who went up
the river last year for the apparent purpose of swindling
the natives, has informed you to a farthing how econo-
mically you can go a-Niling.   I believe on my soul that
his only motive for existing—or trying to get to heaven
—is to see how cheaply it can be done.   If he were
offered his salvation for a dollar, he would ask the vendor
if he wouldn't take fifty cents.   And there was your
other friend, the Reverend Ananias Longbow, who had
so many extraordinary adventures.   He has told you
how to see the cream of Ghawázi, and enjoy everything as
nobody else can, and find choice antiques as he alone
knows how, and hear 'Awalim such as only the good
like him ever hear, and, in short, how to spy out all the
nakedness of the land.   You see that I have sketched
him from life.   He abounds in Egypt.   He is the man
who is always going to show you what only he has seen
—the Old London Particular wonderful wonder of
wonders.   God bless him! for he means well, and I
believe would give you anything he had to show—if he
only had it.

Yet all of this previous "posting-up" does not prevent anxiety.   For the practical part of your journey
you consult guide-books, and all kinds of literary Nilo-
meters, to see how high it will rise in prices, or how

low it will ebb in your purse ; and you study to advantage the different forms of contracts with dragomen—correctly speaking, dragomans. You would not call their wives dragowomen, or their infants dragochildren, any more than you would say Musselwomen or Musselchildren. For "storing your mind" you peruse a quantity of invaluable works, in which the author or authoress carefully records the meals eaten, where they got them—"At Beled-el-Shaïtan our dear good Abderahman again bought us some pigeons"—the interesting state of their digestion, the names of all the natives who entertained them, with perfectly free-and-easy accounts of the ridiculous appearance of their hosts—*pour encourager les autres ;* how dear little Tweedles and lovely accomplished Seedie and Deedie were attacked with the fleas or cholic, or were adored by natives, with all the usual innocent, unconscious advertising of friends. Bah! what a heathen wretch I am not to know that there are abundance of good honest souls, open-hearted gentlemen and gentle ladies, who have as good a right to find their pleasure in this reading, and in their own simple, sober way, as in any other! Dost thou not see, Sempronius, how vastly prone are even we writers, who walk constantly in terror and timidity, yea, in the agony of conscientiousness, for fear of letting drop a tiny syllable of offence, are to offend? Didst thou but know how we make these fine works, expunging two sheets where we write one (like the boy who on his way to school slipped back two paces for every one advanced), for fear of those dragon-flies, the Libels, which light God knows where on our fish-poles, when we are angling for a few pence and a very little fame, thou wouldst pity us wretched gladiators of the pen. O Cæsar, *morituri te salutant!*

Let me see! Gladiators with fish-poles (those must have been a kind of *retiarii*), and dragon-flies slipping back on ice as they expunged two sheets for one.   Does not that sentence prove the insane, Irish agony of fear and contrition into which the author was plunged by one feeble effort at liveliness and sarcasm and style?   Yea, over this stile is the way to Doubting Castle, kept by Giant Despair, who despiseth the King of the Celestial Country, and seeks to destroy his holy pilgrims. "Didn't I hear sumfin drop," as the black man said when he fell out of the sixth-storey window on his head. "Dat was *me*."   "Behold I have Come Down!"

Well, if you have any very natural anxieties; remember this, that you will probably not go up the Nile until you have been a week at Shepheard's, or the New Hotel, or the Orient, or Nil.   And if during that week you do not learn all there is afloat or a-going regarding dahabéahs, dragomans, donkeys, dirt, Denderah, damages, dancing-girls, dervishes, dampness, dollars, and deductions, may I be—dashed!   The first of these *d*'s should have been dress.   "What clothes should I take to Egypt?"   The answer to this is stereotyped—most people have it photographed before they leave.   Plenty of good warm clothing for the cool nights, abundance of

thin clothing for the warm days, and as little as possible
of either, including one dress suit for probable dinners,
opera, and festas. The truth is, that humble, plain
men like you and me will do very well with one light
Oxford grey *pareil partout*, or " ditto " suit, one good
stout London winter suit, and the steel-pen coat, as
Tom Hood, junior, calls it, with its " accomplices."
Should you become a Mahometan, you will of course
order 'a turban, which should be white and made very
full around the ears; but as one renegade is said to be
worse than ten Turks, you had better get at least a
dozen. I was told that what is called a *Circassian* or
Circassienne would be indispensable, but on making inquiry, they informed me that a fair average article of this
kind would cost at least eighty pounds, and so did not
invest. I am inclined to think there must have been
some misunderstanding in the matter. Perhaps I did
not pronounce it correctly. Although the weather is
often hot during the day in winter in Cairo, and very
hot on the Nile—we had it from 95 to 100 in the shade
at the First Cataract—it is still a dry heat, and not nearly
so distressing as that of the hot summer days in England. At all events, make sure of some thick under-
clothing, and plenty of shirts—the more the better. As
for money, letters of credit cost two per cent., and there
is an uncomfortable discount even on Bank of England
notes. Bring all the sovereigns you can come honestly
by—they are always at par—but do not make a display
of handfuls of them. Silver francs are good for shop-

R

ping. When you have Hebrewed a man down to
shillings, he will generally make it francs rather than
lose the sale. Count every piastre you get from your
banker before you leave his office, and look after him
and everybody in all things like a detective. They'll
bear it. As for the expense of going up the Nile, the
dragomans are disinclined to take a boat for less than
two months, though they will arrange for a lesser time;
and for a party of not less than three you will have to
pay not less than two pounds a head per diem. This
will include everything. I have heard of many who did
it for less, and a great many who spent more.

Be as temperate in drinking as you can thin it out.
You can get up more gout in Egypt on less wine than
in any country in the world. It may not come out *there*,
but it will in London. Don't live in immortal dread of
ophthalmia. As it is principally caused by the cold and
damps, and darkness of night after the heat and light
of day, you should keep in your shell of evenings. The
streets of Cairo are elegantly paved with a choice kind
of dirt, consisting partly of natron and partly of donkey-
ammonia. The dust from this is "bad for the eyes"—
as the devil said when a broad-wheeled waggon went
over his nose. Many people suffer from this for a few
days, and think it is ophthalmia, and begin to repent of
their sins, and grieve over their wasted opportunities,
and think of what they might have been. What joy it
will be to those who have read this good little book—
firstly, to think they *did* read it; and secondly, to know

that their perceivers are in no danger! But on coming
in after a walk or drive in Cairo, great care should be
taken to wash the eyes carefully, first with a damp
towel round about them, so as not to rub the circum-
jacent and out-lying dust into the eyes, for this dirt-
irritation, though not deadly, is very annoying, and I
knew one gentleman who was seriously inconvenienced by
it. He thought it good fortune that it wasn't the
ophthalmia — "*Nulla tam bona est fortuna, de qua nil
possis queri*" — "No luck is quite perfect." I never
knew a man to be under fire and come out without being
hit, but what he had scratched or bumped himself in
some way.

Remember what I told you, that at the hotels everybody talks Nile and dahabéahs, and little else, just as
they talk stocks in the City, fishin' at Billingsgate, fashion
in Belgravia, fustian in the ——, and nightingale music
and doves in St John's Wood. If you do not find out
what to get, buy, borrow, beg, cheat, or steal, according
to your wants and your morals, to make yourself comfortable up the river, it will not be for want of advisers
who know all about it. Your chief want will be a decent
dragoman. The only rule is to get one well recommended — but beware even of good recommendations.
Nobody has bad ones—if they had 'em, they wouldn't
show 'em. Some people are so rejoiced at getting back
alive, that they would give a first-rate certificate to the
devil if he were their drag—and I shouldn't wonder if
he were the true shekh of the corporation—though I

have heard that Hassan is, and I must admit I found
him, a very civil, well-behaved, obliging party.   Other
people get their dragomans cheaper for a trip, in consequence of pledging themselves to give a good *téskeri* or
certificate, and obtaining another situation for them when
they themselves depart.   This class of Nile pilgrims
may be known by the warmth and tenderness of their
recommendations—"A very worthy, honest fellow, sir
—one whom I would trust with all my money."   I
heard of one gentleman who said of his dragoman that
he would have trusted his wife to him; and so, I believe,
the poor man would have done, could he have made sure
that the devoted servant would have run away with
her.   But he knew that the devotion would never go so
far as that.

A dragoman should have some firmness and courage
in order to deal with your boatman and the natives.   We
found below Luxor a dahabéah with ladies on board.   It
had been kept there for three days and nights, thermometer 95° in the cabin, because the rascally darkeys
found that as there was no wind they could have their
own way, and declined "tracking" (which is pulling),
or remigating (which is rowing).   A dragoman of energy
would have seen the governor, and the crew would have
seen the *kurbaj* or hippopotamus whip.   But much worse
than the timid dragoman is the arrogant, domineering
one, who affects equality, and directs everybody, and
lectures the children; or the cool saucy one, who ogles
the ladies, and worships them and neglects the gentle-

men : these two kinds have generally been hatched out
by a certain class of travellers already described, who
are nothing with anybody high or low if not violently
familiar or desperately funny. Then there is the magnificent dragoman, who expands on the kings, dukes, and
swells he has travelled with ; his *forte* is expending
money lavishly, and amiably smiling at your wretched
poverty. He is affable, but he has been accustomed to
something much superior to the " likes of yees." From
what depth of slavery, donkey-driving, Neapolitan laz-
zaronism, Ghettos, or Maltese scum he himself ascended,
is not mentioned. But he is great, far above you, oh!
small, untravelled citizen ; and I am not astonished to
hear your feminines talk about our dragoman and his
successes in society as if he were their cousin, and as
if they too got a little reflected light from his higher
aristocratic splendour. Then there is the good, honest
stupid dragoman, whom the children worship, and the
ladies scold just as they scold the children, and who by
a kind of blind fidelity and sense of duty always con-
trives to blunder into lots of luck. Also the jolly little
dragoman, and the deep and silent old-file dragoman,
and the big-nigger dragoman, who is a bigoted Mahometan, and the Syrian and Greek and Jew dragomans.
And there is the first-rate good dragoman as well as the
first-rate bad. They told me of one pious Christian
dragoman—it is needless to say that he was a Maltese.
This man was in great demand, and I heard of one family
with a chaplain trying very hard to overreach another

family with a chaplain in order to obtain him.   But of all, the worst wanted is the magnificent dragoman, by a certain kind of people who talk a great deal of folk who never heard of them.   " We are going to have the cook of the Duke of ——," was the morning and evening hymn of a very good family of whom I heard—*not* in Egypt.   They lived off that cook in more senses than one—they fed on his dishes and devoured his gossip. " Our cook " was their unfailing reference on all occasions when in society, and as they generally talked swells and peerage, cook was valuable.

There are people who, like the magnificent dragoman, will smile at the idea of a pitiful two pounds a day ; some of them are folk who would have smiled twice as much once if they could have got half as much themselves a day, steadily.   I knew a man who said it was impossible for anybody to travel anywhere "like a gentleman " for less than thirty or forty dollars in gold per diem ; but then I must admit that I don't think *he* could have done it for thirty hundred, or thirty thousand either.

Bless my soul !—well !—really !—in telling you how to dress for Egyptian travel, I confined my advice entirely to gentlemen !   Of course I was struck aghast, not knowing what to advise ladies, especially those who go down unto the sea, or up the river, in ships ; and I was beaten much aghaster when I saw something in a sermon lately preached by a Mr Morgan in New York, comparing a woman to a schooner—the whole having a very strong application to ladies and dahabéahs—the

only difference being, that the weaker vessels—I mean
the dahabéahs—have only one sail. Well, "it costs
as much," said Mr Morgan, "to launch a woman on
the sea of life in these times, as it would to fit out a
small schooner. As to her outfit, she has to be freighted
with hats, bonnets, veils, necklaces, ear-rings, pins,
chains, bracelets, rings, ruffles, bows, bands, buttons,
loops, folds, pipings, plaits, silks, muslins, laces, fans,
boots, slippers, parasols, collars, cuffs, nets, chignons,
waterfalls, 'rats,' 'mice,' braids, frizzles, puffs, curls,
pannier, tournure, and Grecian bend. What a cargo,"
ejaculated Mr Morgan, "was this for such a small vessel! Few are the underwriters who take a risk in such
a craft, and few were the young men who would marry
this 'Dolly Varden' walking advertisement." The lec-
ture, we are told, was heard with deep emotion by a
vast concourse of Christian young men, and those parts
of it which referred to women's failings were greeted
with wild applause. After which, as I suppose, all of
the same Christian young men who could went to visit,
worship, flatter, adore, praise, cajole, fawn on, wheedle,
coax, court, get engaged to, or marry as many of these
Dolly Vardent damsels as they could—within the limits
prescribed by law of course—and the more elegantly
rigged the "schooners" were, the more did the Christian
mariners adore them. Which was the end of the deep
emotion and wild applause. '*Fol lol de riddle, diddle,
tol lol de ray!*' Ladies going to Egypt! take whatever
you like!

Those travellers who suffer from nervousness, especially in France or Italy, will find the first two weeks in Egypt very "trying." But after that period of probation, they will sleep well and derive much benefit from the climate, especially if they exercise freely, and inhale as much of the invigorating air of the desert as is possible during the daytime—the night air cannot be too carefully avoided. The same advice will apply to "consumptives." Beware of the night air, and dread all sudden changes of temperature. I observed that many people caught colds in Cairo and on the Nile owing to neglect of this rule. I would also repeat and emphasise what I said of the air of the desert. It is so pleasant and so beneficial that it is to be desired that some physician would establish a sanitarium a few miles from Cairo, out in the sands or among the rocks.

It is not well to drink much wine, beer, or spirits in Egypt, but coffee may be far more freely indulged in than in Europe or in America. As regards smoking, most men come down to cigarettes or mild tobacco in native pipes. It is not a country for strong cigars or strong emotions. Avoid sedulously all causes of irritation or excitement—other and abler writers have preceded me in urging this on strangers in Egypt. Cultivate calmness, equanimity, and cheerfulness—few people are aware of the degree to which they *may* be cultivated here. Live for peace—it was the main temporal object of Christianity, which was founded and perfected between Egypt and Palestine, its neighbour. Laugh at the

natives with their little foolish teasing ways : if I spoke
of them as pests, it was in fun, look you ;—just now I
am in earnest. If you have an eye for the beautiful, or
a love of art, there is inexhaustible material for enjoy-
ment in the graceful folds of oriental garments and in
the varied colours of dresses, tarbūshes, and turbans.
I pity the artist who learns nothing in the East.

If you do not wish to incur the entire expense of a
dahabéah to yourself, remember that there are always
respectable people, English and American, who have the
same wish to economise, and the landlord at your hotel,
or some dragoman, will bring you together and arrange
a party or a trip. Sometimes a notification to this effect
is posted on the bulletin-board:—" A gentleman with
two ladies will be glad to join two "—or three—or four
" others "—according to the size of the boat which they
have taken—" to go to the First Cataract—or Second
—or for two or three months." This may be relied on
during the winter season. Then there are the steamboat
excursion parties, which take you to the First Cataract
and back for, I believe, forty pounds.

Many people are afraid of all kinds of vermin in
Egypt. During the whole time I was there I never saw
but two scorpions, and those Master Snaix was carrying
in his cap, I suppose for luncheon ; for, if I remember
rightly, he also desired violently to eat them alive, for a
consideration. Nor was I once troubled in any way by
anything else except musquitoes. There are fleas, but
—*unberufen!*—they never trouble me. However, I

must admit them; but fleas are too important to be passed over with a mere notice, and so I reserve them for a separate chapter. Arn't you glad, ma'am? You can skip that chapter you know; oh, you 'll go through *this* book bouncing and kiting! Be sure, when you speak of it, to say that you read it all through, "except that horrid chapter on fleas." Bless me! why it's enough to make one creep and crawl all over just to think of it! *Ugh!*

CHAPTER XX.

It is, I believe, generally conceded that the plague of
flies mentioned in Exodus included the blue-tailed and
green-headed varieties (both of which bite), musquitoes,
horse-flies, blue-bottles, carrion flies, the deadly *baal-
tse*, wasps, hornets, yellow-jackets, jiggers, midges,
gnats, gallinippers, and fleas. In support of this
opinion I might quote many of the learned who have
upheld it—as for instance, Salvianus and G. A. Sala,
Suidas and Swinburne, Tertullian and Tennyson, Dio-
dorus Siculus and Darwin, Rabanus Maurus and Charles
Reade, Ludovicus Vives and G. H. Lewes, Ramusius
and the Rosettis, Robertus Expertus and Robert Brown-
ing, Cleanthes and Poet Close, Dionysius Carthusiensis
and Dion Boucicault, Artemidorus and Artemus Ward,
Hartmannus Schedel and Bret Hart, Sartor Resartus
and Bayard Taylor, Maximil and Max Müller, Richardson

and Hepworth Dixon, Riviére and Shirley Brooks, Von Hutten and Tom Hood, Conrad and Cartwheel—I mean Peter Cartwright—Bochartus and G. H. Boker—and with them the entire seventy thousand who have written books really worth reading, and which no gentleman's library should be without, as it has been estimated by somebody who had perused them all at his leisure moments. Mind, I say I *might* quote from all these gentlemen's works what their opinion was of fleas—if they ever wrote it anywhere, and I had read it. But as I never did, I will content myself by asserting that of the entire lot there was none who did not distinctly state in conversation at least, once in his life, that the flea was a plague of Egypt and a high-heeled cuss, or words to that effect. And I here call the reader's attention to the fact that, since writing was invented, no author ever before cited such a cloud of witnesses as I have done to verify my assertion with such absolute certainty of their concurrence.

I must admit, however, that there is one writer who might be counted out of this cloud as neither the friend nor enemy of fleas. I refer to one Jacobus Masenius, who lived somewhere or other in an early rubbish corner of the seventeenth century, or in a late dust-hole of the sixteenth, and who absolutely wrote a book called " Laus et Defensio Pulicum " ("The Praise and Defence of Fleas "), but which he subsequently negatived by publishing a " Vituperium et Damnatio Pulicum " (or " The Vituperation and Condemnation of Fleas "),

rendering himself by this double-shuffle utterly un-
worthy of being ranked anywhere at all.

Nevertheless, as Mascnius stands, as regards elegance
and eloquence, at the head of Latin flea-literature, I
cannot lightly pass him by; and as his astounding conversion and repentance were really ap-paul-ing, I am
confident that the reader will be really charmed to know
what he could have said when he was a sinner dyed in
the wool, or rather in the fleece! He begins his defence
by declaring that as great church clock-makers and ho-
rologists do not consider the watch worn in a ring by
the late Charles V. as a very small potato—or rather
turnip—not worth noticing, but, " on the contrary, quite
the reverse "—admire it; so all great philosophers and
theologians see wonders in insect-animalculæ, as much as
in the works of the starry heavens. Then, with an elegant reference to a story told by Scaliger (*Exercit*,
59 and 320), whom, however he does not name, he
observes—" How many lions led in chains in days of
yore were not considered by any historian as worth
mentioning, while a single flea which was thus fettered
was consigned to immortality as a miracle of nature and
art—a flea, I say, not bound with common ropes like a
thief or malefactor, but with golden links and collars, as
if by ornament, to convey the sense of its distinguished
merit."

Jacob's reason for not giving his authority for this
flea story is because in so doing he would have spoiled
the elegant point and application which he made of it;

for he represents this flea as a great and good one, whereas the German author of the " Floh Geschichten," or "Legends of Distinguished Fleas" (Frankfort, 1007), tells us plainly that it was bad enough to have been the old "wicked flee" himself mentioned in the Bible. It is true that an African Egyptian artist did confine this Egyptian flea with a little gold chain, and that so finely that the captive would jump as far as ever in his fetters, yet not as a reward, but as a punishment for having sucked blood from the jeweller's beautiful young wife till he was full, and then with unexampled impudence laid himself down beside her in bed and went to sleep! And it is this great, greedy, voluptuous vampire, this type of matchless effrontery, whom the subtle Masenius would exalt to a saint, and who would have remained one, had not I, two and a half centuries later, pulled him down and un-sainted him.

Jacob's next step in defending fleas is one of such extraordinary subtleness and gentleness as to be really a curiosity. It is simply that in all his arguments he shall attack nobody, and will accuse no one of ignorance, ingratitude, envy, or malice. "I shall leave to every one untouched his own good opinion of himself and his honour." This is tolerably cool, considering which end of the stick Jacob has hold of, and what sort of clients he appears for; but he very truthfully claims that it is an entirely new and original style of pleading, invented by himself, and never before used. "Right you are, Jacob." I may also add, that, to the best of my know-

ledge, it has never since been employed by anybody, and
it might have remained for ever unknown to man had
I not exhumed it from the depths of an antique little
parchment-bound volume.

We pardon anything to our relations in the way of
familiarity—moralises Jacob—why not fleas, which have
our own blood in their veins? yea, often blood-royal, and
are raised upon it—*ac persæpe principum Regumque
sanguine propagari*—so that fleas are partly human.
And if they do haunt ladies' society continually, they do
not, like Sardanapalus, become effeminate thereby, but
are always active, and, like Achilles under similar circumstances, are continually flaring-up and bursting out
like true warriors, and rushing to bloody warfare, wildly
desiring victory or death. Fleas go in the best society,
yea, they are in the bed-chambers of queens and em-
presses—they are, as it were, a kind of confidential
family doctors, and were undoubtedly the first to practise
phle-botomy! " *Ut phlebotomo chirurgus sanguinem, sub-
tilissime prolicit.*" * And as they have good blood in
their veins, so, as is becoming, they have immense families, and an immense range of relations and connections;
and indeed, when we consider the number that have perished during religious wars and political contests, by
torture and murder, the swarms which still survive must
appear as a miracle, and one to be ranked with the pre-

---

* I have a vague recollection that Southey, in "The Doctor," makes
this point, without reference to Masenius. Somebody does it, I know.

servation of the Jews, by whom it is thought, says another writer, fleas were first brought from Egypt, and disseminated by them even unto the uttermost parts of the earth. Have they not, like Alexander, conquered the world? Is there a city, a village, a hamlet, free from them? Sooner will giants expel Jove from heaven, sooner shall lambs conquer wolves, locusts sheep, a tortoise expel hares from the world, than ye shall exterminate these animalcts, though you had the vigour of Achilles and the strength of Hercules. Solomon says— "Go to the ant, thou sluggard;" but Jacob—I must declare with more sense—sends him to the flea, as a perfect pattern of activity, enterprise, shrewdness, and happy cheerfulness. Taking it altogether, the defence is a blossom and a palm, which is more than can be said of Jacob's "Recantation or Abuse of Fleas," which is flat enough, and, according to the Bible, all that could be expected, since David spoke of hunting down fleas as very small work indeed (Sam. xxiv. 14), with very little point in it.

But if Jacobus Masenius is the ingenious and elegant Macaulay among Flea-writers, Opizius Jocoserius showed himself their Bopp, or Grimm, or "great gun" of stupendous learning in his "*Political Dissertation on what are called the Spiritus Familiares or Familiar Spirits of Women, that is to say,* FLEAS," a work in which, with the exception that he betrays at times a superstitious awe of fleas, verily believing them to be a kind of diabolical imps holding mysterious intercourse with the fair sex;

the author shows that he is a lawyer with a level head
and ready wit. Thus, since fleas haunt all places of
worship in Egypt, as well as in all other countries, it
may be interesting to my lady readers to know whether
it is legal to kill them in church time. It is true, as
regards the affirmative, that Agesilaus once slew such
an animal while sacrificing, exclaiming that a lurking
spy should be slain even at the very altar—"*Insidiator
vel in ipsa ara occidendus.*" But if it be killed for
pleasure or amusement, says Opizius, even during the
dullest sermon, it is wrong according to the ecclesiastical
law, because it distracts the thoughts from sacred things.
Also by the laws of nations, because it is a sacred place;
and finally by all laws ecclesiastical, international, and
civil, because the flea, even as a criminal, has there his
right of sanctuary. Again, it is laid down that "*rix-
antes in templo,*" all fighting in church shall be severely
punished, so that you have no right to "go for" a flea
in church, even though he should have gone for you;
and finally, because the law distinctly prohibits going
à verbis ad verbera, from words to blows.

Again, supposing a lady had caught a whole handful
of these volatile iniquities, would she have a right to
kill them all? See what it is to be a lawyer! Certainly
not, you must not send "the whole caboodle" at a blow
"to the son-in-law of Ceres." For, as Cicero says ("Pro
Cluentio"), "Was it not determined by our ancestors
that if a great outrage had been committed by many
soldiers, certain offenders should be selected by lot, so

s

that fear should fall on all, and punishment only on a few." And Seneca (Liber 2 "De Iracundia," cap. 2) lets off steam to the same tune. But as it would be a difficult matter to draw lots for or conscript certain fleas, the largest and plumpest may be seized for sacrifice, with a conviction that these are the principal culprits.

I would here make a remark of my own. The great Hahnemann deduced all diseases from *psora*, and as it is pretty well known that people who suffer from the cousin to that complaint and bless the Duke of Argyle, are generally familiar with fleas (in fact, Macaulay classes them together), is it not probable that the preacher and practiser of *Similia similibus curantur* got his great idea from what Scaliger says, that by burning fleas alive you cause all the rest to *vamos* the *ranche* and cut for their lives, without so much as looking after their property or turning their heads; nay, they will even leave the flea-wives and flea-lets *in periculo mortis*, and not think of them for an hour after, so great is their terror?

"And let no one who reads wonder that fleas should be regarded as a kind of goblins, fairies, elves, or vampires, since they love the country, and, like poets, affect rural scenes, haunt dark and secret places, lurk in pleasant valleys, ambuscade in shady groves and thickets, hide in lonely grottos by quiet fountains, and are generally wide awake when witches are aflight and dreams hover over the pillow." Like the incubi, they haunt damsels, to their own sorrow sometimes, since

there is a story on record of a nymph who in one day
(in August) killed six thousand of them, counting them
accurately. However, the Church has always recognised
their diabolical nature, as appears by its great and fearful exorcism, which, when read with bell, book, and
candle and plenty of incense (to which I would add lots
of flea-powder), causes them to flee to the uttermost parts
of the Red Sea. And this terrible and sacred spell is
given by Berthier Chassan ("Consil," 2, nam. 124) as
follows :—

✠ 𝔄𝔡𝔧𝔲𝔯𝔬 𝔟𝔬𝔰 𝔓𝔲𝔩𝔦𝔠𝔢𝔰 ✠ 𝔐𝔲𝔯𝔢𝔰 ✠ 𝔏𝔦𝔪𝔞𝔠𝔢𝔰 𝔙𝔢𝔯𝔪𝔢𝔰 𝔢𝔱
𝔬𝔪𝔫𝔦𝔞 𝔞𝔫𝔦𝔪𝔞𝔩𝔦𝔞 𝔦𝔪𝔪𝔲𝔫𝔡𝔞, 𝔞𝔩𝔦𝔪𝔢𝔫𝔱𝔞 𝔥𝔬𝔪𝔦𝔫𝔲𝔪 𝔡𝔦𝔰𝔰𝔦𝔭𝔞𝔫𝔱𝔦𝔞 𝔢𝔱
𝔠𝔬𝔯𝔯𝔬𝔡𝔢𝔫𝔱𝔦𝔞 𝔥𝔬𝔠 𝔦𝔫 𝔱𝔢𝔯𝔯𝔦𝔱𝔬𝔯𝔦𝔬, 𝔢𝔱 𝔭𝔞𝔯𝔬𝔠𝔥𝔦𝔞 𝔫𝔞𝔩𝔲 𝔢𝔵𝔦𝔰𝔱𝔢𝔫𝔱𝔦𝔞, 𝔲𝔱 𝔞
𝔡𝔦𝔠𝔱𝔬 𝔱𝔢𝔯𝔯𝔦𝔱𝔬𝔯𝔦𝔬 𝔢𝔱 𝔭𝔞𝔯𝔬𝔠𝔥𝔦𝔞 𝔡𝔦𝔰𝔠𝔢𝔡𝔞𝔩𝔦𝔰 𝔢𝔱 𝔞𝔡 𝔩𝔬𝔠𝔞 𝔞𝔠𝔠𝔢𝔡𝔞𝔩𝔦𝔰, 𝔦𝔫
𝔮𝔲𝔦𝔟𝔲𝔰 𝔫𝔲𝔩𝔩𝔦 𝔫𝔬𝔠𝔢𝔯𝔢 𝔭𝔬𝔰𝔰𝔦𝔱𝔦𝔰, 𝔦𝔫 𝔫𝔬𝔪𝔦𝔫𝔢 𝔓𝔞𝔱𝔯𝔦𝔰 ✠ 𝔉𝔦𝔩𝔦𝔦 ✠ 𝔢𝔱
𝔖𝔭𝔦𝔯𝔦𝔱𝔲𝔰 𝔖𝔞𝔫𝔠𝔱𝔦 ✠. 𝔄𝔪𝔢𝔫.

The same exorcism may be read to unprincipled and
iniquitous sparrows who manifest their disrespect for holy
places (*contra passeres ecclesiam fœdantes*), and inter-
rupt service by singing, chirping, flirting, helping young
ladies on with their bonnets, and making unhallowed
contributions to the collection-box of brass farthings,
buttons, and lozenges——Bless my soul !—I had quite
forgot myself, and thought I was talking of saucy young
men. I really must have been sleeping in church ! Why,
yes—to be sure ! That's it—ha! ha! ha!

The great poet of fleas was Gripholdius Knick-knackius,
who wrote about the same time as Jacobus Masenius a
Macaronic ode, entitled " *Floia, Cortum versicale de*

Flois smartibus, illis Deiriculis quæ omnes fére Men-schos, Mannos, Weibras-Jungfras, et cetera, behüppere et spitzibus Schnablis stechere et beissere solent." It is a jolly book in Latin-German, with a little English intermixed. It begins thus—

> " Angla floosque canam qui wachsunt pulvere swarto."

And is throughout vivid and startling, full of kicking off the bed-clothes, howling, snapping at, catching, sticking, biting—in fact, a noble work, inspired with life, unequalled in its kind.

The word *pulex*, a flea, is derived, says Bartholinus Anglicus (Lib. 18, cap. 87), from *pultis*, dust, because they are born of the dust. But better authority says it is from *pu*, the first syllable of *puella*, or girl, and *lex* (in German *Lechzt*) or *lix*, " because one always wets the thumb and finger, or *licks* them, before catching a flea." Coarse and vulgar! Yes, these old jokers were not very refined. But the English flea, and his uncle the German floh, both derive their names from a root signifying to fly, since it would appear that two centuries ago fleas were so enormously large and ferocious and active, and had such incredible powers of sustained leaping, that philosophers, such as Socrates, gave up as a bad job the endeavour to measure their leaps or class them as creepers, and so " let 'em fly." And in proof of this, I can show that the old Spanish discoverers in America regarded them as fliers, since Pedro de Victoria having been attacked with his friends by a swarm of

first-class A No. 1 musquitoes and gallinippers, and
nearly frightened to death, went home and told the
astounded people how hundreds of millions of fleas had
come flying in swarms, and inflicted countless wounds
on them as if with gimlets! The singing of fleas was
a new thing to Pedro, and so he attributed it to the
gnashing, grinding, and gritting of their teeth as they
came in ferocious glee to feed. Unfortunately for the
Spaniards, they were all entirely shelled at the time,
having just come out from a swim, and so the "fleas"
had blank sheets to cipher on. I do not know where this
took place in America, but from the horridly tragical
tone of the history, and the agonising quantity of the
musquitoes, I suspect it must have been in New Jersey,
either at Cape May or Long Branch, since it is usual to
go in swimming at both these places. And it is also
to be observed that New Jersey is called New Spain,
which is just the kind of a name which would have
been given by such an old Spaniard as Don Pedro de
Victoria.

I could expand this chapter on fleas to an infinite
extent, such is the mass of learning extant on the subject, and, indeed, I could fill this page merely with the
names of jolly writers on it. But that I am probably
better qualified than any of them to discuss it, will
appear from the fact that until one was caught and
exhibited to me in Cairo by Miss ——, I never saw a
flea in my life, nor have I ever interviewed one since,
being one of the exempt. Now it is well known that

those who are entirely outside of anything and really
ignorant of it, are always the ones who talk most about
it and meddle with it. Did not Claudius the abstemious write the great song of "Rhine Wine?" Does not
—— review poetry in the ——? Does not Shiny Blob,
the great American tuft-hunter, go on his annual war-
path among the aristocracy, bearing back as trophies a
mass of titled names, which, as I hear, he does not invariably pronounce correctly, although he makes up for
deficient quality by quantity, as he always gives them
in full, in the most obliging manner, to everybody?
Does not ——, who never gave the subject an hour's
study, pronounce authoritatively on pictures and art?
On what principle are ——, and ——, and ——, and
—— appointed to office? Why are —— and —— in
the Senate? Lord knows that they have no special
qualification for that business! Why was —— Secretary of ——, unless, indeed, because two negatives
make an affirmative, and he added to incapacity the
higher quality of corruption? And therefore, finally,
why did I write on fleas?

N.B.—As I have not the remotest idea on earth what
names should fill the blank places in the foregoing
sentences and antecedent pages, I leave them for the
present as they are, with full confidence that the superior
intelligence and shrewdness of my readers will fully
supply my ignorance, and that they will have no difficulty in filling to overflowing those measures of iniquity
which I left empty. Moreover, by this ingenious plan,

as you will observe, the author gets and bears all the blame for being sourcaustic, satantalising, gall-usive, spiteful, malignant, and given to applying to a foe what may truly be called a *venom de plume* or *venom de guerre*, when the reader is the really guilty party.

Let it be, however, observed, that unless one comes down to dots, and calls names specifically, he may as well give up all accusation. I thought I had drawn my portrait of the great self-made man with tolerable fidelity in that chapter on asses, and just to treat myself to a "little recognition of merit," I read it aloud to two friends—separately. Of course they recognised him—"capital"—"to the life!" But—whew!—when it came to his name, each had a different man in his eye—and neither of them was *my* man! Well, all the inference to be drawn is that there are many of him, and that he flourisheth as a green bay-tree—so long may he wave! So endeth the lesson on fleas. Let us go up the Nile!

CHAPTER XXI.

As we were casting off to go up the Nile, a cat was
observed on board, and her presence was objected to—
not by a lawyer you may be certain, for he never finds fault
with anything in the fee-line.   So Miss Mouser was removed to a barge near by, where she set up such a series of
caterwailings, curses, remonstrances, and *non come-puss*
miäulings in vulgar Arabic, that our hearts were touched,
and at this auspicious moment the Mahometan gentleman adroitly suggested that as, for aught he knew, our
boat abounded in mice, Puss had better be recalled.
He would not say there were mice—but of rats he had
very little doubt.   There were rats by millions on some
boats—he mentioned no names—and then the sailors
were strangely superstitious, and had ideas that if the
cat left it would probably be their duty to desert.
When he had preached thus far, there was a general

outcry. " In Heaven's name bring her back ! " So a
sailor went full of joy to do so, but scarcely had he gone
three steps returning with Puss, when somebody suggested putting her down as she would certainly find her
way back without assistance. Which she did with about
three frantic leaps of joy, of such tremendous and
incredible size that unless you had seen it you would
never have believed it—which is the reason I tell you
so, having observed that this ingenious and sensible
way of inducing people to believe in a regular whacker,
is in general use among all story-tellers.

" It was not her destiny to stay ashore this trip," I
remarked carelessly to the Mahometan gentlemen.

" No," he replied ; " all the men in the world could
not have kept her away. That is *kad'r* or *kismet*—
destiny ? "

" Well," I said, " if you believe in fatality, why don't
you jump overboard ? If it is fated, you will not drown
a second sooner or later."

" Very good ! but if I am not to be drowned a second
sooner or later, I need not wet my clothes in trying to
find out the time. I should only fare like the suicide
in our Arab story."

" And what was that ? "

" Once there was a man who determined that he would
die on a certain day. So he took a dose of poison, and
with a rope around his neck swung himself off from the
bough of a tree which hung over a deep stream. And
to make sure, he held a loaded pistol in his hand, and

as he dropped, he turned it towards his head, intending to blow his brains out. But the bullet went too high and cut the rope, so that he fell into the water—of which he swallowed so much that it caused him to throw up the poison—and he was saved. *Allah kerim*—God is merciful!"

Of this gentleman I may observe that he, with another one who was with us, fully illustrated a remark in my last chapter, to the effect that the less a man has to do with any subject professionally the more does he work it up as an amateur—or, the less he is "on" it, the more he is "in" it. For it was of him and the other that a third, who was profoundly learned and confoundedly observant, remarked that there were two on board, one a Mahometan and the other a temperance man—the one representing religion and the other principle as regarded abstinence from wine—and the two between them could polish off a bottle of sherry in less time than any couple of gentlemen he had ever met in his life! I ascertained subsequently that this had been done simply as a sacrifice by each for either. The Mahometan gentleman would not have tasted wine for worlds, but being in company with a Christian, he, with the innate politeness of an oriental, drank lest he might be a restraint on the other, while the Christian gentleman, fully appreciating this noble conduct, drank that he might show the Muslim that he too could rise superior to the trammels of mere moral law. I commend this story to all temperance men, for it shows how refining and ennobling are their doctrines. Who but a temperance man—or a Turk—could get "graped" on such magnificent principles?

There is a still deeper moral in this affecting little story, which is, that when you do make up your mind to sacrifice a minor principle to a greater one, do it in a decent wholesale way while you are about it, as you ought to make a present, and don't go to bargaining with your conscience, and try to get off cheaply. Do as the Mahometan did, and polish off your bottle if you must break the precepts of the Koran. Otherwise you will only go farther and fare worse, as once happened in this very land of Egypt to three distinguished Christian saints, whom a certain Egyptian monarch once had caught in the Thebaid, and brought into his presence. Having sufficiently inspected these curiosities, he informed them that as they had evidently lived quite long enough for their own comfort, he thought it but proper to put them to death. The saints vigorously disapproved of this. They antagonised. They polarised.

"It is not an original idea," cried Saint Grummer. "O your Highness! millions of martyrs have perished like such."

"Please don't!" quoth Saint Hummer. "It hurts. Besides, we haven't done nothing."

"And we won't do it again!" eagerly cried Saint Bummer. His real name was Bug; you remember doubtless that there was a Saxon lady saint whose real name was Bugga. She wrote poetry, and, like all poetesses, changed her name without waiting to be married. She was the first who ever did so, and I am the first who ever indicated the origin of the custom. It is the opinion of the learned that she was justifiable, all things considered, in turning poetess, saint, or anything, since she did not marry, to get rid of her unfortunate cognomen.

"Well, if you don't like being put to death," quoth the king, "and have no money to pay your ransom with——"

"Not a rap," said Saint Bummer.

"Nary red," cried Saint Grummer.

"Flat broke," wept Saint Hummer.

"Cat's fishhooks!" cried the king, "you must do something. You must sacrifice——aye, by Termagaunt, that 's it! you must sacrifice food to the idols."

"Oh, no!" cried Saint Bummer.

"Or you must embrace heathen sweethearts."

"Oh, ho!" said Saint Grummer.

"Or else drink wine, consecrated to our gods. Get drunk on it, you know. Corned."

"Oh, woe!" wailed Saint Hummer.

"Well, talk it over among yourselves, gentlemen," said the king, turning away and hitting a wasp on the wing with his sceptre as he did so. "Take your choice, boys! Wine, women, or wittels. It's all one to me. I know men as wise as you that wouldn't require long to decide. Remember, I stand the expense. Everything in this establishment is first quality. Import my own wines, I can recommend our dry sherry; and we boast the prettiest waiter-maids in the city. *Au reservoir*, old coons !"

" He called us old coons !" said Saint Bummer tearfully, as his majesty departed.

"That is because we 're up a tree," exclaimed Saint Grummer lachrimosally.

" And I'm—af-raid—we'-ll—have to co-me dow-wn !" wailed Saint Hummer querimoaniously. "I want—to —go—home !"

So they consulted. Now, since they had to abandon their principles, they should have gone in heavy, and thrown the entire house out of the windows while they were about it, or else died like bricks. But these were a kind of small potato, few-in-a-hill, retail saints, who wanted to get off as cheaply as possible in all manner of expenditures.

"I think," said Saint Bummer, "that to sacrifice to idols is the greatest sin I ever heard of."

"And the —— —— the—young ladies," gasped Saint Grummer, "is certainly the next worst; I can't go them."

"Then we must get drunk," groaned Saint Hummer.

So it was agreed upon that, all things considered, it would be best to try a little of his majesty's fine old dry sherry. Now, to tell the truth, the sin of tippling was no novelty to any of these good men. Before they went into the saint business they had been as exemplary pints' smashers and quarts' crushers as any in the profession on the premises. But they were of that unfortunate sort

who never can drink moderately, or stop short of the
man wi' a poker, so they had been obliged to fly to the
desert, and not only sign the pledge, but to keep it too.
And they had been absteeming now for so many years,
that the first glass would act on them as on Indians, and
make them willing to scalp their grandmothers to get a
second.

Now the wine was served by three remarkably fine,
doosid fine girls.   As Saint Grummer took off his glass,
in the deep abstraction of his sorrow he mechanically
smacked his lips and felt in his pocket for a sixpence.

"It is certainly very fine sherry," said Saint Grummer.

"It is dry," quoth Saint Hummer.

"So am I," cried Saint Bummer.

"Well then, gentlemen," exclaimed Saint Grummer,
with a more amiable expression than he had worn for
many a year, "as things is, suppose we try another horn;
—you haven't got such a thing in the house as a biscuit,
my dear?" he remarked to the doosid fine girl, who was
looking with her great dark magnificent eyes into his
muddy ones like a panther into a pig-pen.

"Or a bit of lemon?" added Saint Hummer.

"Or a shake of bitters?" smiled Saint Bummer.

The young ladies had all of these luxuries.   Then it
occurred to Saint Grummer that they hadn't asked these
Hebes to drink, whereupon his Hebe declared he was a
perfect gentleman, and she couldn't think of drinking a
whole glass, but would love dearly to take a little tiny
sip out of his'n.   After this they all went on dreadful,

drinking healths and singing things from Offenbach, and in short, boozed and flirted to such an extent that another young lady who came in to help, went softly back to the king and reported that it was "all *quite* right and no mistake about it."

Having reached the highest point of conviviality and intimacy, the young ladies suggested supper. "You can have no idea, you old darling," said Damsel No. 1 to Saint Bummer, "what delicious suppers we have here."

"Hoo—ooray!" cried Saint Bummer, "oysters on the shell!"

"Bray—vo!" roared Saint Grummer, "lobsters and Strasbourg pies!"

"En—core! bully!" screamed Saint Hummer.

"All you will have to do, you dear pets," continued the fair enticeress, "will be to put a *little* bit of your suppers on the altar before the idols. You wouldn't mind, Bummer my dear, giving a little to those good idols who bestow everything on us?"

"No; give 'em a whole pie!" yelled Bummer.

"And some 'taters," added Saint Grummer.

"An' a pickle," cried Saint Hummer.

And as a magnificent supper was brought in, the three saints, guided by the three young ladies, began to insanely pile whole dishes on the altars. In fact they had to be choked off, so zealous were they in doing what Saint Bummer informed them was the " p 'plite thing, you k-know, in good s'iety." About four o'clock in the morning, the king softly opened the door and looked in.

The entire party, sound asleep, lay around loose on the heavily-cushioned divans. The great gold French clock solemnly ticked the hour; a great fifty-tune musical box, which was the last thing attended to by the tipsificators, continued to drop and splutter out and repeat, as if it never would have done, a German waltz; and the great Angora cat stole furtively around a vast silver wine cooler, leaving a salmon in which she had made a large hole.

"It is *all* right," smiled the king, as he softly closed the door. "Right as a trivet. Now if I had begun by asking them to sacrifice to the idols, they would have been roasted alive first."

I was reminded of this little story as we sailed up the Nile, and were passing the picturesque Gebel-el-Tayr, or Mountain of the Birds, on the summit of which is a Cophtic convent village, from which, as is well known, monks swim off in a manner which does infinite credit to their muscular Christianity, and jump up into dahabéahs, or steam-boats, to beg. Two made for us, but the current, which is very powerful here, was too much for one of them, and he missed us. The other came clambering up the stern, exclaiming, *Ana Christiano ya Howaga!*— "I am a Christian; oh, gentlemen, give me some brandy!" To this speech—the most natural and sensible one which any man shivering with cold and dripping with wet, could make under the circumstances— our wine-keeper obstinately turned a deaf ear. The

Copht was a fine muscular, copper-bronze coloured man ; and having received a rather handsome amount of small change from us, looked at me artlessly and inquired, *Kam filoos di ?*—"How much money is that?" Which done, he stowed it all away in his mouth, and struck for shore, where I saw him on landing immediately surrounded by several friends, as is usual on such occasions. I wondered if this Copht was a descendant from Saint Bummer or either of his companions.

Our wine-keeper was very penitent after the poor clergyman had swam back, and declared that, when we came down the river, if a poor Copht came on board he would give him two bottles of the best, and all that sort of thing, of course. But no monk ever troubled us again from *that* convent, as you may well imagine. I daresay that they concluded that our Christianity was of a very shaky, heretical sort, and that we were not much better than Muslim—small blame to them !

I am not writing a guide-book for the Nile, nor re-writing old ones; in fact, I have not seen such a thing since I begun work on these pages. As regards criticism or fine-art talk on the tombs or temples, anything but unmitigated praise would be at present unfashionable, and probably unacceptable, as no people care to think they have gone such a long and expensive journey to see anything which was not perfection, and as the "enthusiasts" in art are at the present day delirious over everything Egyptian. Turning over a very "deeply inspired" and immensely "catholic" work on art a few

T

days ago, I learned to my astonishment that the Greeks
were far inferior to the Egyptians as regards true principles and good taste, while another recent writer evidently holds that Egypt was the beginning and end of
all " great " beauty.   I can recall a time when, among
fellow-students in æsthetics and the history of art, there
were very few who felt deep and earnest yet discrimin-
ating admiration of what was really " love-worthy " in
Egyptian architecture, but I believe that the same
would be as solitary to-day.   Yet I am convinced that
these Egypto-maniacs of this generation are of the same
stock, and are occasionally the same persons, who then
pooh-poohed the whole temple with all the idols.   These
all-or-nothing adorers are always in extremes.   But
apart from all this, you who visit the temples naturally
enough wish to admire them as much as possible, and
enjoy everything as much as possible—and why
shouldn't you?   Right you are, O travellers !—may
your enjoyments never be lessened !   Therefore have I,
guided by sober second thought, torn out a certain
number of pages which you would probably have skipped
over, and which would be quite out of place in a sketch-
book of nonsense, which is about as much as this work
pretends to be.   A few remarks may, however, still be
pardoned.   I believe that a Doric column is as beautiful
as a dumpy ten-pin, and that the Parthenon, or York
Minster, or Durham Cathedral, or that of Rheims,
indicate higher culture, with as perfect an unity, and
are replete with more beauty and dignity and real

grandeur, than any temple in Egypt, inspired as the latter may be with stupendous pantheism and awful night. Indeed, it is a strange thing to me that Englishmen of culture, who have not seen one-tenth of the great cathedrals of their own country, go straying all over the earth to look at buildings—not knowing, or not believing, that out of Greece there is nothing in the world so beautiful in architecture as what exists in England and Normandy.

The beautiful in art or nature is not a matter of chance liking or disliking. It has its standard, towards which all men assimilate or approach as they study in a liberal spirit the different periods of civilisation, types of mankind, and natural phenomena. The Hottentot Venus would not be a Venus to a Hottentot who had fairly studied sculpture and humanity, though he might continue to entertain a liking through association of early impressions for his countrywomen. We may often like as picturesque that which we condemn as artistically beautiful. When a scene-painter sets forth fairyland in a Christmas pantomime, I do not at all expect that he shall follow architectural standards. I like to see the home of Giant Blunderbore look like Fingal's Cave slightly reduced to Romanesque order, and the palace of Aladdin or Alla' ad Din, composed of Saracenic Chinese domes and rainbows run mad among sheet-lightning, intermingled with Gothic towers of lapis lazuli, on the sides of which stick gold tourelles. It is true that an exception to this rule occurs to me when I look over the beautiful Romanesque fairy tales illustrated by Mr Marcus Ward, in which Cinderella and the Sleeping Beauty are given in a manner which satisfies dreamy childhood and critical age, but then that Romanesque era was a dreamy age, during which hundreds of heroes went into fairyland.

I have touched on this before when I spoke of the lattice-windows of Cairo, showing that an object may content to excess our romantic sense, while it only pleases to a limited degree artistically. Ordinary admirers do not realise this; people who confound word-painting and "fine feelings" and "gushing" with pure æsthetics, have very little idea of it. They know, they assume, what is correct, therefore whatever pleases them must be correct. This error abounds in all English criticism. He who becomes entangled in this paradox, and supports himself with much practical knowledge of art, has wherewith to keep himself muddled for a lifetime.

Now, from the picturesque side, the ruins of Egypt are incredibly pleasing, calling forth much that is strange and dreamy, out of a thousand old fairy closets and witch-corridors, in that elfin castle of the olden time which exists somewhere among the ever-rustling forests in every man's great estate of Memory. We all own one. Some have a large, rambling pile, with hundreds of clustering towers ivy-grown, and others only a little antique grange or Gothic hunting-box behind the trees : but for all of us it *is*, and while it is we have our right to poetry.

It is a pity that, as this world goes, we are generally alone when company would be most tolerable—as in visiting standard works of the purest art; and are obliged to be with friends of the world when we stray through those dreamy scenes of the picturesque, of which nothing can be said, though much may be profitably felt. The Madonna di San Sisto, despite the mystic ravings of fine writers, was meant and made to challenge criticism and discussion, but no ruins are. A belle or a beau may " make up " for company to any extent, but a venerable patriarch who should dye his hair white and paint wrinkles would be an old humbug. Now it is impossible to be alone in Egypt —in fact there are robbers, and guides, and beggars, and children who take care of that to a maddening extent— and a mob gives an *air de théâtre* to anything ; therefore it is saying much for the wonderful picturesqueness of Egyptian temples that Abydos, in which I found five separate parties of friends lunching, impressed me far beyond my expectations, and took me far behind the forest in my fairyland, so that I found the dreamy past in the waking present. But what would not one believe —or dream—of giant gods in the great hall of Dendera, or among its sculptured passages? It was there I first realised how completely all Egypt of old lived for ever between life and death, counting gods and demons as much more real than themselves, and the present life as a mere brief getting ready for the future. What to us are shadowy phantoms and mere possibilities, were to those worshippers of clouds and abysses something so actual and permanent that all mankind, working for ever, let it do its best, could hardly build and toil and carve enough to prove its belief.

There is a strange book which I was so fond of in my youth that, to obtain possession of it, I once copied it in full. This is the so-called "Hermes Trismegistus," generally supposed to be a Greek forgery of the second or third century. It purports to be a *resumé* of the mystical theosophy of ancient Egypt. Whatever it is, I believe that its author had gone deeply into thought, and that, too, in Egypt; for there is in this, as in its counterpart-forgery, "Ossian," a cloudy grandeur which all the taint of forgery cannot dispel. The same feeling inspires the Book of the Dead. It is vain to say that the religion of ancient Egypt was not mystical, when all its gods were manifestly incarnations of such deep principles that art never sufficed with them, as with the Greeks, to give a literal representation. If it was not so, why is it that, of all reading, the tremendous unformed yearnings of Jacob Böhme, with his terrible "Byss of the Abyss and Out Worlds," and the wandering starry splendour of the "Dyonisiacs" of Nonnus and the "Orphica Carmina," leap up so readily into the soul, and haunt one "in these holy halls?"

Not one of these writers belong to pure art—they are all in place in the library in your fairyland castle. They are of the picturesque. If these Egyptian temples were quite perfect, un-ruined, spick and span new, I grant that the ghosts of old mystics would be

less at home in them. But then if Jacob Böhme had
been cultivated as Swedenborg was—who, in his way,
raised a very perfect Egyptian temple—then he would
have given us a mythology of Isises and Osirises,
Athors and Typhons—iu fact, to the eye of the expert
it is all there, only unhatched. There are minds and
moments in history which coincide before and after
perfection, and sometimes the unfinished looks like the
ruined, and the rising star like the setting; and I once
in my youth mistook a Renaissance church for a Romanesque, and was ashamed of my error till I found it
stated in a book of architecture that it was such a wonderful coincidence that anybody else might do the same
regarding it.

The sympathetic reader may judge of what Karnak
must be, when I say that, as regards picturesque beauty
and all that the multitude, grown weary of the Gothic,
at present admire, Dendera is merely a preparation for it.
It is barbarous but giant-like, gorgeous and magnificent.
I wish that the papyri had yielded us a grand Egyptian
epic, that we might compare it with the Nibelungen and
Mahabharata. It would have been awful. But the Nibelungen song, with all its mossy rudeness, would be (like
the German Romanesque architecture which it reflects)
more artistic, simpler, and truly grander than the Egyptian, just as Odin was grander than the lumbering
Jötuns.

I saw Karnak not only by day, but by full moonlight.
Its splendour and mystery are heightened by the ease

with which one loses the clue to its construction and gets
lost in its forest of vast columns. I especially regretted
here that guide-books and guides insist so industriously
on informing you of the number and size of the great
stones which go to make up these temples. One gets in
time to thinking of it all as an aggregate of so much
mere mason-work, labour, or money. Thank God that
the architects of Europe made their columns and temples
of smaller stones!—we are spared in looking at them
such an amount of prosy, petty, childish amazement at
monoliths by the ton. There are many travellers who
seem to think of nothing but the quarrying and carrying;
yet the truth is, that there is not in all Egypt a single
carved stone nearly as large as the pedestal of Peter's
statue in St Petersburg—which pedestal was brought
over swamps and under difficulties which would have
appalled old Egypt. There are monolithic columns even
in America which nearly equal the largest in Egypt:
there is a cast-iron monument in India more than sixty
feet in length, one-third of which was deeply sculptured
in the cold metal. If the Pyramid of Cheops would build
a wall around France, the pavements of London would
thrice do it. I am told that there is in Japan a wall
several miles in length, the hewn stones of which average each thirty feet in length.

Apropos of the sculpture of the Egyptian temples.
I have a suggestion to make to practical men of science.
It is well known that a mystery exists as to the tools
with which these carvings in the hardest granite were

executed. All of the old Egyptian cutting implements were made of bronze. I believe that no iron has ever been noted among them. You find the chisel lying on the unfinished granite carving as the workman left it— the same which he used to cut it—but try with the mallet to complete his task, and at the first touch the edge turns back like lead. What I would suggest is that the bronze was phosphuretted, which, as is well known, hardens it like steel; and that the volatile phosphorus, or its effect, escapes with time, being incapable, probably, of resisting more than a certain number of variations of temperature. Another possible solution of an old problem in bronze has also occurred to me. In the arms bazaar in Cairo I saw several of those curious bronze mirrors, with Chinese letters in deep relief on the back, which are well known to collectors of *bric-à-brac.* These mirrors are so perfectly polished that no one can detect the least irregularity on their surfaces; yet when they are held in the sunshine, so that the light may be cast against the shade of a wall, the characters on their backs are distinctly seen in the reflection. Now I can remember that many years ago, in America, a daguerreotypist once scored or cut deeply a cross on the back of one of his plates, which, like the mirrors, are made of copper or bronze, with polished silver surfaces; and when this plate by accident was placed at the proper angle in sunshine, it cast a light on a wall, and in the reflection the cross made on the back was quite perceptible, though the face was smooth. Hence I infer that where the cross was cut the metal was made more dense, or harder, and that the surface being of two textures, indicated them by reflection, though the eye could detect no difference. In the Chinese mirror the same effect is intentionally produced by the characters being hammered on, or rather into, the plate.

To return to the temple. Egyptologists may assert as much as they will that the ancient religion of this land was not mystical, and that, hidden away in its depths, there was for the *vere adeptus*, or the initiated of the initiate of the priesthood, a simple rationalistic naturalism. But this was not the religion or the inspiring source of their art. There have been men who believed that Christ and his apostles were also atheistic *illuminati*, but I hardly think that any of them maintain that all the art and preaching and praying and martyrdoms of Christianity were inspired with any such icy extract of "pure reason." As I said before, if the Egyptian religion, as it really was in the aggregate, was not mystical, why was it symbolical to such an extent as to be unnatural? In the Greek, the Romanesque, and Gothic, the representation of divinity is almost always within the limits of art, one might almost say of nature : can this be said of the dog, cat, and owl-headed gods of Egypt? How did this art, in which at the present day critics see only the solemn beauty of the Sphynx, and the sweet placid tranquillity of Hathor, impress contemporaries who certainly lived and breathed among purer sources of inspiration?

> "Quis nescit, Juvenalis ait, quam turpia demens
> Aegyptus portenta colat ? Crocodilon adorat
> Pars hæc : Illa pavet saturam serpentibus Ibim :
> Effigies sacri nitet aurea Cercopitheci
> Dimidio magicæ resonant ubi Memnonæ chordæ :
> Oppida tota Canem venerantur, nemo Dianam."

It is the same sentiment, the same unearthly grandeur, the same brilliant magic which pervades Medinet Abou and the Memnonium. I cannot see in the latter that "grave yet elegant *simplicity*," which a writer on it couples with (what I cheerfully admit) "its gorgeous decorations, consisting of divine figures and symbols imitative of the starry orbs of heaven and the beautiful plants and flowers of the sacred Nile, together with the battle-scenes carved upon the side-walls commemorating the victories of the Egyptian monarchs, or processions to their gods," &c. "It is certainly the most *elegant*, if not the most stupendous, in Egypt."

It is in this bewilderment of the simple, the gorgeous, and the elegant that the error of so much Egyptian "criticism" consists. These people admire it so much that they call it everything all at once. It is "silent, magniloquent, and tumultuous." Now one might as well attribute simplicity to the interior of St Peter's at Rome as to the hall of Memnonium, which is again referred to as "chaste and classical." I do not think that its azure roof studded with golden stars, its gigantic blue-and-green stalks and flowers, and finally its bewildering bas-reliefs of the most conventional and unnatural character, with thousands of grotesque hieroglyphs, giant geese and beetles, owls, snakes, and jackals, chains and hand-mirrors, all of the gayest-coarse colours, could have ever been simple, chaste, or classical, in any sense properly belonging to those much abused words.   It was precisely in the same way that people in old-fashioned times used to praise the above-mentioned St Peter's.   It was pure and simple, and chaste and classical once, so much so, that the difficulty which the eye experiences at first in appreciating its vast size (and which is due to bar-barous blunders in the proportions of decoration) was boldly set down to its very perfection.

There is indeed a strong tendency among Egypto-maniacs to inform those who, like myself, do not find in Egypt the acmé of classical simplicity, and the ideal naturalism which is the soul of pure art, that we do not see and feel it, because we are incapable, prejudiced, narrow-minded, and ignorant.   We are below it.   Our old-fashioned fancies for Greek and Gothic and all such trifling modern trash have disqualified us.   Like the little boy in *Punch* who has been made sick by the penny pie which he had bought of a street-vendor, we are loftily informed "that's becos you ain't used to 'igh livin!"

The author whom I have cited as praising the sim-plicity and purity of Egyptian style and ornament, is one with whom I fully sympathise when he lauds and depicts their vast magnificence and bewildering splen-dour.   But when he speaks of Luxor and Karnak as a perfect wilderness of ruin, "almost outrunning the

wildest imagination or the most fantastic dream," I feel
tempted to ask if this was not almost exactly the effect of
those labyrinthine edifices before their ruin, when in their
pristine splendour, which was most splendid in "the hall
of a hundred and thirty columns with its *superb* roof,
glittering in all the vivid beauty of its paintings, when
thronged with monarchs, and priests, and worshippers,
devoted to splendid and gorgeous ceremonies?" And
what else could it, and everything like it, be devoted to,
save gorgeous and barbaric ceremonies? Truly in all
this "there is none of the divine intellectual harmony
of Grecian art." I believe that the term "wisdom" is
applied very conventionally to ancient Egypt. Wisdom does not mean profound mysticism, or transcendental symbolism, but a rational appreciation of what is
good, beautiful, and true. It was not *wise* to let the
people grovel in onion-and-cat worship, though it may
have been profoundly cunning. What could have been
done was shown by Moses, who at one blow swept away
from his people the tremendous mass of polytheistic
trash which had gathered around them, and led them
intellectually, as well as literally, into a clearer, better
life, out of the darkness and away from the goblin gods
of the Nile-land. Moses was truly wise, in the true sense
of the word, perhaps the first really wise man of genius
that Egypt ever produced, and he was not "Egyptian."
For look you, reader, though I may have had my joke in
my way at the Jews in that chapter on asses, it was only a
joke. But here I am serious, and am parting my beard like

Rabbi Ben Syra. I have only one word more to say on
Egyptian chastity, purity, and wisdom. It is the charming manner in which these are combined in the portrait
of Amun, the presiding deity of Thebes, which we see
at every step. "But this was a symbol," we are eagerly
told, "and people did not *then* attach the ideas to it
which they do now." *Fol-de-rol!* When the bad little
boys even of old Egyptian times, and Christians of the
earliest ages, and Greeks, attacked these sculptures, it
appears from their naïve scratches that they had very
much the same ideas about them as the same sort of
people have now. It is all very well to tell us what the
elect of the mysteries thought of Amun; what did the
multitude of the mud think of it, and where was the
stupendous wisdom of leaving to them such a mass of
gross and ridiculous symbols? Why did not the pure-
minded Initiated keep Amun and all the trash to themselves?

Apropos of the god or worship of fertility. Everywhere in Egypt in the old temples, but especially at the
bases of columns, we find deeply cut niches, of perhaps
half-an-inch or an inch in breadth, and four inches in
length. These were made either in early or modern
times by women, but always with the belief that by so
doing they would have children. In some places they
are so numerous as to constitute a serious blemish to the
sculpture, though, as the sculpture itself, like the
blemish, was only a result of superstition, they appear
harmonious enough to the mere observer of history.

And as Superstition conceives the superstition which
destroys her from her sire, Pride or arrogance, as Sin in
Milton gives birth by Satan to the dogs which devour
her, so did the iconoclast frenzy of early Christianity,
which impelled the saints to destroy all graven images
and everything that had the mark of "the beast," spring
from Egypt herself, fathered by her own insane intoler-
ance. Egypt was the mother of fanaticism, and as she
sowed so she reaped. Even in her great days of pride
she was divided against herself, and the crocodile-wor-
shippers warred with the anti-crocodilists, and set many
an example to the iconoclasts of later days. Those who
see the cruel and deliberate destruction in the temples,
indulge freely in abuse of the early Christians, but in
truth the destruction was an essential portion of the
whole plan.

Talking of religion, we had a pious old party on board
—our Arab reis and steersman. He had a good old face,
a white beard, and eyes in which there always appeared,
not exactly the light, but the glimmer of a smile. He
wore a white turban, in one side of which a cigar was
generally inserted; when I "doned" him another, he
stuck it in the other side, which gave him the air of a
benevolent old Satan, whose horns had inadvertently
come spouting through the muslin. He was religious,
like all the crew, three or four of whom generally stood
by him, all holding the helm. Sometimes I would bring
on deck a box of French bonbons and give one to each
of these mariners. They much preferred it to a glass of

rum, in fact, they would not have had the latter ; and as I gave to each his sugar-plum, he bowed low and solemnly, and smote his breast and his forehead. One day I gave one a candied pear which was a little bigger than the fruits bestowed on his mates, and he felt the honour so keenly that he went through the motions twice, and some time after, when he caught my eye, worshipped me again from afar. When Mohamet wanted a light, he was too great a man to go for it himself, so sent one of his clerks with one of his horns to the cook's fire forward. The messenger always went in a great hurry, but returned slowly with the cigar in his mouth puffing zealously to show his devotion.

One day we went ashore. Observing our steersman, I asked the Mahometan gentleman if "reis" was not pronounced *rice.* He declared that it was.

" But it is also pronounced *race.* "

And he admitted that it might be. We went on. Under the palm-trees—

" A *race*," I observed, " is the master of anything, or its boss."

" He is," said the unwary oriental, as a black camel passed by.

" Especially if he be one of the dominant races." This was casually remarked by His Excellency near an orange grove.

" Certainly," quoth the Mahometan.

"Then, O child of Islam," I continued, "if he superintends a mill, you would call him a mill-race."

" I would," replied the good man innocently. There rose a pyramid in the distance. His Excellency spoke.

" He would not be a mill-race unless he turned the wheel himself." And this brought us to the Tombs. I have known a man to go there for less than this in New York.

It was of the one who was called His Excellency, from the surpassingly dreadful nature of his puns, that the Persian spake in these words :

" He is of that character which he is like one lake; it may be rumpled at the bottom, but it is calm and serene upstairs."

And it was of himself that the Persian spoke this way-ly:

" I am of that character, madame, when anything *pliz* me I am very found of it for two days."

And it was *to* him that I remarked :

" You are of that character which combines the largest vocabulary with the smallest grammar of any gentleman of my acquaintance. It is of your nature that you conquer wider territories than Iskander, and leave them to be governed by the eagles of your fancy. You have the largest armies of words with the least discipline of any general living."

Which was all very fine of me, but I doubt very much whether I or any other man could have absorbed so much language in one-tenth of the time which he took, I do not say to learn it, for he never studied, but simply to receive it—and considering that he spoke about a dozen of the

U

most varied languages really perfectly, and hardly pretended to English, I feel as if my remarks were highly unprincipled. The capacity of cultivated orientals for languages is miraculustrous. I used to observe at lunchtime the progress he had made since breakfast, and his pronunciation would exhibit a marked improvement through the afternoon. Like Mr Weller's young woman in "Pickwick," I could see him a-swellin' wisibly before my werry eyes.

Our table received seven daily, and the enormous extent of our ideas and general intelligence may be inferred from the fact that it required eight languages for us to converse in. At the end three spoke English; the Mahometan gentleman and the Persian conversed sometimes in Persian, but habitually in Turkish; my *vis-à-vis* spoke German to me; our waiters were addressed in French or Italian; the Persian gentleman directed his servant in Armenian, and my *vis-à-vis* and the Mahometan gentleman, when in a hurry, generally found Arabic the most convenient medium. And there was somebody—I forgot who—who used to converse or soliloquise in modern Greek, with somebody else, or by himself. If Homer had been a Frenchman, he would have talked modern Greek. English was, however, familiar to us all, excepting the servants, so that the Babel was pretty well regulated. Talking of languages, there is once in a great while a traveller who thinks it worth while to study Arabic. I always said, as regards going about Cairo, " If you can afford it, *don't* take a dragoman." But to indulge in this luxury you must be rich enough in words to do your own talking. If your object be merely to acquire a little of the ordinary language used in conversation in Egypt, I commend to you the " *Vocabulaire Phraséologique, avec la Prononciation figurée, à l'usage des étrangers en Egypte, par M. Barthélémy, Leipzig, Wolfgang Gerherd."* It is, I believe, the only work of the kind which is of any use in Egypt, where the ordinary dialect is markedly distinct from that of Syria or Algiers. It is a very small, cheap little volume, which can be carried about easily. I find that three-fourths of my copy will go into my waistcoat pocket. After carefully examining a great number of grammars and systems for teaching vulgar Arabic, I have come to the conclusion that a somewhat despised, quite humble, and not at all philosophical-philological work by Bichara Soussa, a Copht of Alexandria, is certainly the most intelligible and practical. It is called a " *Nouvelle Méthode pour apprendre à parler l'Arabe vulgaire en très peu de temps et sans maitre."* The truth is that the so-called vulgar Arabic is both simple and easy, but those who write on it generally soar at once into the classical tongue, and attempt to apply the methods necessary to acquire the latter. The two works of which I spoke are both in the ordinary or Roman letter, so that the student will not find it necessary to learn the Arabic alphabet. There is a very useful vocabulary of Egyptian Arabic given in Murray's " Handbook for Egypt."

I was much pleased with the great courtyard of the temple of Edfou, which being in what is called the Ptolemaic style, exhibits marked indications of Greek influence.   I believe that the regular Egypto-maniacs speak of this temple with contempt, as a specimen of decadence.   I can only say that if so, it was like the Dutchman's bread which descended upwards.

I suspect that ere this more than one of the universalists in the beautiful has felt inclined to inquire what I mean by artistic, and on what grounds I would limit the term "art" to setting forth that which research and comparison show is most correct.   " Is not a work of art as much one when employed to set forth the picturesque, the dreamy and irregular, as the most perfect ideals of natural forms?"   To which I reply, that if we understand by art merely skill or the ability to *make*, then anything is artistic which man produces.   But there is a natural and truthful tendency in all people to regard real or pure art as identical with well-defined originality and accurate excellence.   The product of the mill or machine is never inspired with the true spirit of the artist, and, in its turn, the best mere hand-work or skill in *imitating* any haphazard objects in nature, however romantic, or picturesque, or suggestive, or even in combining them, is less artistic than the same skill guided by the effort to set forth types of beauty.

There is a vast amount of confusion between the two, more 's the pity !   But the mystical, picturesque, and suggestive, like the eccentric, simply indicate genius, or perfect ideas half developed. One final problem remains yet to be settled. Let us suppose that an artist—like many great modern startlers in paint—simply attempts to set forth some natural object—say a grove or a man —in some unheard of and original manner peculiar to himself, which you perhaps do not comprehend at first, but which, when you do, proves to be sufficient to enable you to see the original as the artist saw it. Is this ART? To which I reply that this paradox is almost a dilemma, but truth compels me, however reluctantly, to answer No. All of these methods awaken *suggestiveness ;* and however great the skill displayed, they all need ekeing out in the beholder's creative powers. If the purely artistic exist at all, it must be within the limits of the ideal as drawn from nature, and it must be intelligible.

If any reader complain that I have not given him the regular Nile trip with all its "stoppages" for his money, all I can say is he ought to be envied and congratulated. For of all places on earth there is not one so thoroughly described. It is the only bit of travel in the world which everybody has depicted to absolute perfection. Other rivers and tours were very or a little different from what I anticipated, but the Nile was nothing new. The palm-trees, and desert, and camels, and mud villages, and natives, and incidents—when were any of them ever unknown ? As for the temples, who can describe them ? The painter and photographer—not the writer.

Ne sutor ultra crepidam :—Do not go beyond your business, unless you would appear as *Asinus ad lyram*

(a donkey trying to play the lyre).   Donkeys and saints,
fleas and the Can-can, goblins, mosquitoes, crows and
Cophts, pilgrims, poultry, poetry, pottery, and street
cries have been done to the best of my humble ability:
I have sketched my bits—it is all I can do.   The next
young or old amateur letter-writer who goes up the
Nile will achieve the entire panorama with all the
thrilling details of his or her life on the raging canal to
perfection, even unto the diet.   This alas! is far beyond
my powers, and yet I too want to publish my little book
as much as anybody, and see myself in print.   I haven't
thrown some chance remarks into shape, urged by the
solicitations of numerous kind friends, and I haven't been
reluctantly persuaded to appear in print; on the contrary, I have been in a deuce of a hurry to get it through.
I might say something harrowing about having written
nearly the whole of it with charcoal on the wall, during
a painful attack of illness—but don't, because such pleas
sound uncommonly like "a poem written while standing
on one foot," and I will not offer the work as a curiosity
whose only claim is that it was performed under difficulties.   But I do regret having undertaken to even pen
trifling sketches of such a country as Egypt, without the
aid of more books than I could carry home at a trip in my
pockets, all of them finding room enough on a chair by
me—the result having doubtless been divers and sundry
blunders.   Few books have ever been written with so few.
My real desire was, had I time, to take *Das heutige
Aegypten* for a foundation, and grapple with the tre-

mendous social and industrial problems which this wonderful country presents. With its railroads rapidly
extending into a fertile country of enormous extent,
inhabited by industrious and money-loving races, skilled
in many manufactures, and with a marvellously shrewd
and vigorous man of extremely liberal views at its head,
Egypt should not long remain a dependency, and until
it is entirely free in every respect, it cannot enter as
it should on the great career of progress. It is the
interest of every truly great and enlightened nation, of
England as of America, to aid in every way these advancing nationalities, and wish them God-speed.

The great practical problem of Egypt is, however,
not so much the want of entire independence, as the
want of fuel. In this there is a difficulty of appalling
magnitude, for I have never seen, save on the great
plains of Western America, a country where the people
were so severely put to it to keep their pots boiling.
Fortunately they need very little fire for warmth. But
social progress means coal now-a-days; and as virtue is
nothing but transmuted comfort, so comfort is only the
refined form of industry, and industry of coal. In this
we all steadfastly believe. Virtue is coal, refined through
several stages, so that in the infinite *Signatura rerum*
(which Swedenborg cribbed from my beloved and ever-
perused Böhme) religious zeal may mean carbon in spirit
and in truth. For, as you know,

> " All that is great and good in men
> May be traced to oxygen."

At present England supplies Egypt with coal: how long will she be able to do it? But as this is a problem which must be forced to a favourable solution, even though the Khedivé should be obliged, as the Arkansas captain was in a steam-boat race, to put a few coloured persons * under the "biler," I need not dwell on it. There are one hundred and eighty thousand or million square miles, more or less, of coal in America, of incredible thickness and best quality; and as coal carries itself, I have no doubt that the day is not far distant when some means will be provided of taking it profitably to England and Egypt; unless, indeed, *ad interim,* the great invention should be perfected of bottling up sunshine, or extracting it from cucumbers. Should this fail, I will then, and not sooner, come as *deus ex machina* with my great invention of combined mammoth reflectors, one of which (in a country like Egypt, where the sun shines every day in the year, and where the thermometer amuses itself in mid-winter by climbing up to 100 in the shade) will keep anything warm except your fair refuser's heart, and your enemy's manners. I have spoken so earnestly of fuel, because manufactures with steam are essential to progress, and these constitute the great want of Egypt. May it soon be alleviated!

---

* To my brother philanthropists—*black* is not a colour. Should the Khedivé take to this fuel, I would rather recommend him to begin with several of the yellow Turkish vagabonds, who annoy strangers in Cairo, and who from their greasy appearance would make good kindlings. They are "bound to burn" any way.

APPENDIX.

Since writing the chapter on the pilgrims, I have found the following interesting article referring to the same subject, and describing the fortunate results of the expedition, in the London *Daily Telegraph* of May 9, 1873.

We are very glad to announce that the annual pilgrimage to Mecca has gone off this year with remarkable success. "Glad to announce!" we hear good Mrs Grundy ejaculate ; "why should a Christian newspaper rejoice over the happy conduct and termination of the rites and ceremonies of Mahound !" But the estimable lady in question ought to understand that this great custom of the Moslem world is no longer a matter of indifference to ourselves. The East and the West are now-a-days so closely knit together by commerce and intercourse, that, upon sanitary grounds alone, we have every reason to watch with the utmost interest the accounts from the holy cities of Arabia. Twice has Europe received the plague of cholera from the crowds that throng from all parts of the Eastern world to Mecca and Medina. On many more occasions the breaking up of the great gathering has been the signal for the dissemination of the dreadful disease through the countries which lie adjacent to the Prophet's birthplace. The reason of this is plain enough. Mecca may be described as one of the driest and worst provided places that exist ; so that when we add to the want of water the poverty of many pilgrims, their bad lodging, wretched food, and trying fasts, an outbreak of cholera will appear no more than natural. Thus originated, the terrible scourge has been conveyed by the returning caravans to numerous oriental countries, and more than once even to our European capitals. This year was, above all, to be dreaded, for it was a particular occasion—it was the *hadj-el-akbar*, or "grand pilgrimage." Whereas in ordinary seasons the Islamite palmers number only from 60,000 to 100,000, they were certain to exceed this average greatly in the spring just past ; and they did exceed it. The sheriff of the holy places computes the

x

total of pilgrims recently departed home at 210,000—a prodigious multitude for such a little town as Mecca, and one that would have assuredly bred a pestilence in former days, with the probability that it would have been carried north, south, east, and west, in spite of quarantine and deserts. Happily the Turks have taken a leaf from the book of modern science; they have lately appointed a Frankish "director of sanitary service;" and they have placed under this gentleman—Dr Pasqua by name—intelligent native medical assistants, who have deodorised and disinfected the holy cities, to the affront and amazement of many a true believer's nose, but to the undoubted benefit of his health. During the great "three days" at Arafat— when the mischief used generally to commence—these energetic *savants* have looked after water, food, and general hygiene so success- fully that the choleraic epidemic of last season has not reappeared, and the *hadjis* have gone back to their various abodes without any sign of the old and almost habitual infection. Thanks to these pre- cautions, a threatened outbreak of smallpox was stamped out in the beginning; and much is due to the Khedivé of Egypt, who abso- lutely forbade the Takrouri pilgrims to sail from the Red Sea coasts, because there was sporadic cholera in the Soudan. The British Government also did its part by looking closely after the ships which sailed from Bombay, Calcutta, and Singapore, the excellent result being that this enormous multitude of religious travellers has gone and returned without bringing us back the terror of a cholera year. From whatever other source the ghastly summer-plague may arise, it does not appear that any of the Mecca pilgrims will import it. They have got back to India and Malacca, to Egypt and Turkey, to Persia, Syria, and the Caucasus, with clean bills of health—none the worse, if none the better, for their pious outing.

And if good Mrs Grundy must not hope to see Mecca going out of fashion yet awhile in the Islamite world, she ought to be pleased to have Western science linked—and so happily linked—with this great pilgrimage. It is the best advertisement for cleanlier habits and healthier arrangements throughout the East that could be obtained. In America they placard the mountains of the Hudson River with somebody's sanitary soap; and hygienic science has done a similar thing for orientals by proving in the centre of their reli- gion what cleanliness and carbolic acid will effect. It is hard to convey to Western minds an idea of the fascination, the glory, the dignity, and the sacredness which those cities have for the Mussulman. There is the centre of the world for him; thither he bends his head seven times a day; nothing is so noble and divine on earth as the *Beitullah* in the Prophet's birth- place. Nothing, indeed, ever can or must vie with it! When Sultan Ahmed built his lovely marble mosque at Stamboul, and raised around it six minarets, the Sheik-ul-Islam told his Majesty at once and sternly that it were mortal sin to give any mosque the same number of minarets as that at Mecca, and the contrite Padishah was obliged to build a seventh for the *Beitullah* to make matters right. There, too, is the mystic Kaaba—not, as people suppose, a single stone simply, but a parallelogramatic chamber of grey Meccan marble, into one corner of which the black aerolite, wrongly called the Kaaba, is built. That holiest *adytum* is only opened thrice in the twelve months, and every year the priests of Cairo stitch a new cover of black silk and gold, embroidered with pearls and turquoises, for the precious shrine. The cost of this gift the Sultan defrays himself, and when it undulates in the breeze upon the holy building the *mollahs* say—and the *hadjis* firmly believe—that the angels of Paradise are fanning their wings around it. Seventy thousand of these angels have it in their care; and at the moment when the last trumpet shall sound they will carry it back to the place in heaven from which the black celestial stone fell. Then every lip which has kissed it will be found recorded in the books of the Seraphs of Judgment, and it is a rule of Allah that every good and bad deed counts nine times over if done at Mecca. There is Zem-zem, too, the holy well, which gushed from the dry sand to save Hagar and Ishmael; and only to drink of this is almost as good as salvation, whatever faults Dr Letheby and his microscope might find with its somewhat brackish lymph. Then, again, hard by the holy city is Arafat, the sacred mountain, upon whose summit Adam, led by the Archangel Gabriel, met Eve again, after 200 years' separation, the penalty of their fall. No pilgrim can earn the high title of *hadji*, or wear the green turban of honour, unless he has taken part in the annual procession to this hallowed mount. Here was the grand gathering in the present year, and to it the sanitary authorities devoted their most anxious labours. Like the sagacious pilgrim of Peter Pindar, who "boiled his peas," the doctors have "boiled the water," or kept the supply pure with permanganates and filters. The happy consequence has been that very few comparatively have died at the holy places, and that neither the caravans nor the eighty-seven steamers, twelve barques, and countless *sambouks* and *buggalows* which convey the *hadjis* to and fro, have brought pestilence back to the towns and cities of the Orient.

This, we repeat, is an excellent achievement and a great feather in the cap of Frankish hygienic science. They will talk of it in more places than can be enumerated, and perhaps begin henceforth to be cleaner all over the malodorous East. For though it is a distinguished and advantageous thing to die at Mecca, still it is pleasanter, in an earthly sense, to come back alive to pillaws, kubobs, and the bosom of one's family, there to recount the marvellous sights of the Prophet's birthplace, and to enjoy the sanctified orders of the hadji. The desire to earn that title is almost universal; every sincere Moslem hopes to find cash and the opportunity for the trip at some time or other, but he likes to return in the flesh, and to talk about it. It is indeed curious to note the different parts of the earth which send their pilgrims, and their enormous numbers, taking the cost and trouble of the enterprise into account. Thus, out of the 50,000, more or less, arriving by sea, India furnished in even figures about 13,000; Persia, 4500; Mesopotamia, 3500; Africa, 1300; Egypt and Turkey, 12,000; Algeria, 9000; and the Caucasian regions some 4000. The caravans and the divisions of Arabia constituted the rest—some from immense distances. Many not only arrive, but start, so poor that they depend upon wealthy Islamites for every cake they eat; and there were 2500 of these pious beggars who could not even pay the ten piastres which the judicious Sheriff of Mecca exacts from his visitors. We must perforce admire the religious earnestness that moves all these poor people to leave their sunny corner in the gutters of Damascus, Cairo, or Bagdad, for they, at least, cannot hope to profit by the trade which goes briskly on along with the religious services. Meantime Frankish civilisation is so much enhanced in esteem by these improvements, that there is actually talk of a railway to be constructed to Mecca and Medina, although it will be strictly orthodox, controlled, "financed," owned, and stoked by good Moslem. Europe has but one wish on the whole subject—namely, that the pilgrims should not create a yearly plague and afterwards scatter it abroad. That guaranteed, we shall be happy to make them as many steamboats and railway-carriages for the hadji as they can fill, although it is, perhaps, doubtful what the Prophet would think of such a means of visiting Zem-zem and the Hill Arafat.

www.ingramcontent.com/pod-product-compliance
Lightning Source LLC
Chambersburg PA
CBHW021213270326
41929CB00010B/1105